ADOBE® INDESIGN® CS4
HOW-TOs
100 ESSENTIAL TECHNIQUES

EG39887

JOHN CRUISE

KELLY KORDES ANTON

Adobe

Adobe InDesign CS4 How-Tos
100 Essential Techniques

John Cruise and Kelly Kordes Anton

This Adobe Press book is published by Peachpit.

For information on Adobe Press books, contact:

Peachpit
1249 Eighth Street
Berkeley, CA 94710
510/524-2178
510/524-2221 (fax)

Peachpit is a division of Pearson Education.
For the latest on Adobe Press books, go to www.adobepress.com
To report errors, please send a note to errata@peachpit.com

Project Editor: Susan Rimerman
Production Editor: David Van Ness
Copy Editor: Peggy Nauts
Composition: ICC MacMillan Inc.
Indexer: James Minkin
Cover and Interior Design: Mimi Heft

Notice of Rights

Notice of Liability

The information in this book is distributed on an "As Is" basis, without warranty. While every precaution has been taken in the preparation of the book, neither the authors nor Peachpit shall have any liability to any person or entity with respect to any loss or damage caused or alleged to be caused directly or indirectly by the instructions contained in this book or by the computer software and hardware products described in it.

Trademarks

Adobe, InDesign, Photoshop, and Flash are registered trademarks of Adobe Systems Incorporated in the United States and/or other countries. All other trademarks are the property of their respective owners.

Many of the designations used by manufacturers and sellers to distinguish their products are claimed as trademarks. Where those designations appear in this book, and Peachpit was aware of a trademark claim, the designations appear as requested by the owner of the trademark. All other product names and services identified throughout this book are used in editorial fashion only and for the benefit of such companies with no intention of infringement of the trademark. No such use, or the use of any trade name, is intended to convey endorsement or other affiliation with this book.

ISBN-13: 978-0-321-59094-7
ISBN-10: 0-321-59094-5

9 8 7 6 5 4 3 2 1
Printed and bound in the United States of America

Acknowledgments

Thank you to Peachpit Press, including Victor Gavenda, Susan Rimerman, David Van Ness, and Peggy Nauts for their attention to detail in making sure the book reads well and looks perfect. Dan Brogan, of 5280 Publishing, Inc., generously supplied InDesign sample files to lend a real-world touch to the discussions in this book.

Finally, we thank each other for providing inspiration and information for this revision and for projects we've worked on over the last 11 years.

This book is dedicated to Ryan Cruise, Robert Anton, and Michael Anton.

Contents

CHAPTER ONE

Getting Started with InDesign

InDesign is a powerful page layout program renowned for its ease of use, precision, and integration with other applications in the Adobe Creative Suite. Hallmark features of InDesign include professional type and graphics handling, drawing tools, transparency, and Adobe Photoshop effects. Expert preflight tools help you prevent possible output problems when working on print publications. For online publications, you can export InDesign files that contain movies, sounds, and interactivity as media-rich PDFs and—new to InDesign CS4—you can export interactive SWF files. With powerful creative tools and flexible workflow features at their fingertips, graphic designers around the globe use InDesign to produce all types of print and electronic publications. Many of the publications you see—including magazines, books, newsletters, brochures, posters, and online catalogs—are produced in InDesign, often in concert with Adobe Photoshop and Adobe Illustrator.

InDesign is a mature program with many features. It's possible, after all, to use InDesign to do everything from creating a one-color business card or a five-color poster to exporting XML tags for an automated catalog system. That's why this book breaks down the software into the 100 most essential tasks you need to know to hit the ground running. Whether you're new to page layout software or you're switching from another program, you can use this book to learn InDesign's most important features and start producing your own high-quality publications.

A few notes about this book may help you understand its approach. Although keyboard shortcuts can really streamline tasks, we did not include them. Almost every feature has a keyboard shortcut, so including them for both Mac OS and Windows adds a significant amount of clutter. For the complete keyboard shortcut list, see the InDesign Help file. In addition, InDesign offers several ways to perform almost every task. Rather than attempt to include every method, we present the easiest and most obvious methods.

In this chapter, you'll learn how to customize the software and interface; how to manage the many floating panels; and how to use Help.

#1 Getting Started with the Welcome Screen

When you first launch InDesign, the Welcome screen displays (**Figure 1**). If you're new to InDesign, you can use features of this screen to orient yourself to your new software. If you're ready to launch into a project, however, you can open new and existing files from this screen. The Welcome screen also provides quick access to InDesign and Adobe resources such as user groups and plug-ins.

Opening and Closing the Welcome Screen

To open the Welcome screen, you don't need to relaunch InDesign—simply choose Help > Welcome Screen. The Welcome screen closes automatically when you open a file, and you can click its close button any time you need to get it out of the way.

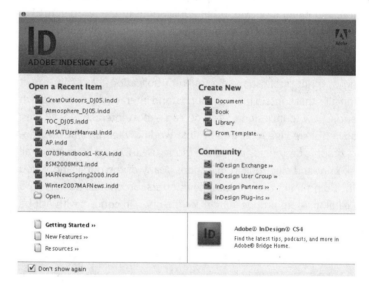

Figure 1 The InDesign Welcome screen provides helpful links and shortcuts.

Opening Existing Files

To open existing InDesign files, use the options in the Open a Recent Item area in the upper-left corner of the Welcome screen.

- **File List:** The Open a Recent Item area lists the last nine documents you opened. To open one of these documents, click its name.

- **Open Button:** To open any InDesign file, click the Open button. This opens the Open a File dialog box to the last location (file path) from which InDesign opened a file (see #12 for more information).

Creating New Files

If you're ready to get started on a new project, use the Create New area in the upper-right corner of the Welcome screen.

- **Document:** This lets you set up the page size and other details for a new document (see #9 for more information).

- **Book:** This lets you create a book file for managing all the documents that make up a single publication (see #84 for more information).

- **Library:** This lets you create a library for quick access to frequently used objects (see #71 for more information).

- **From Template:** This opens Adobe Bridge so you can locate and open a template to use as the basis for a new document.

Exploring InDesign

The lower-left corner of the Welcome Screen provides one-stop shopping for more information about InDesign and other Adobe products:

- **Getting Started:** Click this link to display the Getting Started page of the Help file, which takes you to information about installation, new features, and more.

- **New Features:** Click this link to display the What's New page of the Help file and focus on the differences between CS3 and CS4.

- **Resources:** Click this link for video workshops, free extras such as fonts and templates, customer support information, and the like.

Joining the InDesign Community

The Community links in the lower-right corner of the Welcome screen take you to InDesign information on the Adobe Web site. The links provide:

- **InDesign Exchange:** Download templates, tutorials, plug-ins, and scripts—many of which are free.

- **InDesign User Group:** Read news and participate in discussions.

- **InDesign Partners:** Get information on print providers and trainers.

- **InDesign Plug-ins:** Find useful third-party plug-ins that expand the software's capabilities.

Skipping the Welcome Screen

If you never use the Welcome screen, you don't need to display it. Check Don't Show Again in the lower-left corner of the Welcome screen to keep it from opening when you launch InDesign. If you change your mind later, click Reset All Warning Dialogs in the General pane of the Preferences dialog box.

#2 Modifying Preferences

Preferences let you customize various features in InDesign. For example, you can change the measurement system, the color of guides, and the display quality. If you're working on a document or project and find yourself thinking "I wish InDesign did it *this* way..." chances are you'll find a preference to fulfill your wish.

The most important thing to know about preferences is whether you're changing them for an individual document or for InDesign:

- When no documents are open, changes to preferences affect all new documents; they do not affect existing documents.

- When documents are open, changes to preferences affect only the active document.

To edit preferences, choose InDesign > Preferences > General (Mac OS) or Edit > Preferences > General (Windows). In the Preferences dialog box (**Figure 2**), click an option in the list at left to display that pane. You can also choose an option from the Preferences submenu (such as Type, Grids, or Spelling) to open the Preferences dialog box to a specific pane.

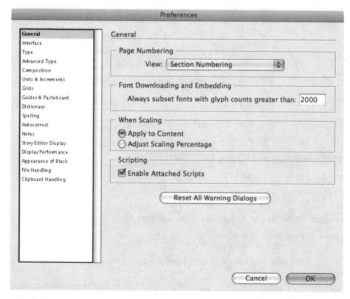

Figure 2 To display different panes in the Preferences dialog box, click an option in the list at left.

With its 17 panes and more than 100 options, the InDesign Preferences dialog box offers more controls than we can cover in this book. However, if a preference setting has a significant impact on how something works, we mention it in the context of that feature. For example, we discuss Spelling preferences in #30. It's definitely worth your time to flip through the panes in the Preferences dialog box to see if there's anything you'd like to change. Preferences with default settings you might want to change include:

- **Type pane:** If you're accustomed to leading being paragraph-based rather than character-based, you can check Apply Leading to Entire Paragraphs while adjusting other typography settings. If you're working with long blocks of text, you might want to turn on Smart Text Reflow, which automatically adds pages and threads text frames to contain all the text in an imported file. (This is similar to auto-page insertion in QuarkXPress.)

- **Units & Increments pane:** If you're not comfortable working in the default measurement system of picas, change it here.

- **Spelling pane:** If InDesign is your primary word processor, you might prefer to have possible misspellings flagged as you type. If so, check Enable Dynamic Spelling.

- **Display Performance pane:** By default, InDesign attempts to optimize speed with quality when displaying type and graphics. You can adjust these settings to see more detail, increase speed, and more. For example, you can choose High Quality from the Default View menu if you prefer to see high-resolution previews of graphic files. You can also decrease the Greek Type Below value to prevent text from displaying as gray bars onscreen.

Resetting Preferences

When you're new to a program such as InDesign, it's often best to start out with the default settings. If you inherit a copy of InDesign from another user, you may want to clear out all his or her changes to preferences. To do this, press the following keys while you start up InDesign: Command+Option+ Control+Shift (Mac OS) or Ctrl+Alt+Shift (Windows). When the alert asks if you want to delete the preference files, click Yes. Note that this deletes all default settings (such as text-for-matting defaults) as well.

#3 Customizing Keyboard Shortcuts

InDesign provides hundreds of keyboard shortcuts to streamline your work. Nonetheless, some features do not have keyboard shortcuts and some of the shortcuts are hard to remember. Fortunately, you can change the keyboard shortcuts to better suit the type of work you do and your manual dexterity. For example, if you frequently use the Change Case commands or the Fill with Placeholder Text command in the Type menu, you can create keyboard shortcuts for those commands. Or, if a command you use frequently has a finger-contorting shortcut, you can replace it with an easier one.

InDesign stores keyboard shortcuts in sets. You can create your own sets of keyboard shortcuts and select a different set at any time while you're working.

Selecting a Shortcut Set

To specify a shortcut set for use with InDesign, choose Edit > Keyboard Shortcuts. Choose an option from the Set menu. If you're familiar with PageMaker 7 or QuarkXPress 4, you can use that program's keyboard shortcuts for similar features. The selected shortcut set is in use for your copy of InDesign—it is *not* saved with the active document.

Editing Shortcut Sets

You can edit the shortcuts for any command in any set—even the Default, PageMaker 7, and QuarkXPress 4 sets. However, it's a good idea to keep these default sets intact. Instead of editing them, create a new set based on one of them, and then edit it. To edit shortcut sets:

1. Choose Edit > Keyboard Shortcuts.

2. Choose an existing set to edit from the Set menu, or click New Set. If you create a new set, enter a name for it and choose an option from the Based on Set menu to specify a source for the initial list of keyboard shortcuts.

3. To locate the command whose shortcut you want to edit, choose an option from the Product Area menu. For example, if the command is in the Type menu, choose Type Menu.

4. Scroll through the Commands list to locate the individual command and select it. For example, if you want to create a shortcut for Type > Change Case > Sentence case, select it (**Figure 3**).

5. If the command already has a keyboard shortcut, it's displayed in the Current Shortcuts field. Select it and then click Remove.

6. Click in the New Shortcut field, and press the new keyboard shortcut you'd like to use for the command. A note under the field lets you know if that shortcut is already in use.

7. If you want the shortcut to work only in certain situations—such as when working with text—choose an option from the Context menu. (Otherwise, leave it at Default.)

8. Click Assign.

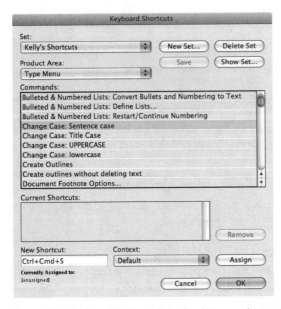

Figure 3 The Keyboard Shortcuts dialog box lets you select a set of shortcuts to use, create new shortcut sets, and edit the shortcuts for individual commands.

While you're working in the Keyboard Shortcuts dialog box, you can click Save at any time to preserve your changes.

Printing Shortcut Sets

If you want to print out a list of shortcuts for the selected set, click Show Set. A list of commands and their shortcuts displays as a text file in a text-editing window. You can save or print this information.

#4 Introducing the Tools

Ninety-nine percent of the time you're working, you will have the Tools panel open so you can create and modify the objects that make up your pages. You'll reach for the Tools panel frequently to switch tools, so you'll want to position it and configure it in a way that's convenient for you.

Positioning the Tools Panel

If the Tools panel isn't displayed onscreen, choose Window > Tools. To configure and position the Tools panel:

- By default, the Tools panel is docked at the left side of the screen. Drag the title bar (the light gray bar) at the top of the Tools panel to reposition it. Once you drag it away from the edge of the screen, the panel is no longer docked. You can dock it again by dragging it to the edge of the screen.

- When the Tools panel is docked, click the small double arrows on the title bar to toggle between a double column and a single column.

- When the Tools panel is not docked, click the small double arrows on the title bar to switch among a double column, a single column, or a single row (**Figure 4a**).

You can also configure the Tools panel by choosing an option from the Floating Tools Panel menu in the Interface pane in the Preferences dialog box. The options are Single Column, Double Column, and Single Row.

Figure 4a Click the arrows on the Tools panel title bar to change its configuration from double column to single column to single row.

Identifying Tools

In the Tools panel, the tools are positioned according to function. Starting at the top (or at left if the panel is horizontal), first you'll find selection tools, and then drawing and type tools. After that, the panel contains transformation tools followed by modification and navigation tools. If you move the pointer over a tool, a tool tip displays the name of the tool and its keyboard shortcut (**Figure 4b**).

If tool tips are not displaying, choose Normal or Fast from the Tool Tips menu in the Interface pane in the Preferences dialog box.

Figure 4b Point at each tool with the mouse to display a tool tip that tells you the name of the tool and its keyboard shortcut.

Selecting Tools

To select a tool, move the pointer over it and click. To use a tool that's hidden in a pop-out menu (indicated by a small triangle next to the tool's icon), click and hold on the tool. When the pop-out menu displays, select another tool (**Figure 4c**). The hidden tool replaces the original tool in the Tools panel.

To quickly switch tools, you can press the keyboard shortcuts shown in the tool tips. For example, you can press P to select the Pen tool or H to select the Hand tool. (If the text cursor is flashing, you cannot use the single-letter shortcuts.)

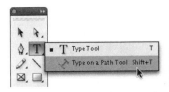

Figure 4c To display and select hidden tools, click and hold on a tool's icon.

Setting Tool Preferences

You can change the default settings for some tools by double-clicking the tool's icon and making changes in the dialog box that displays. For example, double-clicking the Type on a Path tool displays the Type on a Path Options dialog box. Other tools that have preferences include the Position tool, Pencil tool, Polygon tool, Smooth tool, and Eyedropper tool.

#5 Using the Control Panel

Application Bar

InDesign CS4 introduces the Application bar across the top of the screen above the Control panel. Controls on the Application bar include the Zoom Level field/menu for changing magnification, the View Options menu for showing and hiding layout aids such as guides, and a Search field that takes you to information in the Community Help area of the Adobe Web site. On Mac OS, you can choose Window > Application Bar to hide the bar.

The context-sensitive Control panel provides comprehensive options for modifying whatever is currently selected—a graphics frame, text frame, text, graphic, table cells, and more. In fact, if you keep the Control panel open, you are unlikely to need many of InDesign's other panels and dialog boxes. Since the Control panel is so useful, you'll want to keep it handy.

- When you first launch InDesign, the Control panel is docked to the Application bar at the top of the screen. (A panel is "docked" when it snaps to—or automatically aligns with—the edge of the screen or another panel.)

- You can drag the Control panel to any location, such as the bottom of the screen, by dragging its title bar (the vertical gray bar at the far left edge of the panel).

- Click the arrow ▾≡ at the right side of the panel to display the Control panel menu. At the bottom, you can choose Dock at Top, Dock at Bottom, or Float to position the panel.

- To reduce the width of the Control panel (when it is not docked), drag the lower-right corner. Depending on how much you reduce the width, some of its options may be hidden.

- To open and close the Control panel, choose Window > Control.

The options on the Control panel change depending on what you're editing at any given moment (**Figures 5a–5c**). For example, if you select a frame using the Selection tool, a set of options relating to frames displays. For the most part, these options change automatically. When you're formatting text, you can click the character button A or the paragraph button ¶ to control which options display more prominently at left.

As with the Tools panel, point the mouse at any option on the Control panel to display its tool tip and find out what it does.

Figure 5a When text is selected, the Control panel displays either character or paragraph options. The character options allow you to choose a font, size, leading, and other formats for selected characters.

Figure 5b When a line is selected, the Control panel offers controls for sizing and positioning the line.

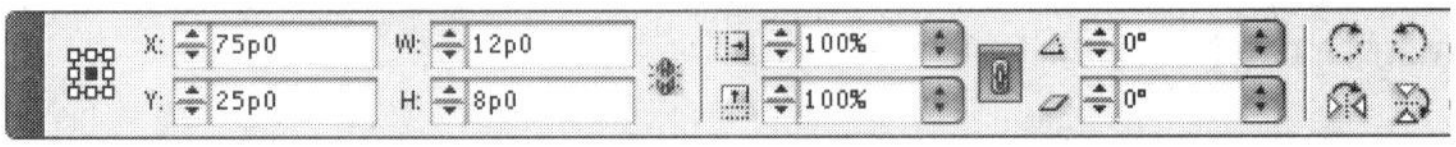

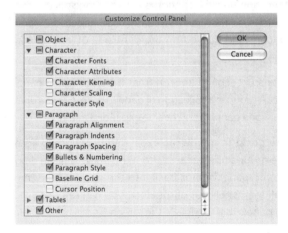

Figure 5c When a graphics frame is selected, the Control panel lets you move it, resize it, scale the graphic, rotate it, and more.

To increase the power—or to reduce the size and complexity—of the Control panel, you can customize it. Choose Customize from the Control panel menu to open the Customize Control Panel dialog box (**Figure 5d**). Click the arrow next to a category of controls (such as Character) to see all the options (such as Fonts, Kerning, or Style). Check any options you want to add to the Control panel and uncheck any options you want to hide. For example, check Paragraph Style to add a menu for applying paragraph styles to the Control panel. When you're finished, click OK.

Figure 5d Choose Customize from the Control panel menu to add controls you need and remove controls you never use.

Quick Access to Even More Power

While the Control panel provides an impressive array of options, it doesn't do everything. For even more control over what you're editing, you can:

● Use the commands on the Control panel menu. For example, when paragraph options are displayed, the panel menu provides Justification, Hyphenation, and Paragraph Rules commands.

● Option-click (Mac OS) or Alt-click (Windows) icons on the Control panel to open any associated dialog boxes. For example, clicking the Number of Columns icon on the Paragraph panel opens the Text Frame Options dialog box so you can edit anything to do with columns.

#6 Customizing the Interface

Reviewing Default Workspaces

InDesign provides a variety of workspaces—such as Interactivity or Typography—that provide quick access to related features and highlight helpful menu commands. New users might try the Getting Started workspace to display short menus and limited panels. If you're an experienced user, use the What's New workspace to highlight new features.

Saving Workspaces

When you quit InDesign, your current interface configuration is saved. The menus and panels will look the same the next time you launch InDesign. If you use a certain configuration for specific projects, you can save it as a workspace. To do this, choose Window > Workspace > Save Workspace. You can then choose that configuration from the Window > Workspace submenu or the Workspace menu on the Application bar.

InDesign's feature set is so rich and sophisticated that it can leave users overwhelmed by the sheer number of panels and menu commands. You can streamline the interface to suit your needs, displaying only the panels and menu commands you need, and configuring panels according to how you work. Once you have the interface set up the way you like it, you can save it as a *workspace*. It's easy to switch to different workspaces and restore the default interface.

Configuring Panels

The panels in InDesign put all the artistic tools you need at your fingertips. As you'll quickly discover, however, the scores of panels can clutter your screen. If you have a second monitor, you can relocate them there, leaving them open and ready to use. But if you don't have that luxury, particularly if you're working on a laptop or you're using a small monitor, you'll need to control which panels are open and their positions onscreen.

The best way to understand the panel-management techniques is to simply click around and play with the panels. Once you get the hang of it, choose Window > Workspace > Reset Essentials (or the current workspace name) to restore the default configuration. You can then set up the panels the way you want them and save the configuration as a workspace. In the default panel configuration, the most frequently used panels are open but minimized into icons and docked on the right side of your screen (**Figure 6**). To manage panels:

- **Working with icons:** To expand an icon from the dock into a panel group, click its icon. A group is a collection of panels that move as a unit. From the dock, only one panel group can be expanded at a time.

- **Working with the dock:** To remove an expanded panel group from the dock, drag the group's title bar away from the dock. You can drag individual panels and panel groups back into the dock in the same way. If you drag all the panels out of the dock, you can re-create the dock by dragging panels to the edge of the screen.

- **Opening and closing panels:** To open a panel, choose its name from the Window menu. To close a panel, click its close button in the upper-left corner or choose its name from the Window menu again.

- **Working with groups:** To display a panel within a group, click its tab. You can also drag a panel out of a group so it stands alone or drag it into another group.

- **Stacking panels:** You can snap stand-alone panels and groups together vertically so they move together as a unit. To do this, drag a panel or group to the bottom of another panel or group. Drop the panel or group when a blue line displays.

- **Resizing panels:** You can resize panels such as Pages, Paragraph Styles, and Character Styles by dragging the lower-right corner.

Instant Panel Open and Close

If you find yourself opening and closing the same panel repeatedly, memorize that panel's keyboard shortcut shown in the Window menu or create one for it (see #3). To quickly hide all open panels, press Tab (when you're not working with text). To display the hidden panels, press Tab again.

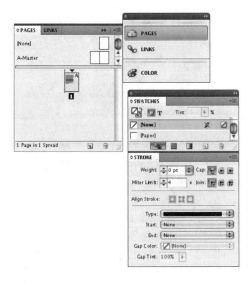

Figure 6 The dock displays icons for open panels. Clicking an icon expands that panel's group (here, the Info panel's group is expanded). The Table panel's group was pulled off the dock as a stand-alone panel group.

Customizing Menus

If the menus are too long or complex for your taste, you can easily remove commands you don't use to shorten and simplify them. You can save edited menus as sets, and save the menu sets in your workspaces.

To customize the menus, choose Edit > Menus. In the Menu Customization dialog box, use the Category menu to specify Application Menus or Context & Panel Menus. Then, locate and uncheck any commands you want to hide. Click Save As to give the menu set a name. Choose the set to use from the Set menu, and then click OK. Anytime you want to switch to the default menus, choose Window > Workspace > Show Full Menus.

#7 Configuring Plug-ins

Plug-ins are software modules that add features to InDesign. Many standard features of InDesign are actually implemented through plug-ins, so they can be easily updated. You can install additional plug-ins from Adobe and other companies to customize InDesign to your workflow. For example, you might purchase a plug-in that adds sophisticated database publishing features for automatically laying out a catalog.

Adobe makes it easy to find third-party plug-ins that meet your publishing needs, and InDesign makes it easy to control which ones you're using at any given time. Features added by plug-ins are integrated directly into the software as menu commands, panels, dialog boxes, and so on.

Finding and Installing Plug-ins

If you have a specific publishing need, check the Adobe Web site for a complete list of third-party plug-ins available for InDesign. (Choose Help > Welcome Screen, and then click InDesign Plug-ins.) If you know that you could save a lot of time if InDesign "just did this," search for a plug-in. You'll find plug-ins for automatically activating fonts as you open documents, for performing math calculations in InDesign, and for creating bar codes, among the many other plug-ins available.

Once you acquire a plug-in, follow the instructions provided with it for installation. If no instructions are provided, drag the file to the Plug-Ins folder within your InDesign application folder.

Configuring Plug-ins

If you buy a lot of plug-ins, you'll be tempted to run them all—all the time. Why get them if you're not going to use them? However, since plug-ins take time to load when you start up InDesign and they sometimes conflict with each other, you might not want to run all of them all the time. To control which plug-ins load, you can create sets of plug-ins, which you can share with other users. (Some plug-ins provided by Adobe with InDesign are required by the program so you can't change their status.)

To configure the plug-ins running in InDesign, choose InDesign > Configure Plug-ins (Mac OS) or Help > Configure Plug-ins (Windows). The Configure Plug-ins dialog box (**Figure 7**) lets you manage plug-ins as follows:

- **Set menu:** Choose a set of plug-ins to edit or to run with InDesign. You cannot edit the default sets (All Plug-ins, Adobe Plug-ins, or Required Plug-ins), but you can duplicate them and then edit the duplicates.

- **Plug-ins list:** Click a check mark to the left of a plug-in name to control whether it loads with InDesign.

- **Duplicate and Rename buttons:** To create a custom set of plug-ins, duplicate one of the default sets and then rename it. For example, you might create a set of plug-ins specifically for production processes.

- **Delete button:** If you no longer need a set of plug-ins, you can remove it by clicking Delete. This does not delete your plug-ins—only the set.

- **Import/Export buttons:** Use these buttons to share plug-in sets in a workgroup; each user needs his or her own copies of the plug-in software as well.

- **Show Info button:** Click this button for information about a selected plug-in such as the version number and vendor.

Note that changes made in the Configure Plug-ins dialog box—including selecting a new set of plug-ins to load—take effect only when you restart InDesign.

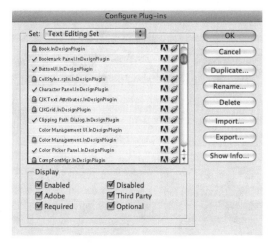

Figure 7 The Configure Plug-ins dialog box lets you create custom sets of plug-ins for specific workflows, projects, and clients. Information in this dialog box also helps with troubleshooting.

#8 Introducing Adobe Help

InDesign CS4 introduces a new, interactive, online InDesign Help and Support Center. Choosing Help > InDesign Help launches your favorite browser and takes you to a special section of the Adobe Web site. This approach has several advantages: Adobe can update the information as necessary; information about all the Adobe Creative Suite products is in one place; and training materials, videos, articles, and troubleshooting tips are consolidated in this area. The most promising aspect of this new system is that you enter an entire community of InDesign users who can provide real-world ideas and assistance as well. The trick is to not become overwhelmed—or sidetracked—by the sheer volume of information.

Opening and Navigating InDesign Help

To get started with InDesign Help:

1. Choose Help > InDesign Help. If you do not have a live Internet connection, see the sidebar at left. The InDesign Help and Support page opens in your preferred browser.

2. To get straight to the answer you need on InDesign, click InDesign Help at right. InDesign-specific Help opens in a new window.

3. Click the options under Using InDesign CS4 at left to display various topics (**Figure 8a**). While reading feature descriptions and steps, you can read user comments and add your own.

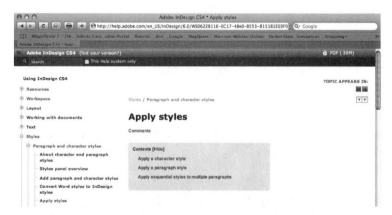

Figure 8a The Using InDesign CS4 Help provides links on various popular topics.

Searching InDesign Help

You might be tempted to search the InDesign Help rather than fumbling through the topics list, attempting to guess where a feature might be covered. However, the Search works like a search-engine search, providing a list of possible resources to wade through. For best use:

1. Type specific keywords in the Search field, which is above the Using InDesign CS4 topics list.

2. Check This Help System Only next to the Search field. This narrows the answers to the InDesign Help rather than the entire Adobe Web site.

3. Press Return/Enter to display links that may help (**Figure 8b**).

4. Click a link to display the information.

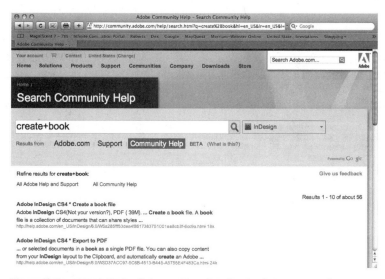

Figure 8b Searching InDesign Help provides a list of topics that you can review.

Tip
Troubleshooting information is provided on the Adobe Help and Support Center home page. For more targeted assistance, click Top Issues, Recent Documents, or Installation Help.

CHAPTER TWO

Working with Documents

In InDesign, a document is an individual file that contains the layout for a publication—an advertisement, brochure, newsletter, book chapter, or magazine article, for example. When you create a document, you specify fundamental aspects of the publication, such as the page size, margins, and number of columns. These settings can be saved as document presets so you can quickly and consistently create documents with all the same settings.

In this chapter you'll learn to create, open, close, save, and navigate documents. Once you create a document, you enter the workspace known as the document window. The document window displays the pages of your publication along with a variety of layout and navigational aids. Within the document window, InDesign provides convenient options for navigating through pages, changing the zoom level, and previewing the output. For ease in file management, InDesign allows you to save metadata such as keywords and creator names with documents. You'll also learn to work within the document window, change the view, preview output, and save metadata.

#9 Creating New Documents

When you start a new project—such as a newsletter—you create a new document that reflects the finished page size, margins, and number of columns. In addition, you can specify the number of pages and whether the document has facing pages (as in a book). As a starting place, it may be helpful to mock up your publication first, even just by roughing it out with pencil and paper. While all these options can be changed after you create the document, designing pages is easier if you know the specifics up front.

To create a new document:

1. Choose File > New > Document. The New Document dialog box that displays (**Figure 9**) lets you set up the document.

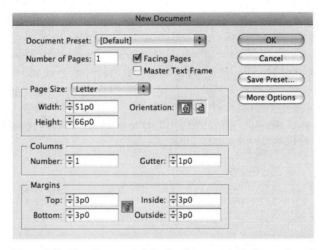

Figure 9 The New Document dialog box lets you specify the number of pages, page size, margins, and more for a new project.

2. Enter a value in the Number of Pages field. You can create documents with up to 9,999 pages.

3. To create a document with two-page spreads as in a book or magazine, check Facing Pages.

4. To automatically place a text frame—a container for text—on the pages, check Master Text Frame. The master text frame will be placed according to the values in the Columns and Margins areas.

Tip

Use the master text frame for publications, such as books, in which text flows continuously from page to page. For magazines and newsletters with multiple stories that may continue on different pages, it's best to manually thread text frames (see #18).

5. Choose an option from the Page Size menu or enter values in the Width and Height fields. To quickly reverse the Width and Height values, click an Orientation button.

6. In the Columns area, enter the number of columns most of the pages will have in the Number field. Enter the amount of space you want between columns in the Gutter field.

7. In the Margins area, enter values in the Top, Bottom, Left, and Right fields to specify margin guides for pages. If you check Facing Pages, the Left and Right fields change to Inside and Outside. If you want all the margin values to be the same, click the Make All Settings the Same button 🔘 between the fields.

8. If a printer asks you to set up bleed or slug areas on pages, click More Options. Specify the size of the areas in the Bleed and Slug fields.

9. Click OK to create the new document.

InDesign creates a new document with the number of pages you specified. Magenta-colored guides on the page indicate margins, and violet-colored guides indicate columns. If you checked Master Text Frame, a text frame (a container for text) is automatically placed within the margin guides; the frame contains the number of columns you specified. Your designs, however, are not constrained by anything you specify for the new document. For example, you can add and remove pages, change the number of columns in any or all of the text frames, and work with the entire page area regardless of the margins.

Entering Values in Different Measurement Systems

The default measurement system for new documents is picas, which are commonly used in graphic design. (A pica is approximately one-sixth of an inch, or 12 points.) You can enter values in any measurement system as long as you include an abbreviation with the values—for example, "in" for inches or "pt" for points. The abbreviations for the supported measurement systems are:

- Agates: ag
- Ciceros: c
- Centimeters: cm
- Inches: i, in, inch, or "
- Inches decimal: i, in, inch, or " with a decimal point
- Millimeters: mm
- Picas: p
- Points: pt (or p before the value)
- Picas and points: p (after the pica value, before the point value)

#10 Saving Presets

If you find yourself in the tedious situation of setting up similar documents over and over—for example, if you create new trifold brochures several times a week—you can save all the settings in the New Document dialog box as *document presets*. You can then select from your document presets in the New Document dialog box. This not only saves you time when creating new documents but it ensures consistency among similar documents. Never again will you wonder about the page size for the book jackets you're working on or the bleed area for a magazine.

Saving Document Presets

To save document presets:

1. Choose File > New > Document. In the New Document dialog box, specify the Number of Pages, Page Size, Columns, Margins, and all other attributes you want in the preset.

2. Click Save Preset. In the Save Preset dialog box (**Figure 10a**), type a name for the document preset in the field.

3. Click OK.

Figure 10a The Save Preset dialog box lets you name and save all the specifications for a new document.

Using Document Presets

To use a preset, select it from the Document Preset menu (**Figure 10b**) at the top of the New Document dialog box. All the settings in the dialog box automatically change to those in the preset. You can also choose one of your presets from the Document Preset submenu in the File menu; this automatically opens the New Document dialog box with the preset selected. If you press the Shift key while you choose an option from the Document Preset submenu, you can bypass the New Document dialog box and immediately create a new document.

Presets and Templates

InDesign provides document presets for ensuring specifications such as page size, column width, and margins are consistent when you're creating similar documents. To create a more sophisticated starting place for new documents, you can make a template that also contains graphics, styles, color swatches, text, and more.

For example, suppose you design business cards for different clients every day. You could save a document preset for a generic business card size as a quick starting place for each new business card job. But, if you are simply updating business cards with new names for the same client, a template is a better starting place. See #13 for more information.

Note

If you select a document preset and then make further changes in the New Document dialog box, the Document Preset menu changes to [Custom].

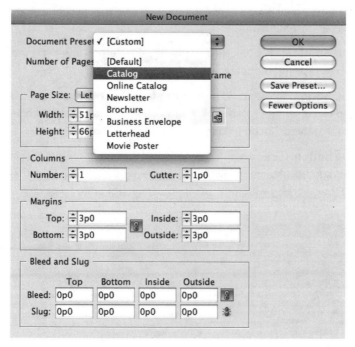

Figure 10b The Document Preset menu in the New Document dialog box lets you create new documents quickly and efficiently by choosing from your list of document setups.

Editing Document Presets

In addition to creating a document preset using the New Document dialog box, you can also use the Document Presets dialog box (**Figure 10c**) to create a preset. To open this dialog box, choose File > Document Presets > Define. The dialog box works as follows:

- **Presets list:** The Presets list shows all your document presets. Click one to see its settings or to edit or delete it.

- **Preset Settings area:** This scroll box shows all the document specifications for the selected document preset.

- **New button:** Click New to create a new document preset. The New Document Preset dialog box (similar to the New Document dialog box) displays so you can name and set up the preset.

- **Edit button:** Click Edit to change the name or specifications of the selected document preset.

- **Delete button:** Click Delete to remove the selected document presets from the list; you cannot delete [Default].

- **Load button:** To use saved document presets, click Load and use the Load Document Presets dialog box to navigate to the location where they are stored. Document presets have the file extension ".dcst."

- **Save button:** Click Save to export selected document presets. Within a workgroup, it's a good idea to share presets so you can ensure that you're all working with the same specifications for similar projects.

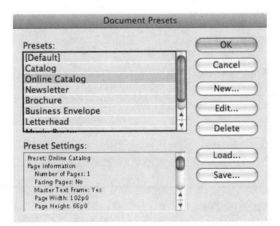

Figure 10c The Document Presets dialog box lets you create, edit, and delete document presets and share document presets with other users.

#11 Understanding the Document Window

The document window is the rectangular space in which the pages of an InDesign layout are displayed. The document window mimics an actual graphic design pasteup board, providing a blank area surrounding pages called the *pasteboard* and layout aids such as rulers, guides, and grids. Within each document window, you can control the zoom level, the quality of the display, and which layout aids are visible. Most of the time, the document window displays the page or spread you are currently working on. Because it may be helpful to see different pages of a document at the same time (or different zoom levels), you can open multiple windows for the same open document.

Reviewing the Document Window

Take a look at a standard document window (**Figure 11a**).

Guides   Rulers   Pasteboard

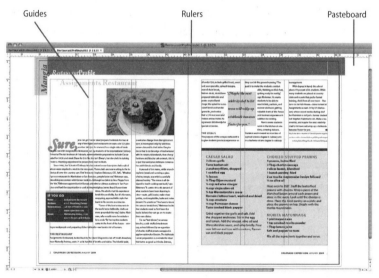

Figure 11a The document window provides a workspace similar to a traditional pasteup board.

Using the Application Frame to Mimic Windows

In InDesign CS4, you can make the Mac OS version act like a Windows application by using the Application Frame. Choose Window > Application Frame to confine all the InDesign interface elements—the Application bar, panels, and open document windows—within a frame that obscures other applications and your desktop. You can minimize and resize the frame as necessary to work with other applications. Since few Mac OS users are comfortable working this way, the Application Frame is off by default.

Customizing the Work Area

You can customize many aspects of the document window using the Preferences dialog box. For example, if you prefer to work in inches rather than points or you can't stand magenta guides, you can change those settings. The Units & Increments pane lets you specify the increments for the rulers and the Guides & Pasteboard pane lets you change guide colors and modify the pasteboard size.

- Rulers display along the top and left side of the document window. The View > Show/Hide Rulers command lets you control whether or not the rulers display.

- A gray pasteboard surrounds each page or spread. Each page or spread has its own pasteboard, which you can use for temporarily storing objects or for creating and formatting objects away from the distractions of the page.

- Different-colored guides and grids may display on the pages depending on the settings in the View > Grids & Guides submenu. Generally, you will see magenta margin guides and violet column guides.

Using Controls on the Document Window

The lower-left corner of the document window provides convenient controls for navigating through documents, reviewing preflight issues, and displaying file information (**Figure 11b**). The preflight controls flag errors such as overset text or missing graphic files that may prevent the document from printing properly.

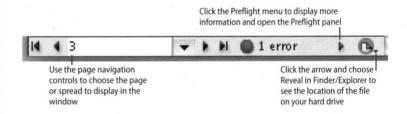

Click the Preflight menu to display more information and open the Preflight panel

Use the page navigation controls to choose the page or spread to display in the window

Click the arrow and choose Reveal in Finder/Explorer to see the location of the file on your hard drive

Figure 11b The lower-left corner of the document window provides controls for switching pages, reviewing preflight issues, and locating files.

Tip
On Mac OS, if you close the Application bar (Window > Application Bar), the Zoom Level field/menu is added to the lower-left corner of the document window.

Managing Document Windows

If you are working on a document and want to see a different view of it—for example, to view the first and last page at the same time or to view the same page at 50 percent and 300 percent—you can open another window for the document. To do this, choose Window > Arrange > New Window.

Once you have multiple windows open, whether of a single document or multiple documents, you create a management issue. The bottom of the Window menu lists all the open document windows so you can choose one to display. To help manage the windows, use commands in the Window > Arrange submenu or the Arrange Documents menu on the Application bar (**Figure 11c**). Point at the icons on the Arrange Documents menu to see what they do.

Figure 11c The Arrange Documents menu on the Application bar provides a visual way to indicate how you want open document windows organized.

Tip

If you choose Window > Arrange > Consolidate All Windows or click the Consolidate All icon in the menu, all the open windows are combined into one tabbed document window. Click the tab of the document you want to display.

Closing Document Windows

To close a document and all its open windows, press Command+Shift+W (Mac OS) or Ctrl+Shift+W (Windows). To close all open documents and their windows, add the Option or Alt key: Command+Option+Shift+W (Mac OS) or Ctrl+Alt+Shift+W (Windows).

#12 Opening Documents

Opening QuarkXPress and PageMaker Files

InDesign CS4 can open files saved by PageMaker 6, QuarkXPress 3.3 and 4.1, and QuarkXPress Passport 4.1. To open files from later versions of QuarkXPress, try the Q2ID plug-in from Markzware (www.markzware.com).

It's easy to open files in InDesign—it's just like opening files in other applications. You can also use Adobe Bridge to open documents. Either way, you are likely to encounter some confusing alerts that you might not be sure how to handle. These alerts may warn you about missing fonts, missing graphic files, and missing profiles—external files that may be required to output the document correctly. Sometimes you can safely bypass these alerts, but other times you really need to pay attention to them.

To open documents:

1. Choose File > Open.

2. Locate and select the InDesign documents you want to open. You can select multiple documents by Command-clicking (Mac OS) or Ctrl-clicking (Windows) the files; Shift-click to select a continuous range of files.

3. At the bottom of the Open a File dialog box (**Figure 12a**), click Open Normal to simply open the selected documents or copies of selected templates.

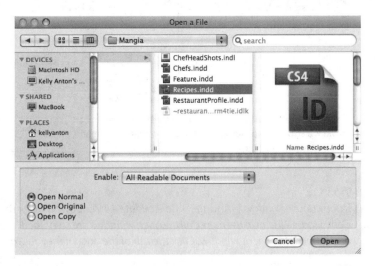

Figure 12a The Open a File dialog box lets you open original files or copies of files.

Tip

You can also click Open Original to open an InDesign template (rather than a copy of it). Click Open Copy to open a new, unnamed copy of selected documents or templates.

4. Click Open.

Fixing Graphic Links

When you import graphics into documents, InDesign keeps track of the location of those graphic files and the last-modified dates and times of those graphics. If you change or move the graphic files, InDesign notifies you when you open the document. If an alert (**Figure 12b**) reports Missing Links or Modified Links when you open a document, you can click Fix Links Automatically to find and update the graphic files. As with fonts, the original graphic files must be available for proper output. If, however, you're simply opening the document to edit text, you need not worry about the links. In that case, click Don't Fix. You can always update the links later using the Links panel (Window menu).

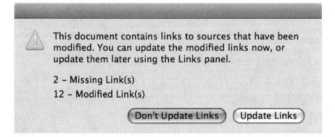

This document contains links to sources that have been modified. You can update the modified links now, or update them later using the Links panel.

2 – Missing Link(s)
12 – Modified Link(s)

Don't Update Links   Update Links

Figure 12b The Missing/Modified Links dialog box warns you if any imported graphic files are missing or have been edited.

Handling Missing Fonts

If the document uses fonts that are not active on your system, the Missing Fonts dialog box (**Figure 12c**) lists those fonts. The best way to handle this problem is to use a font management application—such as Extensis Suitcase Fusion or Linotype FontExplorer X—to activate the fonts listed. Your other option is to click Find Font to display the Find Font dialog box, which lets you replace missing fonts with active fonts and locate font files on your computer. Keep in mind that replacing missing fonts with different fonts can alter the design and cause text to flow differently. You can also bypass the Missing Fonts dialog box by clicking OK. InDesign will substitute a system font until you activate the appropriate fonts.

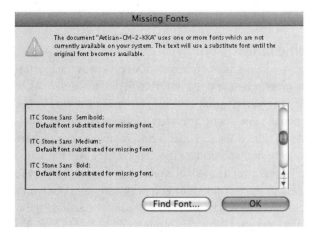

Figure 12c The Missing Fonts dialog box lists fonts used in the document that are not active on your system.

Handling Missing Color Profiles and Plug-Ins

When you open documents, sometimes you encounter alerts about missing color profiles and missing plug-ins. In general, it's OK to ignore alerts about missing color profiles. If you're working in a color-managed environment, however, talk to your systems administrator. If you receive an alert about a missing plug-in, often you can open the document anyway. If the document requires the plug-in, you must obtain and install it to open the document (see #7 for more information).

#13 Saving Documents and Templates

InDesign automatically saves your work and recovers it even if the program unexpectedly quits. Nonetheless, once you create a new document, it's a good idea to name and save it so you know where the file is and what it's called. If you're designing a *template*—a predesigned starting place for a new project—you can save a document as a write-protected template. When you open a template, a new, unnamed, and unsaved InDesign document is created.

Saving Documents

To save the active document:

- To save a new, unnamed document, choose File > Save or File > Save As. Use the Save As dialog box to specify a name and location for the file.

- To save a copy of the document, choose File > Save a Copy. Use the Save a Copy dialog box to specify a different name or location for the file. The active document remains open; you must open the copy to work on it.

- To save your work in progress, choose File > Save at any time. Unlike some other applications, however, InDesign does not require you to save your work obsessively. Changes are automatically saved to a temporary file with the extension .idlk, which is created in the same folder where the document is saved. If InDesign crashes, changes are restored from this temporary file.

Creating Templates

A template is a document that serves as the "skeleton" for a new publication, so it should be as complete as possible. Start by reviewing the document to make sure it includes everything you might need in a template—master pages (preformatted pages), paragraph and character styles (for formatting text), page guides (for positioning objects), colors, and more.

To create a template:

1. Save the document and then choose File > Save As.

2. In the Save As dialog box (**Figure 13**), choose InDesign CS4 template from the Format menu (Mac OS) or Save As Type menu (Windows).

Downsaving Documents

If you need to share a document with an InDesign CS3 user, use File > Export to save the document in InDesign Interchange (INX) format. The InDesign CS3 user will need a free plug-in from Adobe to open the document (choose Help > Updates to locate the plug-in). Note that features from InDesign CS4 may not be faithfully reproduced in the downsaved document.

When working with InDesign, file extensions help you identify the primary file types:

- **.indd** for documents
- **.indt** for templates
- **.indl** for libraries (for storing objects)
- **.indb** for books (for managing multiple documents)

3. Specify a location for the file. If the template is for a workgroup, you might store it on a shared server.

4. Type a name for the template in the Save As field. To identify the file as a template, InDesign adds the file extension .indt.

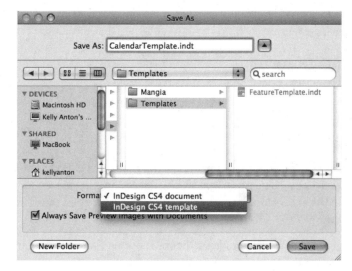

Figure 13 The Save As dialog box lets you name and save documents and templates.

Tip
To quickly create a document from a template, choose File > New > Document from Template or click From Template in the Create New area on the Welcome screen (Help > Welcome Screen). This takes you directly to your Templates folder; you can see the path to this folder at the top of the Adobe Bridge window. Be sure to save your templates in this folder on your hard drive for quick access.

Saving Metadata with Documents

Metadata is information stored with a file that helps you track who created it, who owns the copyright, what it's for, and what's in it. Documents with metadata are easier to find, especially when using Adobe Bridge to manage files—for example, you can save keywords with documents and then search for documents containing those keywords. To store metadata with the active document, choose File > File Info.

#14 Navigating Documents

InDesign offers many ways to navigate within a page or spread and to jump from page to page—so many, in fact, that you're unlikely to remember them all. The best thing to do is figure out your favorite way to navigate and then memorize it. If you're a visual person, for example, you may prefer the Pages panel or the Hand tool. If you're entering edits from hard copy, you may prefer to jump to specific page numbers.

Options for navigating to a specific page number include:

- Press Command+J (Mac OS) or Ctrl+J (Windows) to open the Go to Page dialog box. Type in the page number and press Return/Enter.

- Click the arrow next to the page box to display a list of page numbers to choose from (**Figure 14a**). You can also select the number in the page box, change it, and press Return/Enter.

- Double-click a page icon in the Pages panel, which displays thumbnail previews of the pages (see #82).

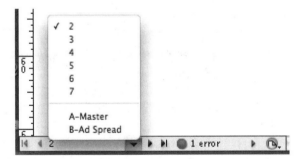

Figure 14a The page box/menu in the lower-left corner of the document window makes it easy to navigate to a specific page.

Options for navigating to different pages and spreads include:

- Use the Layout menu commands: First Page, Previous Page, Next Page, Last Page, Next Spread, Previous Spread, Go Back, and Go Forward. The keyboard shortcuts for these options display in the menu (the symbols shown in the shortcuts refer to the Page Up and Page Down keys on your keyboard).

Absolute Page Numbers

An absolute page number indicates a page's actual position in the document as opposed to the page number assigned to the page using the Numbering & Section Options dialog box (Pages panel menu). When you enter page numbers in fields—such as the Range field in the Print dialog box—you have the option of entering absolute page numbers. To enter an absolute page number, precede it with a plus sign. To jump to the first page of a document, for example, type +1 in the page box on the document window.

• Use the arrows on either side of the page box in the lower-left corner of the document window (**Figure 14b**). From left to right, the arrows work as follows: First Page/Spread, Previous Page/Spread, Next Page/Spread, and Last Page/Spread.

Figure 14b The arrows on either side of the page box let you quickly flip through the pages or spreads in a document.

Options for scrolling include:

• **Scroll bars:** Use the scroll bars in the document window.

• **Hand tool:** Select the Hand tool ![hand tool icon] in the Tools panel. Click and drag to navigate within a page or between pages and spreads. To use the Hand tool without actually switching tools, press the spacebar for temporary access to it. If the cursor is blinking in text, press Option (Mac OS) or Alt (Windows) along with the spacebar.

• **Power zoom:** When using the Hand tool, you can "power zoom." Hold down the mouse button to display a red box that you can drag up and down through the pages (**Figure 14c**). Use the arrow keys on the keyboard to resize the red box. When you release the mouse button, the document window returns to its original zoom percentage.

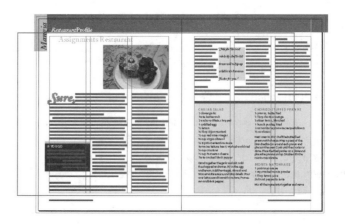

Figure 14c When power zooming, drag the red box to zoom and scroll.

#15 Viewing Documents

To view anything, from a snapshot of an entire document to the curves of an individual character, InDesign lets you adjust the zoom level from 5 percent to 4,000 percent. You can adjust the zoom level—also referred to as magnification or view scale—using a variety of methods. In addition to changing the zoom level, you can control the quality of the display and preview various output options such as bleeds.

Adjusting the Zoom Level

Options for adjusting the zoom level include:

- Select the value in the Zoom Level field in the Application bar. Type in a magnification value and press Return/Enter.

- Click the arrow next to the Zoom Level field to display a menu of zoom percentages to choose from (**Figure 15a**).

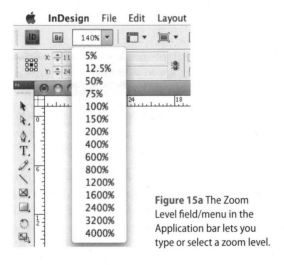

Figure 15a The Zoom Level field/menu in the Application bar lets you type or select a zoom level.

- Choose options from the View menu: Zoom In, Zoom Out, Fit Page in Window, Fit Spread in Window, Actual Size, or Entire Pasteboard. The keyboard commands for these options display in the menu—it's worthwhile to memorize those you use most.

Accessing the Zoom Level Field

On Mac OS, if you hide the Application bar (Window > Application Bar), the Zoom Level field displays on the document window. You can use the shortcut Command+Option+5 to select the Zoom Level field. Then, type a new value and press Return. With this method, you can enter a specific zoom value without removing your hands from the keyboard.

- Select the Zoom tool [🔍] in the Tools panel. Click the Zoom tool on the page to zoom in; each click increases the magnification to the next increment in the Zoom menu (5%, 12.5%, 25%, 50%, 75%, 100%, 150%, etc.). Click and drag to zoom in on a specific area. To zoom out, press the Option key (Mac OS) or Alt key (Windows) while the Zoom tool is selected.

Adjusting the Display Quality

If you feel like pages display too slowly or what you see onscreen looks jagged, you may need to adjust the display quality. You can customize the quality of the display to make it redraw faster or provide more detail. To change the quality, choose an option from the View > Display Performance submenu:

- **Fast Display:** Specifies 24 dpi screen resolution with no transparency; this view is helpful for users with slower computers who may simply need to edit text.

- **Typical Display:** Specifies 72 dpi screen resolution with low-resolution transparency; this view balances speed with quality for most layout work.

- **High Quality Display:** Specifies 144 dpi screen resolution and detailed transparency effects such as drop shadows and feathering; this view is useful for soft proofing—attempting to proof color output onscreen.

You can customize the default display quality in the Display Performance panel in the Preferences dialog box. In addition, if Preserve Object Level Display Settings is checked in the Display Performance submenu (View menu), you can customize the display on an object-by-object basis. To do this, select an object and choose Object > Display Performance. You might, for example, specify High Quality for a specific transparency effect so you can view the text behind it.

Previewing Output

The View menu also provides options for previewing final output:

- **Overprint Preview:** Choose this option to see how spot colors interact with any transparency effects.

- **Proof Setup and Proof Colors:** Use these options when soft proofing (judging colors onscreen). The success of soft proofing depends largely on the quality of your monitor, whether you are using color management (see #77 for more information), and your experience with printing and production processes.

- **Screen Mode:** Use options in the Screen Mode submenu to switch among Normal, Preview, Bleed, and Slug modes. Preview mode hides all nonprinting page elements such as guides and hidden characters so you can see how pages will look when printed. The Bleed and Slug modes both hide nonprinting page elements but show objects in the Bleed or Slug area as defined in the New Document or Document Setup dialog box.

Tip
*You can quickly switch among modes using the Screen Mode buttons at the bottom of the Tools panel and the Screen Mode menu on the Application bar (**Figure 15b**).*

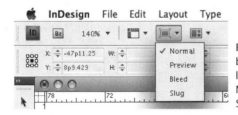

Figure 15b The Screen Mode buttons in the Application bar let you quickly switch among Normal, Preview, Bleed, and Slug modes.

Actual Size

To quickly display a document at 100 percent, or Actual Size, double-click the Zoom tool in the Tools panel. You can also press Command+1 (Mac OS) or Ctrl+1 (Windows).

CHAPTER THREE

Working with Text

InDesign can do everything from serving as your primary word processor to importing text from other programs to automatically applying specialized formatting. In InDesign, text is placed inside text frames or it flows along type paths, both of which can be any size and any shape. Text frames and type paths can be linked (or *threaded*) to each other to flow text through a document.

When it comes to formatting text, you have a variety of options for applying character and paragraph attributes, including *character styles or paragraph styles* for automated formatting. InDesign also provides expert options for setting tabs, creating bulleted and numbered lists, and inserting variable text such as dates and cross references. For word processing, InDesign provides a story editor, spell check features, and search-and-replace functions.

In this chapter you'll learn how to create text frames and type paths, and then how to add, format, and edit text.

#16 Creating Text Frames

Most of the text you see in an InDesign layout—headlines, articles, figure captions, ad copy, and so on—is contained by invisible, rectangular text frames. You can, however, draw text frames of any shape, and you can use the master text frame you specify in the New Document dialog box.

Drawing Text Frames

To create a rectangular text frame, select the Type tool T on the Tools panel. Click and drag to draw a text frame. Use the width and height values shown in the gray box and the rulers to judge the size and placement of the text frame (**Figure 16a**).

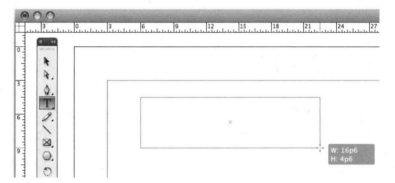

Figure 16a While dragging the Type tool to create a rectangular text frame, you can use the values shown in the gray box and the rulers to judge its size and placement.

To create a round or irregularly shaped text frame, use any of the drawing tools (see #49 for more information). Then, simply click it with the Type tool to enter text (**Figure 16b**). You can also click any frame using the Selection tool or Direct Selection tool and choose Object > Content > Text to convert it to a text frame.

Note

If clicking a frame with the Type tool doesn't convert it to a text frame, check Type Tool Converts Frames to Text Frames in the Type pane of the Preferences dialog box.

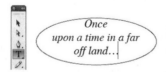

Figure 16b To place text in a round text frame, draw an elliptical graphics frame with the Ellipse Frame tool, click it with the Type tool, and then start typing.

Using the Master Text Frame

If you're importing long blocks of text onto pages—for a book chapter or annual report, for example—you don't have to draw a text frame on each page. You can automatically place a text frame on each document page by checking Master Text Frame in the New Document dialog box (File > New > Document, **Figure 16c**). The values in the Columns areas control the number of columns in the master text frame and the amount of space between columns (the gutter). The master text frame is placed within the boundaries specified in the Margins area.

To enter text in the master text frame on document pages, first select the Type tool. Then, Command+Shift-click (Mac OS) or Ctrl+Shift-click (Windows) the text frame to select it.

Note

The master text frame is placed on pages based on the default master page, A-Master. If you create new master pages, they will contain the master text frame as well (although you can delete it). See #78 for more information about master pages.

Creating Squares and Circles

To create a square text frame, press the Shift key as you drag the Type tool. This constrains the Type tool to creating text frames with four sides of equal length. Similarly, press the Shift key as you drag the Ellipse Frame tool to create a circle.

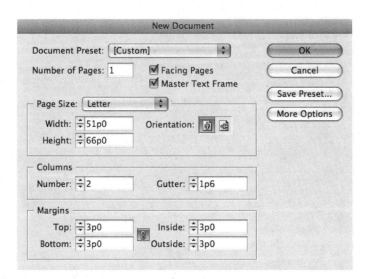

Figure 16c Checking Master Text Frame in the New Document dialog box automatically places a text frame on document pages according to the values in the Columns and Margins areas.

#17 Modifying Text Frames

So what good are text frames, considering that you can't see them? While their primary purpose is to contain text, you can also modify text frames to complement your layout. A magazine article, for example, generally features a rectangular text frame with a stroke around it, two or three columns of text inset from the edges of the stroke, and possibly a fill (background color). To achieve these effects, you can control the positioning of text within text frames (specifying the number of columns, for example), and you can format text frames like any other object (applying a stroke, fill, and drop shadow, for example). To format text frames, select them with the Type tool, the Selection tool, or the Direct Selection tool.

Columns versus Column Guides

When you create a new document, you can specify columns for the pages regardless of whether you use the master text frame. If you don't use the master text frame, InDesign simply draws column guides on the pages that you can use however you want. On the other hand, if you do use the master text frame, it will reflect the number of columns you specified. You can change the columns for a selected text frame at any time.

Setting Up Columns

To modify the number of columns in a text frame, select the frame and choose Object > Text Frame Options. Options in the Columns area in the General tab (**Figure 17a**) work as follows:

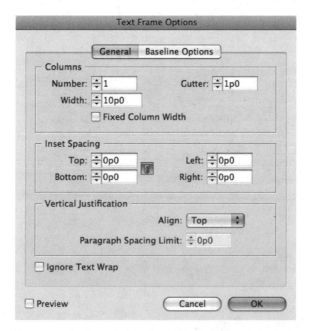

Figure 17a The General tab in the Text Frame Options dialog box lets you specify the position of text within the frame.

1. Enter the number of columns for the text frame in the Number field and the amount of space you want between columns in the Gutter field.

2. If you want the columns to be a specific width, enter a value in the Width field. You don't have to be a math wiz here—if the number of columns, the width, and the gutter you specify won't fit in the text frame, InDesign will automatically adjust the text frame.

3. Check Fixed Column Width to keep the width of the columns the same—even if the text frame is resized. Rather than adjusting column width, InDesign will change the number of columns and the frame will be automatically resized to accommodate the specified column width. For example, suppose you try to make a two-column text frame a tiny bit wider. If Fixed Column Width is checked, when you widen the frame, it will automatically jump from two columns to three columns in width.

Specifying Text Inset and Vertical Alignment

The General tab in the Text Frame Options dialog box also lets you adjust the amount of space between the edges of a text frame and the text. The need for this value is not apparent, however, until you apply a stroke to the edges of a frame and realize that the text is touching the stroke. To adjust text inset, type values in the Top, Bottom, Left, and Right fields in the Inset Spacing area.

Note

For nonrectangular text frames, such as elliptical text frames, you can specify only one inset value.

InDesign provides even more control over the placement of text relative to the top and bottom of the frame. You can specify how lines of the text are placed vertically using the Vertical Justification area in the General tab in the Text Frame Options dialog box. For example, you can specify that text is centered vertically within the frame—an option that works well for cards, invitations, ads, and so on.

Changing Columns

The Control panel provides a quick method for experimenting with columns. When a text frame is selected using the Selection tool or the Direct Selection tool, the far right side of the Control panel provides a Number of Columns field and Gutter field. If you're not sure which field is which, point at them with the mouse to display their tool tips.

Formatting Text Frames

To make a text frame visible in a design, you can apply a stroke to its edges, apply a fill or gradient to its background, add a drop shadow, and more. For more information, see #61, #62, and #63.

Using the Baseline Grid

A baseline grid consists of horizontal lines that text "sits" on. Setting up a baseline grid for an entire document or an individual text frame makes it easy to align text horizontally across columns regardless of varying leading and spacing values before and after paragraphs. Generally, the distance specified between gridlines in the baseline grid is the same as the leading value for body text (around 12 points, for example). Some graphic designers swear by the baseline grid for carefully positioning text, whereas others sneer at its use, likening it to a paint-by-the-numbers painting.

You can set up a baseline grid for a document in the Grids pane in the Preferences dialog box. In addition, you can use the Baseline Options tab in the Text Frame Options dialog box to set up grids for individual text frames. Once you set up a baseline grid, you still need to "snap" paragraphs to it by selecting them and clicking Align to Baseline Grid in the Paragraph panel or Control panel (**Figure 17b**). The View > Grids & Guides submenu lets you show and hide the baseline grid.

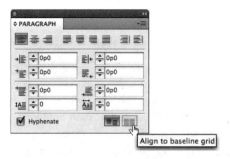

Figure 17b When you choose Show Options from the Paragraph panel menu, the Align to Baseline Grid button displays in the lower-right corner.

#**18** Threading Text Frames

Right away you'll notice that all your text doesn't always fit into one frame. Plus, you may not want all your text crammed into a single frame. To solve this dilemma, InDesign lets you link text frames to each other through a process called *threading*. When text frames are threaded, one long block of text—such as a newspaper story or a series of one-paragraph catalog descriptions—flows from one frame to the next.

All the text within a series of threaded frames is referred to as a *story*. Working with a story—as opposed to multiple unthreaded text frames containing text—has many advantages. You can edit stories in the Story Editor; limit a spell check or search-and-replace function to only the text in a story; or select all the text in a story to reformat it, export it, or copy and paste it. All the advantages of working with stories make threading text frames particularly important.

You can thread two or more empty text frames, and you can thread text frames to an existing frame. You cannot, however, add text frames that already contain text to a thread. Unlike other text-related activities, which require the Type tool, you thread text frames using the Selection tool or the Direct Selection tool.

Preparing to Thread

To start threading text frames, you need to be able to see them to understand what you're doing. Choose View > Show Frame Edges to see outlines of the text frames. Then, choose View > Show Text Threads so you can see the links between frames. With the Selection tool, click a text frame to make its *in port* and its *out port* visible (**Figure 18a**). You'll use these ports to link one text frame to another.

Viewing Text Threads

To see existing text threads in a document, choose View > Show Text Threads.

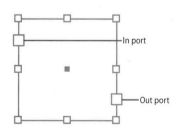

Figure 18a The upper-left corner of each text frame contains an in port and the lower-right corner contains an out port.

Threading Two Frames

To thread text frames, click the out port of the first text frame and then click the in port of the second text frame.

1. To thread two existing text frames, click the Selection tool or the Direct Selection tool.

2. Click the text frame you want to start threading from—this frame may or may not contain text.

3. Click the text frame's out port in the lower-right corner; the loaded text icon ▦ displays.

4. Navigate to the second text frame, even if it's on another page. When the cursor is over another text frame, the thread icon 🔗 displays.

5. Using the thread icon, click anywhere in the text frame that you want to add to the thread (**Figure 18b**). In addition to clicking an existing text frame, you can also click and drag to create a new text frame that is threaded to the first frame.

6. Notice the line (or thread) between the two text frames (**Figure 18c**). To link additional text frames, repeat this process.

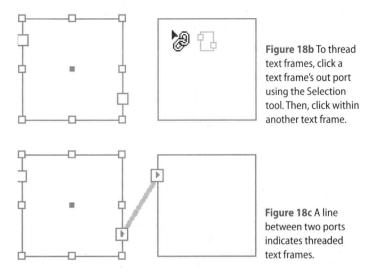

Figure 18b To thread text frames, click a text frame's out port using the Selection tool. Then, click within another text frame.

Figure 18c A line between two ports indicates threaded text frames.

Tip
Threading is not limited to text frames. You can thread type paths to each other, thread type paths to text frames, and thread text frames to type paths. For example, you can flow a headline along a type path and then thread it to a text frame containing an article.

Working with Threaded Text Frames

Once you thread text frames, you're not stuck with the sequence you've created—you can add frames within a thread, reroute threads, delete threaded text frames without losing text, and break threads.

- **To insert a text frame** into a series of threaded frames, simply click the out port of the preceding text frame and click in the new text frame.

- **To reroute threads**, click an out port and then click in the frame to which you want to reroute the text.

- **To delete a frame** within a series of threaded text frames, select it and choose Edit > Clear. Text is automatically reflowed into the remaining threaded text frames. Deleting a text frame from a series of threaded frames does not delete the text within the frame.

- **To break a text thread**, double-click an out port or an in port. The thread between the two text frames will be broken, and the text after the broken thread will become overset (see the Overset Text sidebar).

The master text frame, specified in the New Document dialog box (File > New > Document), is automatically threaded from page to page.

Adding Pages While Flowing Text

InDesign CS4 introduces auto-page insertion similar to the behavior of QuarkXPress. When you import or type text into a master text frame, additional pages are automatically added to contain all the text. The new pages are based on the existing master page. To create a master text frame, check Master Text Frame in the New Document dialog box. (You can also thread text frames on master pages to create additional auto-flow text frames.) To confirm that the feature is enabled, make sure Smart Text Reflow is enabled in the Type pane of the Preferences dialog box.

Overset Text

If you import or enter more text into a text frame than the frame can hold, the text you can't see is referred to as *overset text*. A small red plus sign in a text frame's out port indicates overset text. Generally, overset text is considered a bad thing that needs to be fixed. In fact, by default InDesign's preflight tools will warn you to resolve this problem. To fix overset text, try one of the following:

- Enlarge the text frame.
- Thread the text frame to other frames.
- Choose Edit > Select All to select all the text, and then decrease the font size.
- Edit the text in the Story Editor (Edit > Edit in Story Editor). The Story Editor displays all the text and indicates where the overset text begins.

#**19** Creating Type Paths

Text is not restricted to placement inside frames: You can flow text along any shape path, including along a straight line, a curved line, or a circle or square. Once text is on the path, you can create special effects by flipping the text, creating a stair-step or rainbow effect with the characters, and more (**Figure 19a**).

Figure 19a Using the Type on a Path tool, we flowed text along a line formatted with a stroke and tint.

Placing Type on a Path

You can use any InDesign object, created with any tool, as a type path. Simply draw the shape and fill it or apply a stroke to it if you want (see Chapter 5 and Chapter 7 for information about drawing and formatting objects). Once you have a path, click and hold the Type tool to display a pop-out menu, and then select the Type on a Path tool (**Figure 19b**).

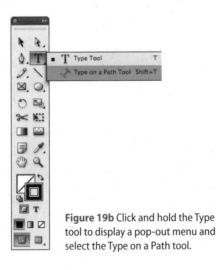

Figure 19b Click and hold the Type tool to display a pop-out menu and select the Type on a Path tool.

With the Type on a Path tool selected, click the path where you want to start the text. While this sounds simple, it works only when the cursor is directly over a path and a plus sign is displayed next to it (**Figure 19c**). Once the blinking text insertion point displays, start typing to add text. Change the font, size, color, alignment, and indents as usual (see #23 for more information).

Figure 19c To create type on a path, select the Type on a Path tool and point at a path. When a plus sign (+) is displayed to the right of the cursor, click to start adding text to the path.

In addition to typing to add text to a path, you can import a text file (File > Place) or you can paste text from the clipboard. You can use either the Type on a Path tool or the Type tool to work with type on a path.

Positioning Type on a Path

To create various effects, you can control where the text is placed relative to the path. Select the path with either the Selection tool or the Type on a Path tool and choose Type > Type on a Path > Options. The Type on a Path Options dialog box lets you choose a special effect for the characters, change how the text aligns with the path, adjust the spacing of characters, flip the text to the opposite side of the path, and more (**Figure 19d**).

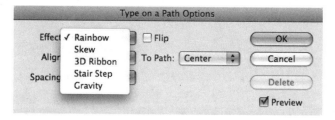

Figure 19d The Type on a Path Options dialog box lets you control how text is oriented to the path, including creating special effects, such as Rainbow, with the characters.

Creating Margins for Type on a Path

When you create type on a path, you can specify the boundaries, or margins, for the text. To do this, click and drag the Type on a Path tool on the path rather than simply clicking it. As you drag, blue brackets display to indicate the start and endpoints of the type path.

To adjust where text starts on the path, click the path with the Selection tool. Notice the blue bracket on each end of the text. These are similar to text frame edges in that they establish the left margin and the right margin for the text. You can drag these brackets with the Selection tool to reposition the start point or endpoint of text on the path (**Figure 19e**). There is also a center bracket, which you can drag across the path to flip text to the other side of the path or along the path to move all the text.

Tip

You may need to zoom in to see and select the brackets.

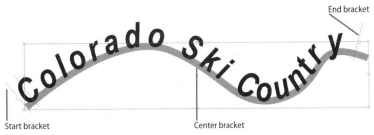

End bracket

Start bracket   Center bracket

Figure 19e To change the starting position of text on a path, drag the start bracket to the left of the text. You can also drag the end bracket to compress the text area.

Deleting Type on a Path

If you decide you no longer want type on a path, you can simply select the text and delete it. When the path is selected with the Selection tool or Direct Selection tool, you can choose Type > Type on a Path > Delete Type from Path. The text is deleted but the path remains on the page. If you don't want to keep the type or the object, select the object and press Delete or Backspace.

#20 Importing Text

Since most people compose documents in word processors, InDesign makes it easy to import Microsoft Word files and other text files. When importing text, you can customize how the text is imported (with or without formatting, for example), and you have several options for flowing it through a document. You can do almost anything from importing raw text with no formatting to bringing in fully formatted text that includes inline graphics, tables, a table of contents, an index, and footnotes.

Placing a Text File

You can import text into an existing frame or type path—the frame doesn't even have to be a text frame because InDesign will automatically convert it. In addition, you can "load" the cursor with the imported text and create a new text frame. To import a text file:

1. If you want to import text into an existing object, select the Type tool or the Type on a Path tool. Click in the frame or on the text path that you want to contain the text. Otherwise, you can select any tool—just make sure no objects are selected.

   Note
   To flow text into the master text frame, press Command+Shift (Mac OS) or Ctrl+Shift (Windows) to select it.

2. Choose File > Place. In the Place dialog box (**Figure 20**), locate and select the Microsoft Word or text file.

   Tip
   You can select multiple files to import. To select a range of files, Shift+click the first and last file. To select noncontinuous files, Command+click (Mac OS) or Ctrl+click (Windows) the files. InDesign will "load" the cursor with all the selected text files and let you place them one after the other.

3. To customize how the text is imported, check Show Import Options. This gives you control over which formats and other elements are imported with the text.

4. If the selected frame contains text or a graphic and you want to replace it, check Replace Selected Item. If you uncheck this option, InDesign loads the cursor so you can create a new text frame.

5. Click Open.

Supported Text File Formats

InDesign lets you import text files in .doc, .txt, and .rtf format. If you try to import a file from an unsupported version of Word, you will get an error message. Save the file as .rtf and reimport it—most of the formatting is still retained. InDesign also lets you import files from Microsoft Excel and in its own Adobe InDesign *Tagged Text* format. Tagged Text is exported from InDesign with proprietary tags that can be converted to actual formatting. Using Tagged Text is helpful for sharing formatted text among InDesign documents.

If the Missing Font alert displays when you import text, you can click OK to bypass the alert if you plan to use formatting specified in InDesign. If, however, you plan to use the formatting in the file, note which fonts are missing and activate them using your font manager. You can also click the Find Font button to replace the fonts with active fonts.

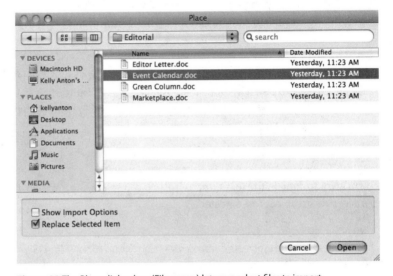

Figure 20 The Place dialog box (File menu) lets you select files to import.

Tip
In addition to using the Place command (File menu), InDesign lets you import both text and graphics files by dragging file icons from your computer desktop onto a page. If a frame is selected, the text or graphic is imported into the frame. If nothing is selected, a text frame is automatically created roughly where you drop the file.

Setting Import Options

If you check Show Import Options in the Place dialog box, the Microsoft Word Import Options or Text Import Options dialog box displays. For Microsoft Word, you can use this dialog box to control whether the table of contents, inline graphics, formatting, and styles are imported along with the text and to resolve any style conflicts. In addition, you can map styles in the Word document to styles in the InDesign document, automating formatting to some degree. For text files, you can clean up the text by removing extra paragraph returns and specifying other options.

Selecting Text

To select text using the Type tool or the Type on a Path tool, click and drag the mouse. Other options include:

- Click twice in a word to select it.

- Click three times to select a line.

- Click four times to select a paragraph.

- Choose Edit > Select All to select the entire active story.

> **Tip**
> *You can also select a range of text starting from the insertion point to another point in the text. Click in the text and then Shift-click in another location, and the range of text is selected.*

Editing Text

When text is selected, you can use standard Edit menu commands to Cut, Copy, and Paste the text to different locations. In addition, you can use the mouse to drag and drop text to different locations. Drag and drop is on by default for text in the Story Editor but off for text in layouts. To turn it on, open the Preferences dialog box, select the Type pane, and check Enable in Layout View in the Drag and Drop Text Editing area.

To drag and drop text, first select it. Then, point at the text with the mouse to display the drag-and-drop icon ►T. Drag the text to a new location indicated by the insertion point, and release the mouse button to drop it. When dragging and dropping text, you can create a new text frame or drop a copy of the text.

- To create a new frame for the text, press Command (Mac OS) or Ctrl (Windows) while you click and drag to create a new frame.

- To drop a copy of selected text, press Option (Mac OS) or Alt (Windows) when you release the mouse button to drop the text.

Triple-Clicking to Select Paragraphs

If you rarely select a single line but often select entire paragraphs, you can streamline the paragraph-selection process. In the Type pane in the Preferences dialog box, uncheck Triple Click to Select a Line. When this option is unchecked, clicking three times selects a paragraph (rather than a line).

#22 Applying Character and Paragraph Attributes

Modifying the Basic Paragraph Style

When you start typing in a new text frame or on a new type path, InDesign applies the formatting specified in the default paragraph style, which is called Basic Paragraph. To modify the Basic Paragraph style, double-click it in the Paragraph Styles panel (Type menu). Make any changes and click OK. When no documents are open, changes you make to the Basic Paragraph style apply to all new documents. When a document is active, changes affect only that document.

Here's where the fun starts—you get to start picking fonts, sizes, styles, and alignment to jazz up your text. InDesign's text formatting comes in two distinct flavors: character attributes and paragraph attributes. Character attributes are attributes such as font and type size that you can apply to individual characters. In fact, each character in a document can have its own unique formatting, although this sort of ransom-note style is not generally what graphic designers are aiming for. Paragraph attributes are attributes such as indents and tabs that apply to entire paragraphs as opposed to individual characters. (If you can't tell where paragraphs begin and end, choose Type > Show Hidden Characters and look for the paragraph symbol ¶.)

Character attributes and paragraph attributes generally work together to complement the actual content. For example, weekly newsmagazines often use serif fonts and justified text to indicate authority, whereas an invitation to a fundraiser might be centered in a script font for an elegant look. While character attributes account for the basic look of text—size, serif or sans serif font, style—the formatting you apply to paragraphs largely controls the "color" of the type. This is not literally "color" as in whether it's black or blue, but the overall appearance (or value) of the type when you glance at a document or even look at it upside down. Are the blocks of text light and airy or dark and dense? Paragraph attributes achieve these results by controlling alignment, indents, space between paragraphs, hyphenation and justification, and more.

Applying Character Attributes

To apply character attributes, select the text using the Type tool. Or, you can simply click in a text frame or on a type path and set character attributes. The attributes will be applied when you start typing. All the character attributes are available in the Control panel's character options (**Figure 22a**). If you're not sure what an option does, point at it with the mouse to display its tool tip. Additional character formatting options are available in the Control panel menu.

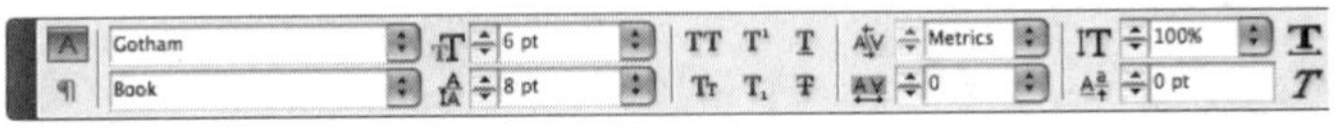

Figure 22a The character options in the Control panel (shown abbreviated here) provide quick access to all the character formatting controls available in InDesign.

If you prefer to work with the Character panel (Type menu), it offers a convenient place to specify basics: Font, Size, Leading, Kerning, and Tracking. Choose Show Options from the panel menu to expand the panel with more advanced options such as horizontal or vertical scaling and skewing (**Figure 22b**). The remaining character formatting options are available in the panel menu as well. The only character attributes you won't find here are color and stroke (see #33 for more information).

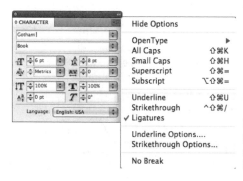

Figure 22b The Character panel (Type menu) provides comprehensive character formatting controls.

Applying Paragraph Attributes

To apply paragraph attributes, use the Type tool and click in a paragraph to select it or select multiple paragraphs. All the paragraph attributes are available in the Control panel's paragraph options (**Figure 22c**). If you're not sure what an option is, point at it with the mouse to display its tool tip. Additional paragraph formatting options are available in the panel menu. Most of the paragraph attributes are similar to those available in a word processor. InDesign, however, has a superior method of *composing* type, which is explained in #23.

Figure 22c The paragraph options in the Control panel (shown abbreviated here) provide quick access to all the paragraph formatting controls available in InDesign.

In addition to using the paragraph options in the Control panel, you can use the Paragraph panel (Type menu). At its default size, it offers only alignment and indent controls, but you can choose Show Options from the panel menu to display more paragraph formatting controls.

What Is Leading?

The vertical distance between lines of text in a paragraph—called *leading*—is usually specified as a paragraph attribute. In InDesign, however, it's applied to characters. On the one hand, this is nice because most of the time you will modify size and leading in relation to each other—and in InDesign, the Font Size and Leading fields are next to each other so you can tab between them. On the other hand, the reason leading is usually applied as a paragraph attribute is that most of the time you want a consistent amount of space between lines in a paragraph. You don't want the space to vary based on individual characters.

InDesign offers the best of both worlds. While you always set leading as a character attribute, you can make it a paragraph attribute by checking Apply Leading to Entire Paragraphs in the Type pane in the Preferences dialog box.

#23 Composing Type

Many of InDesign's character and paragraph formatting options are familiar to you from using a word processor—or even your e-mail program. But what really sets InDesign apart is its sophisticated method of text composition—of adjusting spacing and hyphenation to achieve evenly spaced type in a paragraph. The method is called the Adobe Paragraph Composer, and it works by considering spacing, hyphenation, and line breaks in all the lines in a paragraph in relation to each other. By contrast, the Adobe Single-line Composer and most other programs consider only one line at a time (**Figure 23a**).

Adobe Single-line Composer	Adobe Paragraph Composer
What really sets InDesign apart is its sophisticated method of text composition—of adjusting spacing and hyphenation to achieve evenly spaced type in a paragraph. The method is called the Adobe Paragraph Composer, and it works by considering spacing, hyphenation, and line breaks in all the lines in a paragraph in relation to each other. By contrast, the Adobe Single-line Composer and most other programs consider only one line at a time.	What really sets InDesign apart is its sophisticated method of text composition—of adjusting spacing and hyphenation to achieve evenly spaced type in a paragraph. The method is called the Adobe Paragraph Composer, and it works by considering spacing, hyphenation, and line breaks in all the lines in a paragraph in relation to each other. By contrast, the Adobe Single-line Composer and most other programs consider only one line at a time.

Figure 23a Although the difference between the Adobe Paragraph Composer and the Adobe Single-line Composer is subtle, the single-line method is more likely to produce inconsistent spacing. In this example, you can see that the Single-line Composer produces a much rougher right rag—with some lines nearly touching the margins and gaping holes after other lines—than the Adobe Paragraph Composer. When text is justified, you'll notice the difference in spaces between words.

The three primary factors affecting composition—Hyphenation, Justification, and Composer—are all paragraph attributes, and they are discussed here.

Hyphenation

InDesign gives you far more control over automatic hyphenation than just turning it on and off for a paragraph. You can specify a limit to the number of lines in a row that end in hyphens, whether capitalized words can be hyphenated, the minimum number of letters a word must have to be hyphenated, the number of letters that must precede and follow a hyphen, and more. While these decisions affect the look of the text, they also have editorial implications, so you may want to set them with the help of an editor. For example, whether capitalized words should be hyphenated is often covered in the publisher's style guide and is not at the designer's discretion.

To set hyphenation, first select paragraphs with the Type tool. Then, choose Hyphenation from the Paragraph panel menu (Type > Paragraph) or from the Control panel menu when paragraph options are displayed. The Hyphenation Settings dialog box (**Figure 23b**) lets you customize settings for the selected paragraphs. To see how changes affect the paragraphs, check the Preview box.

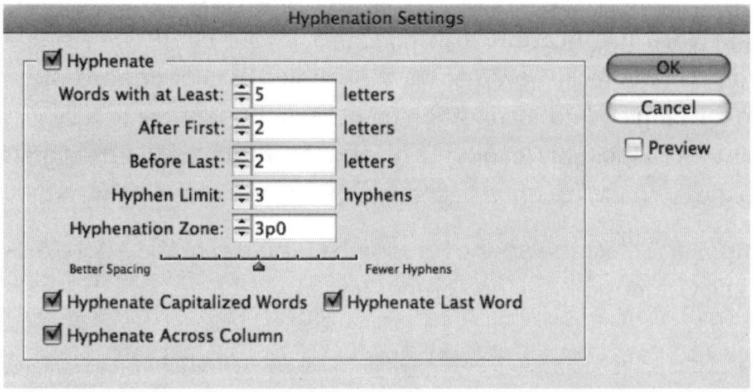

Figure 23b The Hyphenation Settings dialog box provides a slider for striking a balance between Better Spacing and Fewer Hyphens.

Tip
The paragraph options in the Control panel provides a Hyphenate check box so you can quickly turn hyphenation on and off.

Setting Justification

The Justification settings in InDesign control how spacing is adjusted in justified text, the leading, and which composition method is used. To set hyphenation, first select paragraphs with the Type tool. Then, choose Justification from the Paragraph panel menu (Type > Paragraph) or from the Control panel menu when paragraph options are displayed. In the Justification dialog box (**Figure 23c**), be sure to check Preview so you can see how your settings affect the text.

Use the Single-line Composer

Because the Adobe Paragraph Composer is continually considering spacing and line breaks throughout a paragraph, typing in a paragraph with it on can be slow and disconcerting. Text is continually reflowing, making it hard to concentrate on the words. To prevent this, edit the text in the Story Editor, which does not compose as you type (see #29).

- **Word Spacing, Letter Spacing, and Glyph Scaling:** These fields control how spacing is adjusted and how characters are scaled when justifying text. (Therefore, these values do not apply to paragraphs that are right, left, or center aligned—only justified.)

- **Auto Leading:** This field controls the amount of space between lines in the selected paragraphs—if they use auto leading. The value is a percentage of the type size in use. So, if the Font Size is 10 points, and Auto Leading is 120%, the Leading is set to 12 points.

- **Single Word Justification:** In justified text, if a line consists of a single word, you can specify how that word is handled by choosing an option from the Single Word Justification menu. Your options are to fully justify the word (possibly leading to giant gaps within the word), align it with the left margin, center it, or align it with the right margin.

- **Composer:** Select the Adobe Paragraph Composer or the Adobe Single-line Composer from the Composer menu.

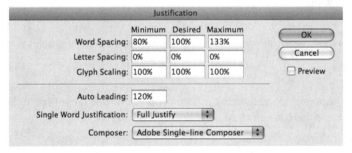

Figure 23c The Justification dialog box lets you fine-tune the spacing within justified paragraphs.

Choosing a Composition Method

When paragraphs are selected with the Type tool, you can choose the Adobe Paragraph Composer or the Adobe Single-line Composer from the Control panel menu. You can also choose a composition method from the Composer menu in the Justification dialog box. The Adobe Paragraph Composer generally leads to better spacing, particularly in justified paragraphs.

#24 Creating Bulleted and Numbered Lists

Lists are a great way to break up blocks of text and keep the reader interested with quick bits of information (**Figure 24a**). With features similar to those in Microsoft Word, InDesign makes it easy to create bulleted and numbered lists automatically. The feature, called Bullets and Numbering, is actually lifted from PageMaker. Aside from saving you the time of entering a bullet or number for each paragraph, formatting it, and specifying a tab and indent, the Bullets and Numbering feature creates lists that are easy to edit. For example, as you add paragraphs, bullets are added or numbers are inserted as necessary.

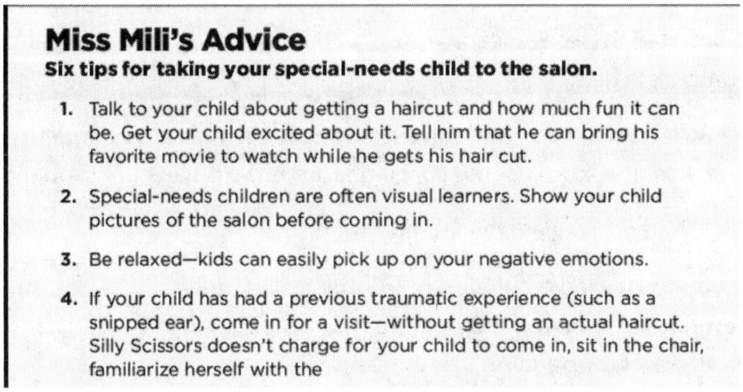

Miss Mili's Advice
Six tips for taking your special-needs child to the salon.

1. Talk to your child about getting a haircut and how much fun it can be. Get your child excited about it. Tell him that he can bring his favorite movie to watch while he gets his hair cut.

2. Special-needs children are often visual learners. Show your child pictures of the salon before coming in.

3. Be relaxed—kids can easily pick up on your negative emotions.

4. If your child has had a previous traumatic experience (such as a snipped ear), come in for a visit—without getting an actual haircut. Silly Scissors doesn't charge for your child to come in, sit in the chair, familiarize herself with the

Figure 24a Clicking the Numbered List button in the Command Bar (Window> Object & Layout) created this list.

To create a bulleted or numbered list:

1. Select the paragraphs with the Type tool.

2. Display the paragraph options in the Control panel.

3. Click the Bulleted List button or the Numbered List button to apply the default formatting.

4. To fine tune the formatting of the list, keep the paragraphs selected and choose Bullets and Numbering from the Control panel menu.

5. In the Bullets and Numbering dialog box (**Figure 24b**), if you need to change a bulleted list to a numbered list or vice versa, choose an option from the List Type menu at the top: Bullets or Numbers.

Customizing Bullets and Numbers

When you click the Bulleted List or Numbered List button on the Command Bar or the Control panel, the default list formatting is applied. To open the Bullets and Numbering dialog box while creating the list, Option-click (Mac OS) or Alt-click (Windows) the Bulleted List or Numbered List button. (To open the Command Bar, choose Window > Object & Layout > Command Bar.)

6. Decide on the format of the bullets or numbers your list will use:

- **Bullets:** Select an option from the Bullet Character area or click Add to access other bullet characters (including bullet characters in other fonts). Use the Text After field and pop-out menu to specify the characters to follow the bullet (such as an em space or tab).

- **Numbers:** When defining a numbered list, you can specify a format (Arabic or Roman numerals, for example), use the Number field to define separator characters (such as a period and a tab), and choose a starting number from the Mode menu.

- **Character Style:** You can choose a character style for bullets and numbers in lists.

7. In the Bullet or Number Position area, specify the Alignment, Indents, and Tab Position to adjust the spacing around the bullets or numbers.

8. Check Preview to review the list, and then click OK.

After you've created a bulleted or numbered list, you can change any of the settings by selecting the paragraphs and opening the Bullets and Numbering dialog box again.

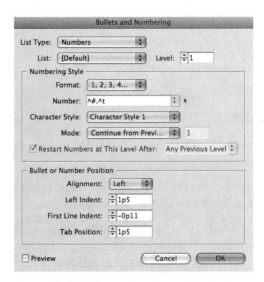

Figure 24b The Bullets and Numbering dialog box lets you customize the formatting of automatic bulleted and numbered lists.

#25 Setting Tabs

You're no doubt familiar with tabs from your typewriter days—if you are old enough to have experienced those days—but tabs are even more important in a page-layout environment. To align text, it's important to use tabs rather than spaces for precision alignment. Unlike characters on a typewriter, the width of characters and spaces in computer fonts can vary, making it impossible to precisely align text.

InDesign provides default tab settings at every half inch, but you're not stuck with those. You can override the default tabs and customize each tab stop by specifying how text aligns with it and adding *leader* characters (**Figure 25a**).

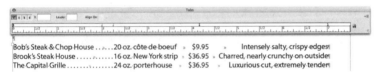

Figure 25a This text is divided into three columns with three different tab stops. The first tab stop is left aligned with a dot leader; the second tab stop aligns to the decimal point in the prices; the third tab stop is right-aligned.

Specifying Tab Stops

Tabs are paragraph attributes, so they apply to selected paragraphs rather than to individual lines selected within a paragraph or to selected characters. To set tabs:

1. Choose Type > Show Hidden Characters to view tab characters in text. They look like double arrows.

2. Select the Type tool.

3. Select the paragraphs for which you want to set tabs.

4. Choose Type > Tabs to open the Tabs panel.

5. Click one of the alignment buttons at top left to specify how text aligns with the tab stop: left-justified, center-justified, right-justified, or align to decimal. If you click align to decimal, you can actually specify any alignment character, such as a comma, in the Align On field at right.

6. If you want to fill the white space created by the tab with a repeated character, you can enter up to eight characters in the Leader field. For example, if you want periods to lead the eye from a table of contents entry to its page number, enter a period in the field. For more space between the periods, enter a period and a space.

7. Click above the ruler where you want to place the tab. The X field displays the position. Once you set a tab stop, all the default tab stops to the left of it are cleared.

Repeating a Tab Stop

If you want to create a series of tab stops that are a specific distance apart, you can use the Repeat command in the Tabs panel menu. For example, if you have a tab stop at .75 inches and you'd like another one at 1.5 inches, select the tab stop at .75 and choose Repeat. The alignment and any leader characters are copied as well.

Modifying Tab Stops

To modify a tab stop, click its icon on the tab ruler and change any of its settings (for example, click a different alignment button). To delete a tab stop, drag its icon off the ruler. To delete all tab stops, choose Clear All from the Tabs panel menu.

Creating a Right Indent Tab

InDesign provides a Right Indent Tab, which forces text over to the paragraph's right-indent value. The Right Indent Tab is particularly useful for positioning an "end of story" character or an author's initials (**Figure 25b**). To insert it, choose Type > Insert Special Character > Other > Right Indent Tab.

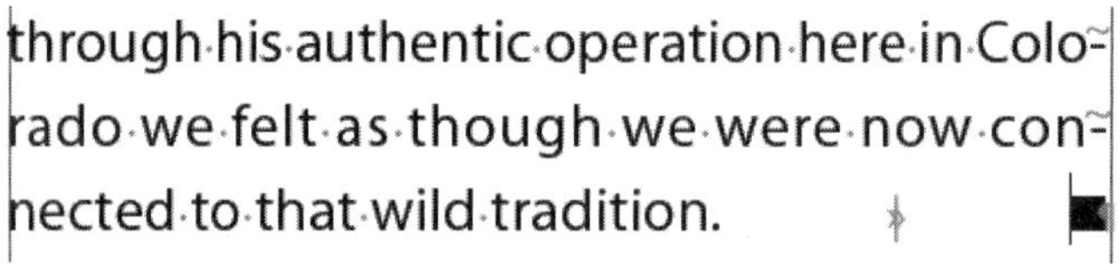
through his authentic operation here in Colo-
rado we felt as though we were now con-
nected to that wild tradition.

Figure 25b To automatically align an "end-of-story" character with the right-indent of the paragraph, insert a Right Indent Tab rather than a standard tab.

#26 Working with Fonts

As you no doubt know from working on a computer, fonts define the look of characters. If you're an experienced graphic designer, you may not need to know much about fonts other than how they're handled in InDesign. If you're new to graphic design, however, we'll cover the basics of fonts for you.

Applying a Font

Fonts are character attributes that you apply as follows:

1. Select the Type tool.

2. Select the text you want to apply a font to.

3. Choose Type > Character.

4. At the top of the Character panel (**Figure 26**), choose an option from the Font menu or enter a font name in the field. The menu displays a preview of the font next to the name so you can see what it looks like.

5. Below the Font menu, you can choose an option from the Style menu—for example, Bold, Semibold, Italic, or Oblique. These are the styles available for the font that are activated on your system—they are not produced by InDesign.

You can also choose fonts from the equivalent menus when the character options are displayed in the Control panel.

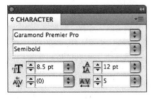

Figure 26 The first two menus on the Character panel let you choose a font and style.

Checking Fonts

When you open a document, InDesign checks to see that all the fonts used in the document are active on your system. If they're not, you're notified so you can activate or replace them. When you're ready for output, use File > Package to have InDesign collect copies of fonts to provide to the printer.

Using an Auto-Activation Plug-In

Font managers such as Suitcase Fusion and FontAgent Pro offer free plug-ins that automatically activate fonts as you open documents. This can be a significant benefit of purchasing a font manager rather than using the utility provided with your system to activate fonts. If you're looking to buy a font manager, check to see if it provides an auto-activation plug-in for InDesign CS4.

Applying OpenType Features

Font designers may include a variety of special features in OpenType fonts. These features may include fancy typographic effects such as Fractions, Discretionary Ligatures, Slashed Zero, and Proportional Old Style numerals. To see which features are available for the active font, choose Open-Type from the Character panel menu. Any features displayed in brackets in the OpenType submenu are not available for the font. You can choose the other features as applicable—for example, if Fractions is available, you might apply it to "1/2" but not to words. Some OpenType fonts will have all the features available in the submenu and others will have none.

You can identify OpenType fonts by the black-and-green "O" preceding the font name, and the name often ends with "Pro."

Tip
If you need to change a document's fonts, you can use Type > Find Font to display a list of the fonts used in the document. You can then replace any missing fonts with fonts that are active on your system.

Font Basics

If you've ever uttered the sentence, "My computer doesn't have that font" (and you're not sure what's wrong with saying that), this section is for you. Since many fonts come with your computer and even more come with programs you buy, it's easy to think that fonts are part of the computer or a specific program. But it's not true. Fonts are independent files that you can turn on (activate) and off (deactivate) through your system or a font management program. You can buy additional fonts from vendors such as Adobe, Linotype, and Bitstream and add them to your system.

Fonts come in a variety of formats, including PostScript, OpenType, and TrueType. Currently, the most widely used and accepted fonts are PostScript Type 1—in fact, you may encounter complaints from other users and printers if you don't use them. OpenType fonts, however, are gaining ground rapidly because they can contain thousands of characters and are cross-platform (meaning the same file can be used on Mac OS and Windows systems).

Whichever fonts you use in whatever format, the most important thing to remember is consistency. It's likely that your computer has multiple versions of the same font—Times, Helvetica, Palatino—in various formats from different vendors. To prevent text from reflowing, the exact fonts you use to design a document should be used each time you edit it. In addition, you need to send those same fonts to the printer with your documents (File > Package).

#27 Using Paragraph and Character Styles

When formatting an entire document, you're certainly not expected to remember and consistently apply the hundreds of paragraph and character attributes InDesign provides. Instead, you can create paragraph styles and character styles to apply multiple attributes to text with a single click or keyboard shortcut. And, if you change an attribute in a style, it's changed everywhere the style is used. For example, you can change a font in a style and it will automatically change throughout a document. Using styles has so many benefits in terms of speed and consistency that you'd never want to work on a long document such as a book, magazine, or newsletter without them.

Creating Styles

Paragraph styles are applied to entire paragraphs and include both paragraph attributes and character attributes. Character styles, on the other hand, specify only character attributes and are applied to selected text. Character styles are useful for local formatting within paragraphs. For example, corporate stock symbols in body copy are often formatted to stand out through the use of small caps, a sans serif font, and maybe a different color. You create paragraph and character styles in the same way, but from different panels.

Generally, the best way to create paragraph and character styles is to first format sample text that includes all the different styles you will need for a document, such as heads, subheads, indented paragraphs, paragraphs with no indent, bulleted lists, and so on. Then, use the formatted text as a basis for the styles. To create a style based on formatted text:

1. Using the Type tool, select formatted text.

2. Choose Type > Paragraph Styles or Type > Character Styles.

3. From the Paragraph Styles or Character Styles panel menu, choose New Paragraph Style or New Character Style.

4. In the Paragraph Style Options dialog box (**Figure 27a**) or the Character Style Options dialog box, enter a name for the style.

5. To apply the style using a keyboard shortcut, click in the Shortcut field and press the shortcut keys you want to assign. Generally, it's best to use the modifier keys and the numbers on the keypad as shortcuts.

Arranging Styles in Groups

By default, styles are listed alphabetically in the Paragraph Styles and Character Styles panels. You can, however, drag styles to new locations in the list. For example, you might list Headline, Subhead, and then Body in the Paragraph Styles panel.

For more complex documents, you might have scores of styles associated with different sections, master pages, content, and more. To manage styles, you can organize them into named groups, which look like collapsible folders. You can then drag any styles you want into each group, organize them, and open the groups as needed. To create a group, click the Create New Style Group button at the bottom of the Paragraph Styles or Character Styles panel.

6. All the options are already set according to the formatted text as summarized in the Style Settings area. Click in the scroll list at left to display panes of options and change any of the formatting.

If you're not working with formatted text, you can create a new style by clicking the Create New Style button at the bottom of the Paragraph Styles or Character Styles panel. This creates a new style in the panel called Paragraph Style 1 or Character Style 1. The number reflects the creation order. Double-click the new style to name and modify it.

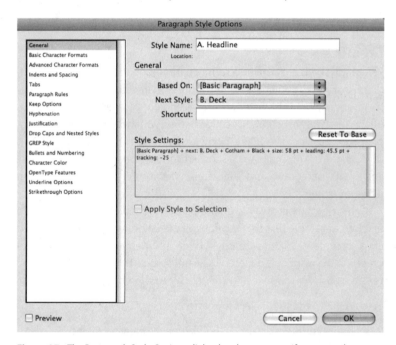

Figure 27a The Paragraph Style Options dialog box lets you specify a name, shortcut key, and formatting for a new paragraph style.

Tip
Character styles do not need to specify all possible character attributes; they can specify only what you want to change. For example, a character style might specify nothing but the color red. You can then apply the character style to any text you want to be red—without changing the font, size, or other character attributes of the text.

Applying Styles

Applying styles is easy: Select the text and click the style name or press its keyboard shortcut.

- To apply a paragraph style, click in a paragraph or select several paragraphs with the Type tool. Click the style name in the Paragraph Styles panel (**Figure 27b**) or press the keyboard shortcut shown for it.

- To apply a character style, select text with the Type tool. Click the style name in the Character Styles panel or press its keyboard shortcut.

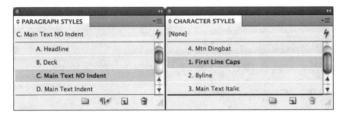

Figure 27b Click style names in the Paragraph Styles panel (left) and the Character Styles panel (right) to apply them to selected text.

Occasionally, you will modify a paragraph's formatting after applying a paragraph style—and then change your mind about the changes. For example, you might try different indents or alignments, or you might tighten the tracking. Any formatting that does not match the style is called an "override." To force a paragraph's formatting to match its original paragraph style, select it and choose Clear Overrides from the panel menu. You can also Option-click (Mac OS) or Alt-click a style name. Note that this does not remove character styles applied within the paragraph.

Modifying Styles

To change the attributes specified in a style, you can double-click the style name or select the style name and choose Style Options from the Character or Paragraph panel menus. Or, as a shortcut, reformat some of the text that is formatting with the style, and then choose Redefine Style from the panel menu. The Character and Paragraph panel menus also provide options for duplicating, deleting, importing, and exporting styles.

Basing a Style on Another Style

When you create paragraph or character styles, you have the option of basing the formatting on an existing style. You can then make slight changes to the new style. Any changes made to the original style affect both styles. For example, if you have a "Body Text" style, you can base "Body Text-No Indent" on that style. Then, if you change the font in "Body Text," it is automatically changed in "Body Text-No Indent" as well.

#28 Inserting Variable Text

Variable text is text that automatically updates itself as needed. For example, you can insert a text variable for Modification Date so the current date is inserted in text every time you open and modify a document. You can also use a text variable to automatically update running headers and footers, add a file name and output date to the slug area when printing, or insert a cross reference to the last page in a document. InDesign provides a variety of variable text definitions for these purposes. You can also define custom variable text for use as a placeholder—for example, if you're designing a birth announcement for an unnamed baby, you can insert variable text; one quick change to the variable text definition and the baby's name appears everywhere it should.

Inserting Text Variables

Text variables are inserted into text just like other characters:

1. Select the Type tool and click in text.

2. Choose Type > Text Variables > Insert Variable.

3. Choose one of the default text variables in the submenu such as Creation Date (**Figure 28a**). This inserts the current date (according to your system settings) in the default format of MM/DD/YY.

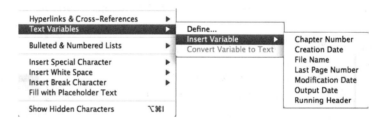

Figure 28a The Text Variables submenu lets you insert text variables into text.

Default Variables

InDesign provides a set of default variables with all new documents. You can modify the default variables to better suit your needs—for example, you can add explanatory text before and after the Creation Date variable, and you can modify the format of the date itself. The default variables work as follows:

- **Chapter Number:** Inserts a chapter number you define; this is useful for cross-references, headers, and footers.

- **Creation Date:** Inserts the date/time the document was first saved.

- **Modification Date:** Inserts the date/time a document was last saved; this is useful for tracking edits.

- **Output Date:** Inserts the date/time an output operation such as printing or PDF export started.

- **File Name:** Inserts the file name of the active document.

- **Last Page Number:** Inserts the last page number in document; this is useful for references such as "page 20 of 100" when the last page number is a moving target.

- **Running Header:** This inserts text from a specified paragraph or character style used to format heads; as the name implies, it is useful for creating running headers and footers.

Editing Text Variable Definitions

To edit a document's text variable definitions, choose Type > Text Variables > Define. Use the New, Edit, and Delete buttons in the Text Variables dialog box (**Figure 28b**) to create, modify, and delete variables in the list.

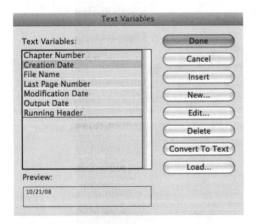

Figure 28b Use the Text Variables dialog box to customize the default text variables and create new ones.

Loading Text Variables

Text variables are document specific, so if you open a document from a previous version of InDesign, it will not even contain the default text variables. In addition, any changes you make to the default text variables and any custom text variables you create are not reflected in your other documents. To share text variables among documents, use the Load button in the Text Variables dialog box (Type > Text Variables > Define).

#29 Using the Story Editor

Part of the beauty of working in InDesign is the way you can truly see your pages coming together—the way the type and graphics work together to communicate a message. However, sometimes you need to revise the text of the message, and all those graphics can get in the way. To get around this, InDesign provides the Story Editor, which lets you edit plain text in a separate window. If you've ever worked in PageMaker or reviewed galleys, the Story Editor will be familiar to you.

Using the Story Editor is particularly helpful when you're working with overset text, reverse type, complex text wraps, or text placed behind other semitransparent objects. Anytime you're having trouble working with text, select a text frame in the story and choose Edit > Edit in Story Editor (**Figure 29**). All the text in the story is displayed in a separate window that includes a list of paragraph styles applied to text, a vertical depth ruler, and an overset text indicator.

When you're editing text in a Story Editor window, the Type tool is automatically selected so you can edit the text as usual. You will see only the most basic formatting attributes, such as bold and italics; tables, inline objects, footnotes, and the like are represented by icons. While you're editing text in the Story Editor, you can see changes in the layout as well.

You can open multiple stories in their own Story Editor windows, including opening a Story Editor for a type path. The Story Editor windows work as follows:

- Drag the Story Editor window and document window as necessary for the most convenient positioning. For example, you might place them side by side to see how text changes affect a column in the layout.

- Each open Story Editor window is listed at the bottom of the Window menu. If the window you're working on goes behind the document window, choose it from the Window menu to bring it forward.

- If you're working with a text frame containing overset text, a line indicates where the text no longer fits in the frame.

- Use the View > Story Editor submenu to control what displays in the Story Editor: Style Name Column, Depth Ruler, and Footnotes. These commands affect all open Story Editor windows.

- If the Style Name Column is displayed, you can drag the divider to adjust the column width.

When you're finished working in a Story Editor window, close it or choose Edit > Edit in Layout.

Figure 29 The Story Editor (Edit > Edit in Story Editor) makes it easy to focus on editing text while seeing the impact of the edits on the layout.

Customizing the Story Editor

If you don't like the Story Editor's font or background color, you can change it in the Story Editor Display pane in the Preferences dialog box. You can further customize the Story Editor by changing the font size, line spacing, text color, anti-aliasing setting, and cursor type.

#30 Checking Spelling

InDesign's spelling checker is incredibly sophisticated. You can check anything from a text selection to multiple documents, check against spelling dictionaries in most major languages, customize the spelling dictionaries, and more. In addition to flagging words that do not appear in its dictionaries, InDesign also flags duplicated words and possible capitalization errors. We have to warn you, though, that the spelling checker is not foolproof. It doesn't know what words you intended to use—there, their, or they're, for example—and it doesn't understand context. When making decisions about possible misspelled words, it's best if you work with a copy editor or proofreader.

Performing a Spelling Check

You can check spelling in selected text, to the end of a story, in an entire story or document, and in all open documents. If you want to check a limited amount of text, you must first select a range of text with the Type tool, click within a story to check it from that point forward, or select a text frame to check the entire story.

To check spelling, choose Edit > Spelling > Check Spelling. Choose an option from the Search menu to specify the scope of the spelling checker: All Documents, Document, Story, To End of Story, or Selection. Then, click Start. When a word displays in the field at the top of the Check Spelling dialog box (**Figure 30a**), handle it as follows:

- **If the word is spelled incorrectly:** Select a word in the Suggested Corrections list or enter the correct spelling in the Change To field. Then, click Change to fix the first instance of the word or click Change All to fix all instances of the word without reviewing them.

- **If the word is spelled correctly:** Click Skip to continue to check spelling. If you know the word is used multiple times in the document and you don't want to click Skip repeatedly, click Ignore All. To add the word to the dictionary, click Add.

The Check Spelling dialog box is actually a panel, so you can jump into the document and edit the text without closing it. When you're finished checking spelling, click Done.

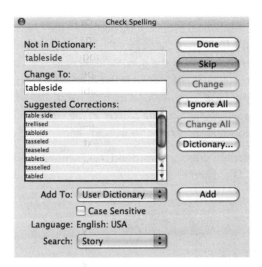

Figure 30a The Check Spelling dialog box helps you find the correct spelling for words.

Customizing the Dictionary

If we know anything about a spelling checker, we know that it's not infallible. For one thing, the dictionary rarely recognizes all the unique words in your content, including the names of people, places, brands, foods, and more. If you frequently work with the same content—and are constantly skipping or ignoring the same words—you can add those words to the document's dictionary or to your user dictionary. Customizing the dictionary not only results in fewer flagged words, but it also helps ensure that you don't misspell proper names.

You have two options for customizing the dictionary:

- While you're in the Check Spelling dialog box, click Add. The word in the Not in Dictionary field is added to the dictionary listed in the Add To field. By default, this is your user dictionary, but you can choose to add the word to a dictionary that is unique to the active document. If the word requires specific capitalization—such as "LoDo," the abbreviation for Denver's Lower Downtown neighborhood—make sure Case Sensitive is checked when you click Add.

Checking Spelling in Different Languages

InDesign is not limited to checking spelling in English. To tell InDesign which language dictionary to use for a word or a range of text, select the text and then choose an option from the Language menu when the Control panel is displaying character attributes. For example, if you select "crème brûlée" and then choose French from the Language menu, InDesign will consult its French dictionary and determine that it is spelled correctly.

- Choose Edit > Spelling > Dictionary (or click Dictionary in the Check Spelling dialog box). In the Dictionary dialog box (**Figure 30b**), choose whether to edit the user dictionary or the document dictionary from the Target menu. Enter correctly spelled words in the Word field, check Case Sensitive or uncheck Case Sensitive, and then click Add. (When Case Sensitive is checked, the capitalization pattern in the Word field is added to the dictionary and used when checking spelling.)

To edit words in the dictionary, select the word and click Remove. Then retype the word in the Word field and click Add.

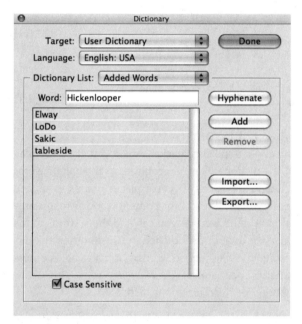

Figure 30b The Dictionary dialog box lets you customize the user dictionary or the document's dictionary.

Setting Spelling Preferences

By default, the InDesign Check Spelling command flags words that it thinks are misspelled, words it thinks should be capitalized, and duplicate words. If this results in too many flagged words, you can customize Check Spelling in the Spelling pane in the Preferences dialog box. The controls work as follows:

- **Misspelled Words** flags words that do not match words in the current language dictionary.

- **Repeated Words** flags duplicate words such as "in in."

- **Uncapitalized Words** flags words that are capitalized in the dictionary but not in the document.

- **Uncapitalized Sentences** flags lowercase words following a period, exclamation point, or question mark.

You might, for example, uncheck Uncapitalized Words and Uncapitalized Sentences if a design-intensive document uses all lowercase text for a special effect.

#31 Correcting Spelling Automatically

If you've ever used Microsoft Word's AutoCorrect features, you've probably noticed that as you're typing it will fix blatant mistakes you make and underline words it doesn't recognize. For example, if you type "teh," it changes the text to "the." If you type "InDesign," it underlines it to let you know that it might be misspelled. InDesign works the same way—except the automatic spelling correction and the underlining of possibly misspelled words are both turned off by default. You can easily turn these features on and off as you need them, and they are both customizable.

Using Autocorrect

To automatically correct common misspellings as you type, choose Edit > Spelling > Autocorrect. You can also check Enable Autocorrect in the Autocorrect pane in the Preferences dialog box. The Autocorrect pane lets you edit InDesign's default list of common misspellings as well. Note that Autocorrect is not retroactive—it will not go through existing text and correct it. It works only as you type.

Underlining Unrecognized Words

To have InDesign underline potential spelling errors, choose Edit > Spelling > Dynamic Spelling. By default, squiggly red underlines indicate potential spelling errors and squiggly green underlines indicate duplicated words and potential capitalization errors. For potential misspellings, you can Control-click (Mac OS) or right-click (Windows) the word to display a context menu (**Figure 31**). You can choose from a list of suggested spellings, add the spelling to the user dictionary, or ignore all instances of the spelling. If you choose Add or Ignore All from the context menu, the word is no longer underlined.

Note
When the display is set to Preview (View > Screen Mode > Preview), you cannot see the Dynamic Spelling marks.

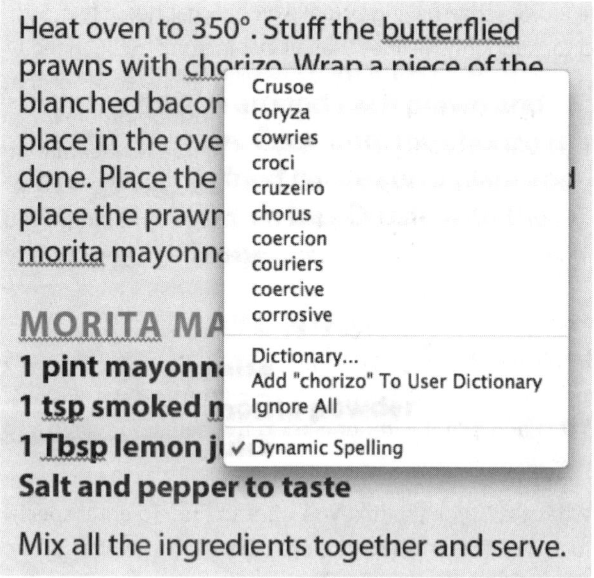

Heat oven to 350°. Stuff the <u>butterflied</u> prawns with ch<u>orizo</u>. Wrap a piece of the blanched bacon place in the ove done. Place the place the prawn morita mayonna

| Crusoe |
| coryza |
| cowries |
| croci |
| cruzeiro |
| chorus |
| coercion |
| couriers |
| coercive |
| corrosive |

Dictionary...
Add "chorizo" To User Dictionary
Ignore All

✓ Dynamic Spelling

MORITA MA

1 pint mayonn
1 tsp smoked n
1 Tbsp lemon ju
Salt and pepper to taste

Mix all the ingredients together and serve.

Figure 31 InDesign does not recognize the names of many ethic foods—such as "chorizo" shown here—and abbreviations used in cooking such as "tsp" and "Tbsp." Displaying a context menu lets you choose a different spelling, add it to your dictionary, or ignore it.

Using Autocorrect as a Macro

While Autocorrect is handy for fixing mistakes, you can also use it as a poor man's macro to save yourself keystrokes. If you type the same phrase over and over—"at 5,280 feet in the mile-high city," for example—you could have InDesign Autocorrect instances of "a5ft" to actually read "at 5,280 feet in the mile-high city."

#32 Searching and Replacing Text

Nothing is more tedious than having to make global changes in text. Suppose that an editor suddenly decides that all instances of "5280" need to be "5,280." Then suppose the designer decides that all instances of that text need to be in Cheltenham Red. The quickest, most foolproof way to handle these changes is through InDesign's Find/Change Text feature.

You can also use Find/Change to search and replace GREP expressions (alphanumeric strings and patterns), Glyphs, and Object formatting. If you use the same or similar Find/Change operations repeatedly, you can save the criteria as queries.

Using Find/Change with Text

To open the Find/Change panel, choose Edit > Find/Change. The panel lets you click in text and edit it without closing the panel. To search and replace text:

1. In the Find What area, type the text you want to find. To enter special characters such as a Tab or Wildcards, click the @ to the right of the field to display a menu. You can combine text with options from the menu—for example to search for a "1" followed by a tab character. To simply change formatting, leave the field blank.

   ### Tip
   If you want to find multiple variations of text, select a Wildcard character from the @ menu. For example, to find "run" and "ran," replace the vowel with the Wildcard for Any Letter. The text will look like this: r^?n.

2. In the Change To area, type your replacement text. As with the Find What area, you can click the @ menu to specify special characters such as Quotation Marks and Break Characters.

3. Choose an option from the Search menu to specify the scope of your search: All Documents, Document, Story, To End of Story, and Selection. (If necessary, you can jump into the document and click in text to specify a starting point, select a story, or select text to search.)

Using Default Find/Change Queries

A query is a set of predefined Find/Change criteria that you can quickly select for use with any document. The Query menu at the top of the Find/Change panel provides a variety of useful default queries, including Dash Dash to Em-dash, Multiple Return to Single Return, Multiple Space to Single Space, and Phone Number Conversion (Dot Format). You can select any of these queries and fine tune it or simply put it to work.

In addition to using the default queries, you can save your custom Find/Change criteria as queries as well. To do this, click the Save Query button 🖫 next to the Query menu. Name the new query and click OK to save it.

4. To further refine the scope, click the buttons under the Search menu:

- Click the following buttons to include the text in these areas in a search: Include Locked Layers ⬚, Include Locked Stories ⬚, Include Hidden Layers ⬚, Include Master Pages ⬚, and Include Footnotes ⬚. Point at the buttons to display their tool tips.

- Click the Case Sensitive button ⬚ to find only text with the exact capitalization pattern shown in the Find What field. When this option is checked, the capitalization in the Change To field is used for changes.

- Click the Whole Word button ⬚ if you don't want to find variations of the Find What text (such as plurals).

5. If you want to consider character and/or paragraph formatting in the search, click the More Options button to expand the Find/Change panel (**Figure 32**).

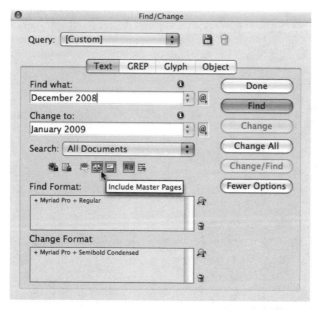

Figure 32 This search will find all instances of "December 2008" formatted with Myriad Pro Regular in the document (including the master pages) and replace them with "January 2009" in Myriad Pro Semibold Condensed.

Specifying Find What and Change To Information

Since Find/Change relies on your accuracy in entering information in the Find What and Change To fields, you can paste text into both fields. (If drag and drop is enabled for the layout, you can also drop text in the fields.) If the text is formatted, its formatting is automatically selected in the Find Format and Change Format areas. Pasting is particularly helpful when you want to Find/Change special characters such as tabs. The Find What and Change To fields also include menus that list your most recent operations.

6. Click the Specify Attributes to Find button ⚎ next to the Find Format field to specify the attributes to find. The attributes you specify are listed in the Find Format field.

7. Click the Specify Attributes to Change button ⚎ next to the Change Format field to specify the new attributes. The attributes you specify are listed in the Change Format field.

8. Click Find to start the search. When you locate the found text, click Change to replace it with the Change To text and formatting or click Find Next to skip it.

9. Click Find Next to continue the search. After you click Change and confirm that the changes are correct, you can click Change All to change all instances within the search scope.

When you're finished with the Find/Change panel, click Done.

CHAPTER FOUR

Typography and Tables

It's hard to say when you go from "working with text" to focusing on "typography," where your primary concern is the appearance of the text. Some of the basic decisions you make, such as font and size, affect typography, but the real reason you use InDesign is for all its fine-tuning options. This includes text within tables, which are often ideal for presenting information. Judicious use of features discussed in this chapter can give your projects a professional edge.

In this chapter, you'll learn how to apply special effects such as scaling type, creating drop caps, anchoring objects in text, wrapping text around objects and images, and more. In addition, you'll look at features for creating and formatting tables that save you time and enhance your designs.

#33 Special Effects for Type

The look of type is largely dependent on the typeface you select, the style (such as bold or italic), and the size. The spacing between characters, words, lines, and paragraphs affects the design as well. But for serious impact, you might experiment with some of InDesign's special effects, such as stroke, color, scale, and skew. (Note that two special effects are discussed in other chapters; see #19 for type on a path and #65 for drop shadows and other effects.)

see #19 for type on a path and #65 for drop shadows and other effects.

Applying a Style

When type is selected, you can apply a style to characters by clicking buttons in the Control panel's character options: All Caps, Small Caps, Superscript, Subscript, Underline, and Strikethrough (**Figure 33a**). All these commands are available in the Character panel menu as well.

Figure 33a The character options in the Control panel include buttons for styles such as Small Caps and Underline.

> ### Note
> *If you do not see all the character formatting controls, choose Window > Workspace > Advanced or Window > Workspace > Typography. In the Character panel, choose Show Options from the panel menu.*

Applying a Stroke and Color

When text is selected with the Type tool, you can *stroke,* or outline, its edges and change its color. To apply a stroke to text, enter a value in the Weight field in the Stroke panel (Window menu). To change the color of text, click a color swatch in the Swatches panel (Window menu). The Fill/Stroke button on the Swatches panel and the Tools panel controls whether the color applies to the stroke or body of the characters (**Figure 33b**).

Figure 33b The Stroke panel lets you outline selected characters, and the Swatches panel lets you apply a color to them.

Less Is More

Special effects generally work best with smaller blocks of text such as headlines or pull quotes. You wouldn't, for example, apply a stroke to an entire page of body text unless you wanted to give your readers a headache.

Scaling Text

To achieve certain design effects, you might want to horizontally scale (expand) or vertically scale (condense) text. Since scaling distorts text, it is usually reserved for increasing the visual impact of display type such as headlines. Some designers, however, will scale text a tiny bit (such as 97% horizontally) for copyfitting purposes. You have two options for scaling text, numerically or visually:

- Using the Type tool, select a range of text and then enter a percent value in the Horizontal Scale or Vertical Scale field in the Character panel (**Figure 33c**) or in the character options in the Control panel. If you end up with overset text from scaling characters, resize the text frame.

Figure 33c The Vertical Scale and Horizontal Scale fields let you condense and expand text, respectively.

- Using the Scale tool 🔧, drag a corner of a text frame to resize it (**Figure 33d**). All the text scales automatically, scaling vertically if you change the frame width and scaling horizontally if you change the frame width. As a shortcut to selecting the Scale tool, you can press Command (Mac OS) or Ctrl (Windows) while using the Selection tool to resize a text frame.

Figure 33d Dragging the corner of a text frame with the Scale tool scales the text as you resize the frame.

Skewing Type

InDesign can *skew*, or slant, type to somewhat mimic italics. To do this, select text with the Type tool and enter a value in the Skew field in the Character panel (**Figure 33e**) or in the character options in the Control panel. Skew is expressed in degrees with positive values skewing text to the right and negative values skewing text to the left.

Figure 33e The Skew field lets you enter a value in degrees to slant type to the right or left.

Converting Type to Outlines

If you cannot achieve the look you want by adjusting the font, stroke, color, scale, or skew of type, you can convert the characters to a frame of the same shape. You can then add a stroke or fill color—or you can fill the frame with text or a graphic. To do this, select the text with the Type tool (you can only convert one line of text at a time) and choose Type > Create Outlines.

Tip
When you use Create Outlines, the new frame is automatically anchored in the surrounding text. To remove an anchored frame, select it with the Selection tool, choose Edit > Cut, and deselect the containing text frame. Then, choose Edit > Paste to place the unanchored frame on the page. To create an unanchored frame, press Option (Mac OS) or Alt (Windows) while you choose Type > Create Outlines.

#34 Setting Up Drop Caps and Nested Styles

Look at the first paragraph of a story in just about any magazine. Usually, at least the first letter is enlarged and embellished in some way to draw your eyes into the paragraph. In graphic design, this is referred to as a *drop cap*. In addition to the drop cap, the first few words or the first line might look different, often with all caps or small caps, although a font switch is becoming more common. InDesign refers to this as a *nested style*.

Although they appear to be applied to specific characters, both drop caps and nested styles are paragraph formats. The benefit of this is that you can use a paragraph style to apply both formats with a single click—and the formats are not dependent on any specific text. You can edit text and even delete the first character of a paragraph, and the drop cap style remains. The nested style formatting might be set up to change the font of the first four words, for example, or to change the font and size of all the words in the first sentence. Again, editing the text will not remove the nested style formatting.

Creating Drop Caps

To create a drop cap:

1. Click in a paragraph with the Type tool to select the paragraph.

2. In the Paragraph panel (Type menu) or in the paragraph options in the Control panel (**Figure 34a**), locate the Drop Cap Number of Lines and Drop Cap One or More Characters fields.

3. In the Drop Cap Number of Lines field, enter the number of lines you want the drop caps to drop into. For example, if you enter 3, the drop caps become large enough to drop down into the first three lines of the paragraph.

4. In the Drop Cap One or More Characters field, enter how many characters you want to become drop caps.

Generally, you will only see one-character drop caps, but sometimes the number is adjusted based on the context. For example, it might be modified so the entire first word of a paragraph becomes the drop cap (and therefore you have to set the value for each paragraph). Or, if you usually use one drop cap but the first character is an open quotation mark, you might adjust that paragraph to have a two-character drop cap.

For quick and consistent application of drop caps and nested styles, save the settings in a paragraph style. Be sure to create any character styles you will need first (for additional drop-cap formatting or for the nested style formatting). In the Paragraph Style Options dialog box, use the Drop Caps and Nested Style panel to set up how the first few characters and/or lines of the paragraph should look. See #27 for more information about paragraph styles.

Once you have created drop caps for a paragraph, you can still select those characters and apply additional character attributes. It's pretty common to see a font or color change in a drop cap.

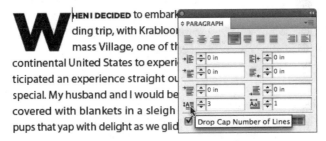

Figure 34a The Paragraph panel provides control over how many characters are treated as drop caps and how deep they drop into the paragraph.

Creating Nested Styles

The Drop Caps and Nested Styles dialog box (**Figure 34b**) lets you create a drop cap, apply a character style to it, and apply a character style to the beginning of the paragraph—for example, to change the first sentence to all caps—all in one place. You can also apply character styles to specific lines—such as every third line—in a paragraph using line styles. To set up this formatting, first create any character styles you will need for the drop caps, nested styles, and line styles. Then click in the paragraph and choose Drop Caps and Nested Styles from the Control panel menu or Paragraph panel menu.

- **Drop Caps area:** Set up the drop cap in the Lines and Characters fields. To apply additional formatting to the drop caps through a character style, choose it from the Character Style menu.

- **Align Left Edge check box:** Certain characters, often in sans serif fonts, might appear to be out of alignment with the rest of the paragraph. If this is the case, check Align Left Edge.

- **Scale for Descenders check box:** In tight leading situations, some drop-cap characters may overlap text below in the paragraph. If this is the case, check Scale for Descenders.

- **Nested Styles area:** To specify formatting for the beginning of the paragraph, click New Nested Style. Select the character style for the text first, and then use the next three fields to specify how much text to apply it to. For example, you might apply a bold font to the first three words in a paragraph. Or, you might apply a different color up to an em space. You can create more than one nested style for a paragraph, which is helpful for formatting single-line paragraphs in a table of contents, for example.

- **Line Styles area:** This area works much the same as the Nested Styles area. To get started, click New Line Style. Select a character style to specify the formatting for the line. Then, specify the number of lines for that formatting. To create a pattern of formatting, such as every other line, create additional line styles.

Note that you do not have to use drop caps, nested styles, and line styles: You can specify only what you need.

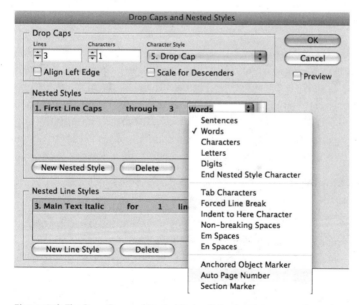

Figure 34b The Drop Caps and Nested Styles dialog box lets you easily apply formatting within paragraphs, including drop caps and style changes such as small caps or bold.

Repeating Nested Styles

InDesign provides the option to repeat, or loop, two or more nested styles. You might do this to apply an italic font to every other word or every third word in a paragraph, for example.

To loop nested styles, create a new paragraph style. In the Drop Caps and Nested Styles pane of the New Paragraph Style dialog box, click New Nested Style, and then choose the first character style you want to apply from the list of character styles. Modify the settings as needed. Add new nested styles in the desired sequence. To loop the nested styles, click New Nested Style, choose Repeat from the list of character styles, and then specify the number of character styles you want to include.

#35 Inserting Special Characters and Glyphs

Many of the special typographic features within fonts—from bullets and em dashes to fractions and ligatures—cannot be found on the keyboard. InDesign provides quick access to common special characters through the Insert Special Character submenu in the Type menu. To see all the characters in a font, use the Glyphs panel. (A *glyph* is a form of a character; for example, some fonts include several different versions of an ampersand. The smallest unit of a font is actually a glyph, not a character.) If you frequently access the same glyphs, you can save them as glyph sets.

Inserting Common Special Characters

From the Insert Special Character submenus (Type menu), you can insert commonly used characters. For example, the Symbols submenu lets you insert a Bullet •, Copyright Symbol ©, Ellipsis …, Paragraph Symbol ¶, or Registered Trademark Symbol ®; the Hyphens and Dashes submenu lets you insert an Em Dash — or En Dash –. The character is inserted at the text insertion point and formatted with the active font. If you end up inserting these characters often, you might want to learn and remember their standard keyboard shortcuts or create your own (see #3).

Inserting Glyphs

To access every variation of every character within a font, choose Type > Glyphs to open the Glyphs panel (**Figure 35**). To insert a glyph at the text insertion point, scroll through the panel to locate the glyph and then double-click. The glyph is inserted and formatted according to the surrounding character formats. The Glyphs panel provides access to all the fonts currently active on your system and offers the following controls:

- **Recently Used:** The most recent glyphs you access are listed across the top of the Glyphs panel for quick insertion.

- **Show menu:** You can limit the glyphs shown in the panel by choosing an option from the Show menu such as Alternates for Selection or Standard Ligatures. The options vary according to what is built into the font, with OpenType fonts generally offering the most options.

- **Font menu:** By default, the Glyphs panel displays the font in use at the text insertion point. You can select a different font from the menu in the lower-left corner of the panel. The menu next to it lets you choose a variation of the font such as Bold or Italic.

- **Scale buttons:** Click the scale buttons 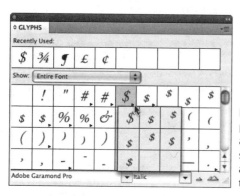 in the lower-right corner of the panel to increase or decrease the size of the glyphs shown. This makes it easy to find the right glyph but does not affect the size of the character you insert.

- **Alternates indicator:** Some glyphs have *alternates*, or different visual forms, from which you can choose. If you see an arrow in the lower-right corner of a glyph's field, click it to view and select alternates.

Figure 35 The Glyphs panel provides quick access to all the glyphs within the selected font. Double-click a glyph to insert it in text at the text insertion point.

Creating Glyph Sets

If you use certain glyphs frequently—for example, if you're working on a cookbook and need to access various fractions—you can save them as a glyph set for quick access. Glyph sets are saved with your copy of InDesign. To create a glyph set:

1. Choose New Glyph Set from the Glyphs panel menu. Name the set and click OK.

2. To add glyphs to the set, select a glyph in the Glyphs panel, and then choose Add to Glyph Set from the panel menu. If you have more than one glyph set, select the appropriate set from the submenu.

3. To view glyphs in the set, choose the set from the Show menu at the top of the Glyphs panel. You can also choose View Glyph Set from the panel menu and select the set you want to display.

    As with other glyphs, you can insert a glyph from a set by double-clicking it.

Saving Fonts with Glyphs

By default, when you add a glyph to a glyph set, InDesign associates the current font with it. This is useful for unusual glyphs that may not exist in every font. However, for more common glyphs, such as 1/2 fractions or bullets, you may not want to associate a font with each glyph. To save glyphs without font information, choose Edit Glyph Set from the Glyphs panel menu, and select the set you want to edit from the submenu. In the Edit Glyph Set dialog box, you can select a glyph and uncheck Remember Font with Glyph.

#36 Anchoring Objects in Text

If you have pictures or other graphic elements that need to flow with related text, you can *anchor* the objects in the text. This prevents you from having to manually reposition objects such as charts, sidebars, or graphics every time text reflows. Any type of object or group can be anchored in text, including text frames, picture frames, paths, and tables. When you anchor objects, you can position them inline with text, above text, or in a custom position such as out in the margin (**Figure 36a**). You have precise control over each object's position, including the ability to fine-tune placement with the mouse.

Figure 36a Anchored objects flow with text. At left, an Inline object is positioned at the baseline of text at the text insertion point. In the center, an Above Line object is positioned above the line containing the text insertion point. At right, an object with Custom positioning is placed outside the text frame, relative to the spine, margins, and more.

Anchoring Existing Objects

You have two choices for anchoring objects: You can anchor existing objects or you can anchor placeholder objects. To anchor an existing object in text:

1. Select any object or group using one of the selection tools.

2. Choose Edit > Cut or Edit > Copy.

3. Select the Type tool and click in text to position the insertion point where you want the anchored object.

4. Choose Edit > Paste.

By default, the object is anchored Inline, but you can reposition it using the Anchored Object Options dialog box. If the object is larger than surrounding text, it may overlap the text; in that case, you may need to adjust the leading or insert line breaks.

Anchoring Placeholder Objects

If you haven't created the object that will be anchored—or if its content is not ready—you can create a rectangular placeholder and anchor it in text. To do this:

1. Select the Type tool and click in text to position the text insertion point.

2. Choose Object > Anchored Object > Insert.

3. In the Object Options area at the top of the Insert Anchored Object dialog box, specify the Content for the object (such as Text or Graphic).

4. Select an Object Style to specify the object's formatting (if you've created any object styles).

5. Select a Paragraph Style for the text it will contain (if the object is a text frame).

6. Enter a Height and Width for the object.

You can also specify the position of the anchored object, as discussed in the next section.

Positioning Anchored Objects

To change the positioning of an anchored object, click it using a selection tool and choose Object > Anchored Object > Options. The controls in the Anchored Object Options dialog box are the same as those for positioning in the Insert Anchored Object dialog box. Choose an option from the Position menu at the top:

- **Inline or Above Line:** Select this option if you want to anchor the object inline with the text or above a line of text.

- **Custom:** Select this option if you want to anchor the object in a different position, such as outside the text frame.

Copying and Pasting Anchored Objects

Anchored objects and anchored object markers function just like characters when it comes to selecting, cutting, copying, and pasting them with the Type tool. If you need to copy and paste a story containing anchored graphics to a different location, for example, the anchored graphics will come right along with it.

Prevent Manual Positioning of Anchored Objects

In addition to all the positioning settings in the Anchored Object Options dialog box, you can drag anchored objects using the selection tools. If you're creating a template and don't want users to be able to move anchored items, check Prevent Manual Positioning.

If you choose Inline or Above Line from the Position menu, the Anchored Object Options dialog box (**Figure 36b**) lets you specify which type of anchoring you want and then further fine-tune the positioning.

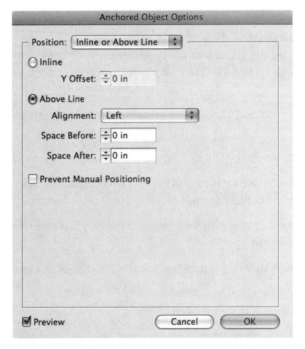

Figure 36b When Inline or Above Line is selected from the Position menu, the Anchored Object Options dialog box lets you specify the position of anchored objects that are flowing with text or above lines of text.

- **Inline:** To position the object inline with text, click Inline. Enter a value in the Y Offset field to move the object up or down from the baseline of the text.

- **Above Line:** To position the object above the line containing the text insertion point, click Above Line. Choose an option from the Alignment menu to specify how the object is positioned within the text frame: Left, Center, Right, Towards Spine, Away from Spine, or Text Alignment (which matches the alignment of the paragraph). Enter values in the Space Before and Space After fields to control the amount of space above and below the anchored object.

If you choose Custom from the Position menu, the Anchored Object Options dialog box (**Figure 36c**) lets you specify precisely where the object should be placed.

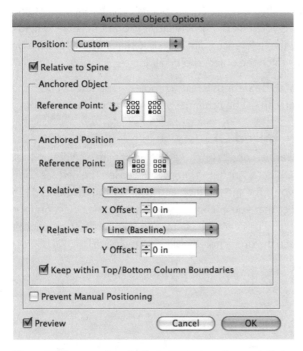

Figure 36c For an anchored object with Custom alignment, the Anchored Object Options dialog box lets you position the object in relation to the columns of text, the page, and more.

- **Relative to Spine:** Check this option if you want the object's placement to be different for right-facing and left-facing pages. For example, if a book has a wide outer margin, you might place anchored objects in the margin. When text reflows from left to right pages, you'll want the anchored objects positioned accordingly.

- **Anchored Object Reference Point:** This option specifies what part of the anchored object should align with the page, text frame, or margins (as specified in the Anchored Object Position area below). For example, if the lower-right corner of the object should align with the text frame, click a box on the lower-right corner.

- **Anchored Position:** In this area, the X Relative To menu and X Offset field control the horizontal placement of the anchored object. The Y Relative To menu and Y Offset field control the vertical placement of the anchored object. The reference points available vary according to the selections you make in the X Relative To and Y Relative To fields, but essentially the Reference Point you click indicates the location on the page with which the object should align.

The interplay of these settings is fairly complex, so be sure to check the Preview box so you can see any changes you make as you make them.

Releasing Anchored Objects

If you no longer want an object anchored, select it with a selection tool, and then choose Object > Anchored Object > Release. (The Release command is available only for anchored objects with Custom alignment.) To unanchor an object that you anchored, select it with the Selection tool, choose Edit > Cut, and deselect the containing text frame. Then, choose Edit > Paste to place the unanchored object on the page.

#37 Wrapping Text Around Objects

The interplay of text and images in a layout contributes significantly to the overall message. You achieve a lot of this interplay by wrapping text around objects such as text frames or lines or around contours within a graphic such as a clipping path or an alpha channel. You specify text wrap for the object that the text will wrap around. For example, if text will wrap around a picture frame, you specify text wrap for the picture frame. The object that text wraps around is called the *wrap object* (**Figure 37a**).

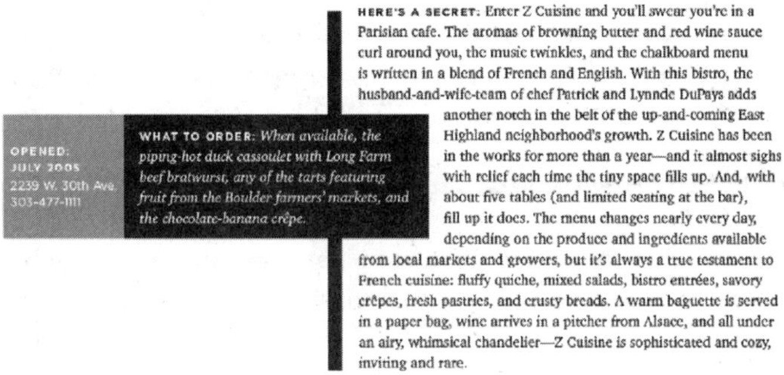

HERE'S A SECRET: Enter Z Cuisine and you'll swear you're in a Parisian cafe. The aromas of browning butter and red wine sauce curl around you, the music twinkles, and the chalkboard menu is written in a blend of French and English. With this bistro, the husband-and-wife-team of chef Patrick and Lynnde DuPays adds another notch in the belt of the up-and-coming East Highland neighborhood's growth. Z Cuisine has been in the works for more than a year—and it almost sighs with relief each time the tiny space fills up. And, with about five tables (and limited seating at the bar), fill up it does. The menu changes nearly every day, depending on the produce and ingredients available from local markets and growers, but it's always a true testament to French cuisine: fluffy quiche, mixed salads, bistro entrées, savory crêpes, fresh pastries, and crusty breads. A warm baguette is served in a paper bag, wine arrives in a pitcher from Alsace, and all under an airy, whimsical chandelier—Z Cuisine is sophisticated and cozy, inviting and rare.

OPENED: JULY 2005 2239 W. 30th Ave. 303-477-1111

WHAT TO ORDER: *When available, the piping-hot duck cassoulet with Long Farm beef bratwurst, any of the tarts featuring fruit from the Boulder farmers' markets, and the chocolate-banana crêpe.*

Figure 37a The black text frame is the wrap object here. An offset value of 9 points keeps the text from touching the wrap object.

To wrap text around an object, select the wrap object with one of the selection tools. Choose Window > Text Wrap to open the Text Wrap panel (**Figure 37b**). To add Wrap Options and Contour Options to the Text Wrap panel, choose Show Options from the panel menu.

- **Wrap shape buttons:** Click one of the first three buttons to indicate the shape of the text wrap—No Text Wrap ▣, Wrap Around Bounding Box ▣, or Wrap Around Object Shape ▣. None places the object on top of text or flows text over the object. Bounding Box wraps text around the rectangular bounding box of the object, and Object Shape wraps text around the contours of the object within the box.

- **Jump Object:** If you don't want text on either side of the object (only above or below it), click the Jump Object button ▣.

Preventing Text Wrap for a Frame

If you want to prevent text from wrapping around objects regardless of their text wrap settings, you can check Ignore Text Wrap for the text frame in the Text Frame Options dialog box (Object menu).

Flowing Text into Shapes

To flow text *into* a wrap object rather than around it, check Invert in the Text Wrap panel. For this to have any effect, the wrap object must be a text frame or type path.

- **Jump to Next Column:** If you want text below the object to flow to the next column rather than under the object, click the Jump to Next Column button .

- **Offset fields:** Enter values in the fields to specify the amount of space between the wrap object and the text.

- **Wrap Options:** If you click Wrap Around Bounding Box or Wrap Around Object Shape, the Wrap To menu lets you specify where the text wraps. By default, text wraps to the left and right of the object. You can choose from Right Side, Left Side, Both Right & Left Sides, Side Towards Spine, Side Away from Spine, and Largest Area.

- **Contour Options:** If you want to wrap text around contours within a graphic, click the Object Shape wrap button. From the Type menu, select any alpha channel or Photoshop path saved with the graphic file. If you've selected a clipping path for the graphic in the Clipping Path dialog box (Object menu), you can wrap text around it by choosing Same as Clipping. For a graphic with a lot of contrast between the foreground and background, you can use the Detect Edges option to create a text wrap contour.

- **Include Inside Edges:** If you're wrapping text around an image contour, you can flow text into any holes in the contour. For example, if you have a picture of a doughnut, you can flow text around the edges and into the white space in the center. To do this, check Include Inside Edges in the Contour Options area. (If the check box is not available, the selected contour has no holes.)

Once you have a text wrap specified, you can edit the contour using the Pen tool or the Direct Selection tool.

Figure 37b The Text Wrap panel lets you fine-tune the interplay of text and objects on the page.

#38 Applying Optical Margin Alignment

In typography, there is a difference between text that is numerically aligned and text that is *optically aligned*. When text is left aligned or right aligned, the aligned edges still look ragged sometimes due to the shape of the characters. For example, punctuation such as quotation marks, commas, and em dashes often cause this problem as do some letters such as "W" and "A." To fix this, InDesign provides *optical margin alignment*—also known as hanging punctuation—which "hangs" the edges of offending characters slightly outside the margins to produce a smoother looking edge (**Figure 38a**). This is a special effect that you will generally use sparingly for text such as pull quotes; it is not generally used for body text.

"The cutting board"
starter is a sampling
of rare Italian meats
and cheeses.
—We want to cater
to suits and baseball
caps, says Frizzi

"The cutting board"
starter is a sampling
of rare Italian meats
and cheeses.
—We want to cater to
suits and baseball caps,
says Frizzi

Figure 38a At left, the text is left aligned, but the left edge looks ragged due to the opening quotation marks and the em dash. At right, the text has optical margin alignment, so the quotation marks and em dash hang slightly outside the margin.

Optical margin alignment is an attribute of a story—which consists of all the text in a series of threaded text frames—so you cannot apply it to selected paragraphs. However, you can select paragraphs and specify that they ignore optical margin alignment.

Applying Optical Margin Alignment to a Text Frame

To apply optical margin alignment to a text frame:

1. Select a text frame with the Type tool or either selection tool.

2. Choose Type > Story.

3. Check Optical Margin Alignment in the Story panel (**Figure 38b**).

4. Specify how much the text should hang outside the margins by entering a point size in the field. (In general, select the point size of the text itself.)

Figure 38b Use the Story panel to create hanging punctuation for the selected text frame.

Setting Paragraphs to Ignore Optical Margin Alignment

If you have headlines and body text in the same text frame, you might want to set optical margin alignment for the text frame so the headline appears properly aligned. You can then specify that the body paragraphs ignore the optical margin alignment setting. To do this, select the paragraphs with the Type tool and choose Ignore Optical Margin from the Paragraph panel menu (Type menu).

#39 Importing Tables from Word and Excel

In most workflows, data that will be presented in a table—whether it's financial data for an annual report or a price list for a catalog—is born in another program. It might be extracted from an accounting system and stored in a Microsoft Excel spreadsheet, or it might be a table a writer produced in Microsoft Word. Either way, InDesign makes it easy to handle tables created elsewhere: You import them like you import other text files. See #20 for more information about importing text.

Note

In InDesign, tables are always anchored in a text frame and always flow with surrounding text. For more information about anchored objects, see #36.

Importing Tables

To import tables from Word or Excel:

1. Choose File > Place.

2. In the Place dialog box, navigate to and select the Word (.doc) or Excel (.xls) file.

3. Check Show Import Options.

4. Click Open. The Microsoft Word Import Options dialog box or the Microsoft Excel Import Options dialog box opens.

5. For Word files, make sure Preserve Formatting from Text and Tables is selected in the Formatting area in the Microsoft Word Import Options dialog box. For Excel files, make sure Formatted Table is selected from the Table menu in the Formatting area (**Figure 39**).

6. Click OK.

7. Since the table is treated like text, the table is either imported at the text insertion point or the cursor is loaded and you click in an existing text frame or create a new one.

Importing Tables without Formatting

Just because you can import formatted tables and spreadsheets from Word and Excel doesn't mean that you should. Given the formatting limitations of the software involved—and the possible design limitations of the people involved—you might just want to create and format the tables in InDesign. You will probably end up reformatting all the text and the tables, and you may find that it's quicker and easier to simply import unformatted text and convert it to tables. In a large project with many tables, you might want to experiment with a couple and decide how you want to handle them.

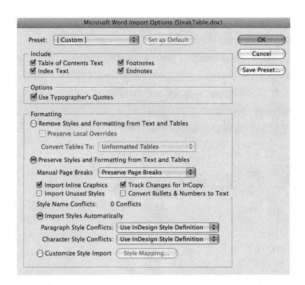

Figure 39 The Microsoft Excel Import Options dialog box lets you customize how Excel tables are imported into InDesign.

Linking Tables

When you import tables, spreadsheets, and text files, you have the option to link to the original file. If any changes occur in the original file, you can update the link in InDesign (using the Links panel) and the table or text is automatically updated. This is similar to updating the link to a graphic file, which InDesign maintains automatically. If you want to do this, check Create Links When Placing Text and Spreadsheet Files in the Type pane in the Preferences dialog box before you import the table. Then check the Links panel to see if a table needs to be updated. See #58 for more information about managing links.

Linking to tables sounds great, right? How many times do writers and accountants make changes after you have formatted their text and tables? But linking is really not as great as it seems, because if you update the link between InDesign and the original file, any formatting you applied in InDesign is lost. And why would you be using InDesign if not to make the table look better? Use this feature only if you're *not* planning to make formatting changes to the tables in InDesign.

#40 Creating New Tables

If you need to build a table in InDesign from scratch, you can easily create one with the number of rows and columns you need. In addition, you can add header rows for labeling the table and footer rows for details and such. Since tables are always anchored in text, you need to click in a text frame to create a table. The table will automatically match the current column width, so if you need to create a text frame to contain a table, make it approximately the width you want for the table. (See #36 for more information about anchored objects.)

To create a table:

1. Select the Type tool.

2. Click in a text frame to position the text insertion point wherever you want the table.

3. Choose Table > Insert Table.

4. In the Insert Table dialog box (**Figure 40a**), enter the number of horizontal rows you need for basic table data in the Body Rows field.

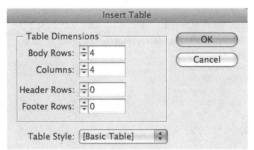

Figure 40a The Insert Table dialog box lets you specify how many rows and columns you want in a new table.

5. Enter the number of vertical columns you need in the Columns field.

6. If you need header rows for the table (to contain a table head and column heads, for example), enter the number of rows in the Header Rows field.

7. If you need footer rows for the table (to contain a citation, for example), enter the number of rows in the Footer Rows field. The advantage to creating official Header Rows and Footer Rows is that they automatically repeat if the table splits across columns or pages.

8. If you have created any table styles, you can choose one from the Table Style menu. See #44 for more information.

9. Click OK to create the table.

The table is anchored in text at the text insertion point. The height of the rows is based on the formatting of the text insertion point, whereas the width of the columns is calculated according to the width of the text frame and the number of columns specified (**Figure 40b**).

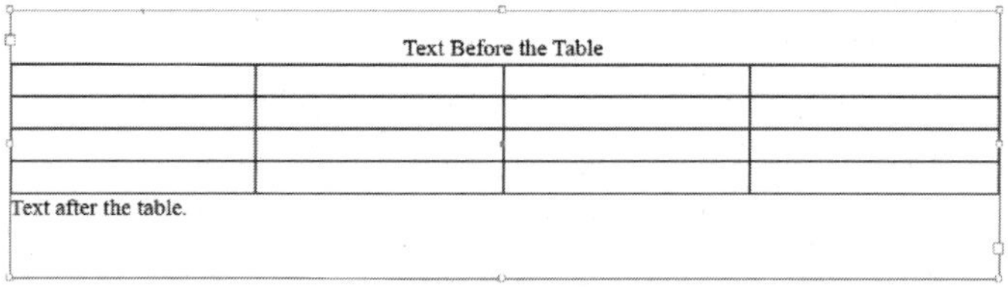

Text Before the Table

Text after the table.

Figure 40b New tables are automatically anchored in surrounding text so if the text reflows, the table moves accordingly.

#**41** Converting Text to Tables

The text that needs to go in a table often already exists, usually in a *tab-delimited format* (meaning that the cells of information for the table are separated by tabs and paragraph returns). You do not need to retype this text into a new table; you can easily convert it into a table. To do this:

1. If necessary, import the text into a text frame.

2. Choose Type > Show Hidden Characters to determine how the text is currently separated (**Figure 41a**). Usually, you will see tabs between "columns" of information and paragraph returns between "rows" of information. Check that all the columns have the same number of tabs between them; it doesn't matter if the tabs don't line up and the text looks messy. All that matters is consistency in the separation characters used.

```
Where To Go       House Specialty   What You'll Get¶
Bob's Steak & Chop House   20 oz. côte de boeuf ($39.95)       Intensely salty, crispy edges.¶
Brook's Steak House       16 oz. New York strip ($36.95)       Charred, nearly crunchy on
outside.¶
The Capital Grille  24 oz. porterhouse ($36.95) Luxurious cut, extremely tender.¶
Del Frisco's Double Eagle Steak house       8 oz. filet ($28.95) Dense and velvety, dark
woody flavor.¶
Elway's  13 oz. bone-in filet ($36)    Tender enough to eat with a spoon.¶
The Keg Steakhouse       10 oz. filet ($25.95) Tender and seasoned to a T.¶
Morton's,
The Steakhouse   24 oz. porterhouse steak ($42)       Buttery and hearty, fat cooked to
crackling. ¶
The Palm 18 oz. New York strip ($35.50)       Huge and hearty. ¶
Ruth's Chris Steak House   14 oz. filet ($34.95)       Sweet and firm.¶
Steakhouse 10    14 oz. New York strip ($28)  Airy texture, smoky.¶
```

Figure 41a Before converting text to a table, choose Type > Show Hidden Characters to determine what is separating columns (usually a tab) and what is separating rows (usually a paragraph return).

3. Select the Type tool and select the text to convert to a table.

4. Choose Table > Convert Text to Table.

5. In the Convert Text to Table dialog box (**Figure 41b**), confirm the selections for the Column Separator and Row Separator. If necessary, you can change the separators by choosing Tab, Comma, or Paragraph from the menus or by entering a different separation character (such as a semicolon) in the fields.

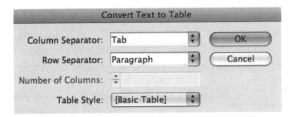

Figure 41b The Convert Text to Table dialog box lets you specify the characters used to separate columns and rows in the text.

6. If you choose the same separation character for columns and rows, you can clarify how many columns you need by entering a value in the Number of Columns field. Otherwise, this field is unavailable.

7. If you have created any table styles, you can choose one from the Table Style menu. See #44 for more information.

8. Click OK to create the table.

You may need to manually adjust the column widths (**Figure 41c**), and you can add header and footer rows as necessary.

Where To Go	House Specialty	What You'll Get
Bob's Steak & Chop House	20 oz. côte de boeuf ($39.95)	Intensely salty, crispy edges.
Brook's Steak House	16 oz. New York strip ($36.95)	Charred, nearly crunchy on outside.
The Capital Grille	24 oz. porterhouse ($36.95)	Luxurious cut, extremely tender.
Del Frisco's Double Eagle Steak house	8 oz. filet ($28.95)	Dense and velvety, dark woody flavor.
Elway's	13 oz. bone-in filet ($36)	Tender enough to eat with a spoon.
The Keg Steakhouse	10 oz. filet ($25.95)	Tender and seasoned to a T.
Morton's, The Steakhouse	24 oz. porterhouse steak ($42)	Buttery and hearty, fat cooked to crackling.
The Palm	18 oz. New York strip ($35.50)	Huge and hearty.
Ruth's Chris Steak House	14 oz. filet ($34.95)	Sweet and firm.
Steakhouse 10	14 oz. New York strip ($28)	Airy texture, smoky.

Figure 41c InDesign converts the selected text to a table, but it's likely that you'll have to adjust the column widths based on the content.

#**42** Adding Content to Tables

Tables consist of individual cells, which function like miniature text frames. You can enter text in individual cells, or you can anchor graphics in them. The one thing you cannot do is flow text through table cells as if they were threaded. If text already exists that you'd like to flow through a table, you're better off converting it to a table (see #41).

Adding Text to Tables

To add text to a table cell, click in the cell with the Type tool. You can then type in that cell, paste text into the cell (Edit > Paste), or import text into the cell (File > Place). To navigate between cells, press the Tab key to jump to the next cell and press Shift+Tab to jump to the previous cell. Row height will adjust automatically to accommodate the amount of text you type in the cell.

Adding Graphics to Tables

Since table cells function like small text frames, to place graphics in them you anchor the graphic in text. With tables, it's easiest to size the graphic appropriately first, before you anchor it. That way, you can ensure the graphic will fit in the cell. To anchor a graphic in text, select it with the Selection tool and choose Edit > Cut or Edit > Copy. Select the Type tool, click in a cell where you want the graphic, and choose Edit > Paste (**Figure 42**). You can also click in a cell and choose Object > Anchored Object > Insert to anchor a placeholder for a graphic.

Figure 42 You can combine text and graphics in the same table cell by anchoring a graphic in text like the steak shown here.

Adding Tabs to Cells

When working with tables, pressing the Tab key jumps to the next cell. If you need to enter an actual tab character into a cell—for example, if you need to align text in the table on a decimal tab—you need to choose Type > Insert Special Character > Other > Tab.

#43 Formatting Tables

With the table formatting options, you can create eye-catching, easy-to-read tables by automatically applying strokes and fills to alternating rows or columns of information, specifying different strokes and fills for individual cells, applying a border to the entire table, and much more. To access the formatting controls, you need to select all or parts of a table with the Type tool. All the formatting commands are available in the Table menu and the Table panel menu (Window > Type & Tables > Table). When cells are selected, frequently used table-formatting options are available in the Control panel as well.

Formatting an Entire Table

To format an entire table as opposed to individual cells, click anywhere in the table with the Type tool. Then choose Table > Table Options > Table Setup. The Table Setup tab (**Figure 43a**) lets you change the number of rows and columns, add a table border, and specify the amount of space before and after the table.

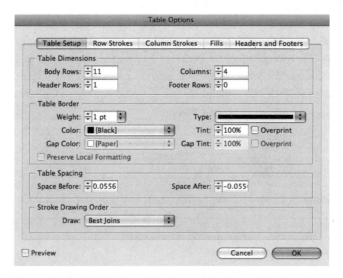

Figure 43a The Table Options dialog box provides formats for the entire table such as a table border and spacing before and after the table.

Aligning a Table within a Text Frame

To position the table within the text frame that it's anchored in—for example, to center the table in the text frame—first use the Type tool to select the paragraph that the table is anchored in. Then, click one of the alignment buttons in the Control panel's paragraph options.

Formatting Rows and Columns

In the Table Options dialog box, the Row Strokes, Column Strokes, and Fills tabs (**Figure 43b**) let you apply a pattern of strokes and/or fills such as applying a fill to every third column. You can also apply a table style to a selected table (see #44). For information about the Headers and Footers tab, see #45.

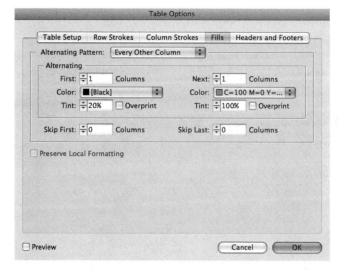

Figure 43b The Fills tab automates the process of creating a pattern, such as applying a tint to every other column, to improve a table's legibility.

Formatting Cells

To format cells, you first need to make a selection—a single cell, multiple adjacent cells, or the entire table. You can then specify how the text is positioned within the cell, specify strokes and fills for the cell, and even select cells with a pattern of diagonal lines. To make a selection, use the Type tool and then do one of the following:

- Click in a single cell to select it.

- Click and drag to select multiple cells.

Formatting Text in Tables

To format text in tables, select the text with the Type tool as always. To select entire rows or columns, move the pointer over the edge of the table until it turns into an arrow, then click or click and drag. Then use the standard text formatting controls: the Control panel, the Character and Paragraph panels (Type menu), and the Character Styles and Paragraph Styles panels (Type menu).

- Move the pointer over the left or top edge of the table until it turns into an arrow. Click the arrow to select an entire row or column; click and drag to select multiple rows or columns.

- Choose an option from the Table > Select submenu, including Cell, Row, Column, or Table.

Once you have cells selected to format, choose Table > Cell Options > Text. The Text tab in the Cell Options dialog box (**Figure 43c**) lets you change Cell Insets, Vertical Justification, First Baseline, Clipping, and Text Rotation within the cells. The Strokes and Fills, Rows and Columns, and Diagonal Lines tabs let you specify cell sizes and add strokes and/or fills to the cells for emphasis or clarity. You can also apply cell styles (see #44).

Figure 43c The Cell Options dialog box lets you specify the text placement, strokes, and fills for selected cells.

Using the Table Panel

The table formatting options used most often are also available in the Table panel (**Figure 43d**). To open the panel, choose Window > Type & Tables > Table. Point at the controls on the panel to display their tool tips and see what they do. The Table panel menu provides quick access to most of the commands in the Table menu.

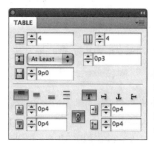

Figure 43d The Table panel provides quick access to commonly used table formatting options such as number of rows and columns, and text inset within cells.

Using Table Options in the Control Panel

When table rows or columns are selected, the Control panel provides quick access to common table formatting options (**Figure 43e**). These include options for formatting text in selected cells, rotating text, adding rows and columns, merging cells, and more. You can also apply styles to selected cells or the entire table (see #44).

Figure 43e When you select rows or columns in a table, the Control panel offers options for formatting the text, cells, and table.

#44 Using Table and Cell Styles

With the array of table-formatting options in InDesign, you can create impressive-looking tables. The process, however, can get tedious if you're working on a document with many tables or applying the same table attributes over and over. To quickly format tables, InDesign lets you create table styles and cell styles. Similar to paragraph styles and character styles, table styles and cell styles let you apply multiple attributes with one click. In addition, changes you make to table styles and cell styles are reflected in any tables and cells to which the styles are applied. So if you decide that cells need a larger text inset or tables need a stroke, you can make that change globally in multiple tables. You can apply a table style when you create a table.

Creating Table and Cell Styles

Table styles apply to entire tables and include both table formatting options and cell styles. For example, a table style might include a table border, a cell style for header rows, and an alternating pattern of row strokes. Cell styles include options such as text inset, baseline, and fills.

Generally, the best way to create styles is to first format a sample table or sample cell. Then, use the formatted table or cell as a basis for the style. To create a style:

1. Using the Type tool, select a formatted table.

2. Choose Window > Type & Tables > Table Styles or Cell Styles.

3. From the Table Styles or Cell Styles panel menu, choose New Table Style or New Cell Style.

4. In the Table Style Options (**Figure 44a**) or Cell Style Options dialog box, enter a name for the style.

5. All the options are already set based on the formatting applied to the selected table or cell as summarized in the Style Settings area. Click in the scroll list at left to display panes of different options and change any formatting.

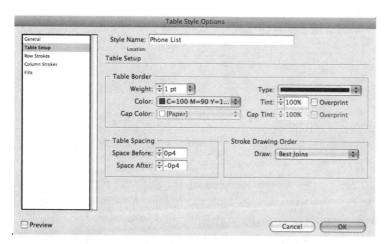

Figure 44a The Table Style Options dialog box lets you specify a name and shortcut key in the General pane and table formatting in the Table Setup, Row Strokes, Column Strokes, and Fills panes.

If you're not working with a formatted table or cell, you can create a new style by clicking the Create New Style button at the bottom of the Table Styles or Cell Styles panel. This creates a new style in the panel called Table Style 1 or Cell Style 1. The number reflects the creation order. Double-click the new style to name and modify it.

Applying Table and Cell Styles

You can apply a table style when you create a table (Table > Insert Table) or convert text to a table (Table > Convert Text to Table). In addition, you can select tables and cells and apply styles from the Control panel, Table Styles panel, and Cell Styles panel.

- **Table style:** To apply a table style, click in a table with the Type tool. Click the style name in the Table Styles panel (**Figure 44b**). If rows or columns are selected in the table, you can choose a style from the Control panel as well.

- **Cell style:** To apply a cell style, select the cell, cells, rows, or columns with the Type tool (see #43 for more information about selecting rows and columns). Click the style name in the Cell Styles panel or the Control panel.

Creating Style Groups

By default, styles are listed alphabetically in the Table Styles and Cell Styles panels. You can, however, drag styles to new locations in the list. In addition, you can manage styles by grouping them in the panels.

To create a group, click the Create New Style Group button at the bottom of the Table Styles or Cell Styles panel. Click on the new group's folder icon to rename it. You can then drag any styles you want into each group, organize the groups, and open the groups as needed.

Create New Style Group   Clear Overrides in Selection

Figure 44b Click a style name in the Table Styles panel to apply it to selected text.

Once you apply a table style, you're not stuck with that formatting. You can continue to modify the table's formatting as you wish. Any formatting that does not match the style is called an "override." After applying overrides, if you need to revert a table's formatting to exactly match the formatting in its style, choose Clear Overrides from the Table Styles panel menu. You can also Option-click (Mac OS) or Alt-click a style name. If rows or columns are selected in the table and you only want to clear overrides in the selection, click Clear Overrides in Selection at the bottom of the Table Styles panel. These same techniques work for clearing overrides in selected cells.

Tip

Cell styles do not need to specify all possible cell attributes; they can specify only what you want to change. For example, a cell style might specify nothing but Cell Insets. You can then apply the cell style to any cells you want to change—without changing the other attributes of the cell.

Modifying Styles

To change the attributes specified in a table style or cell style, double-click the style name or select the style name and choose Style Options from the Table Styles or Cell Styles panel menus. Or, as a shortcut, reformat a cell or table, and then choose Redefine Style from the panel menu. The Table Styles and Cell Styles panel menus also provide options for duplicating, deleting, importing, and exporting styles.

#45 Adding Headers and Footers to Tables

For a table to be useful, it generally needs row and column headings—so you know what kind of information the cells contain. This is easy to accomplish with a row at the top of the table containing column headings and a column down the left containing row headings. A problem occurs, however, if the table is split across several columns, text frames, or pages. The first row, which contains the column heads, can become separated from the columns, leaving the reader to guess what's in them. Fortunately, InDesign provides a simple solution with its header rows feature that automatically repeats the necessary rows whenever the table splits across columns, frames, or pages. In addition, if you need a footer in the table (to contain a disclaimer or source, for example), footer rows repeat as well.

In the following sample table (**Figure 45a**), the first row is designated as a header. So if we add 20 more steakhouses and need to continue the table on another page, the column heads will repeat. The last row is designated as a footer, so it will repeat as well.

Where To Go	House Specialty	What You'll Get
Bob's Steak & Chop House	20 oz. côte de boeuf ($39.95)	Intensely salty, crispy edges.
Brook's Steak House	16 oz. New York strip ($36.95)	Charred, nearly crunchy on outside.
The Capital Grille	24 oz. porterhouse ($36.95)	Luxurious cut, extremely tender.
Del Frisco's Double Eagle Steak house	8 oz. filet ($28.95)	Dense and velvety, dark woody flavor.
Elway's	13 oz. bone-in filet ($36)	Tender enough to eat with a spoon.
The Keg Steakhouse	10 oz. filet ($25.95)	Tender and seasoned to a T.
Morton's, The Steakhouse	24 oz. porterhouse steak ($42)	Buttery and hearty, fat cooked to crackling.
The Palm	18 oz. New York strip ($35.50)	Huge and hearty.
Ruth's Chris Steak House	14 oz. filet ($34.95)	Sweet and firm.
Steakhouse 10	14 oz. New York strip ($28)	Airy texture, smoky.

Figure 45a In this table, the first row is a header and the last row is a footer. These rows will repeat as necessary if the table flows across pages.

Converting Headers and Footers to Body Rows

If you decide you no longer need information in a header or footer row to repeat, but you want to keep it in the table, you can convert it back to a *body row*, or standard table row. To do this, select the rows and choose Table > Convert Rows > To Body.

Creating Header and Footer Rows

You have two choices for creating header and footer rows: You can convert existing rows, or you can add new rows.

- **Converting Rows:** In many cases, you will format your own rows to serve as header or footer rows—then realize you need the "official" header or footer rows because the table will actually continue in a different column, text frame, or page. In that case, you can convert the rows containing the header and footer information into actual header and footer rows. To do this, select the rows containing the header or footer information. (Using the Type tool, move the pointer over the right or left edge of the table until it turns into an arrow. Click to select the row, or click and drag to select multiple rows. Choose Table > Convert Rows > To Header or Table > Convert Rows > To Footer. If you're using both headers and footers in a table, you'll have to convert the rows separately.

- **Adding New Rows:** To add new rows for headers and footers, choose Table > Table Options > Headers and Footers. In the Headers and Footers tab (**Figure 45b**), enter the number of header rows to add in the Header Rows field. Enter the number of footer rows to add in the Footer Rows field.

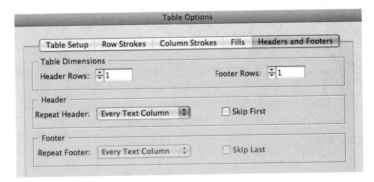

Figure 45b The Headers and Footers tab lets you add header and footer rows to the selected table and control how often the rows repeat.

- **Headers and Footers Options:** Whether you convert existing rows or add new headers and footers, you can control how often they appear in the Headers and Footers tab. Use the Repeat Header and Repeat Footer menus to specify whether the row should appear every time the table flows to a new column, to a new text frame, or only to a new page. If the start of the table contains column headings or footer information in a different format, such as a graphic, you can remove the header and footer from the start of the table. To do this, click Skip First in the Header area or Skip Last in the Footer area.

If you change your mind about header and footer rows, you can select the rows and delete them or decrease the number of Header Rows or Footer Rows in the Headers and Footers tab.

Editing Header and Footer Text

When you edit content in rows designated as headers and footers, the text and graphics automatically update wherever the header and footer is used. (As a result, do not insert words such as "continued" in the header of the continuation of a table because it will show up on the first part of the table as well.) To quickly jump to a header or footer row to start editing it, choose Table > Edit Header or Table > Edit Footer.

#46 Editing Tables

When it comes to tables, change is inevitable. You will find yourself constantly adjusting column widths and row heights, adding rows and columns, deleting rows and columns, and so on. Both the Table menu and the Table panel menu provide many options for editing tables.

Adding a Row

A quick way to add a row to a table is to press Tab when the insertion point is in the last cell in the table.

Inserting Rows and Columns

You can insert blank rows and columns within a table whenever you need them. To insert rows and columns, first select the Type tool.

- **Inserting rows:** To insert rows within a table, click in a row above or below where you want the new rows. Choose Table > Insert > Row. In the Insert Row(s) dialog box (**Figure 46a**), enter the number of rows to insert in the Number field and then click Above or Below to indicate the position.

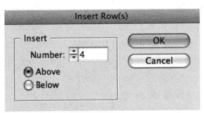

Figure 46a The Insert Row(s) dialog box lets you specify how many rows to insert and where to insert them.

- **Inserting columns:** To insert columns within a table, click in a column to the left or right of where you want the new columns. Choose Table > Insert > Column. In the Insert Column(s) dialog box, enter the number of columns to insert in the Number field and then click Left or Right to indicate the position.

Adding Rows and Columns

You can add rows to the bottom of a table or add columns to the right side of a table at any time. First, click in the table somewhere with the Type tool, then do one of the following:

- Change the values in the Body Rows field or the Columns field in the Table Setup tab (Table > Table Options > Table Setup).

- Change the values in the Number of Rows field or the Number of Columns field in the Table panel (Window > Type & Tables > Table).

- Change the values in the Number of Rows or Number of Columns field in the Control panel (available when rows or columns are selected).

Deleting Rows, Columns, and Tables

The Delete key will eliminate just about any selection in InDesign—selected text and objects, for example. It will not, however, delete selections within a table but will delete the contents instead.

To delete parts of a table or an entire table, make a selection first. With the Type tool, click in a row, column, or table that you want to delete. Choose Table > Select, and then choose Row, Column, or Table. You can also click outside the table when the arrow pointer displays to select a row or column (**Figure 46b**). Drag the arrow pointer to select multiple rows or columns. Once you've made a selection, choose Table > Delete, and then choose Row, Column, or Table.

Note
If you decrease the number of rows or columns in fields in the Table Setup tab or the Table panel, rows will be deleted from the bottom of the table and columns will be deleted from the right side of the table.

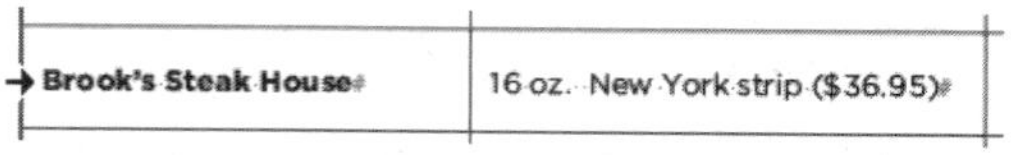

| Brook's Steak House | 16 oz. New York strip ($36.95) |

Figure 46b When you point outside a table with the Type tool, the arrow pointer lets you select entire rows and columns to format, cut and paste, or delete.

Resizing Tables, Rows, and Columns

If the initial column widths and row heights are not quite right—and they rarely are—they are easy to adjust. Using the Type tool, you can drag the gridlines between rows and columns to adjust the sizes (**Figure 46c**). You can also drag any edge of the table to resize the table height or width in any direction.

To "clean up" a table so the columns are the same width and the rows are the same height, choose Table > Distribute Columns Evenly or Table > Distribute Rows Evenly. You can also specify a height for selected rows and a width for selected columns in the Table panel and in the Rows and Columns tab in the Cell Options dialog box (Table menu).

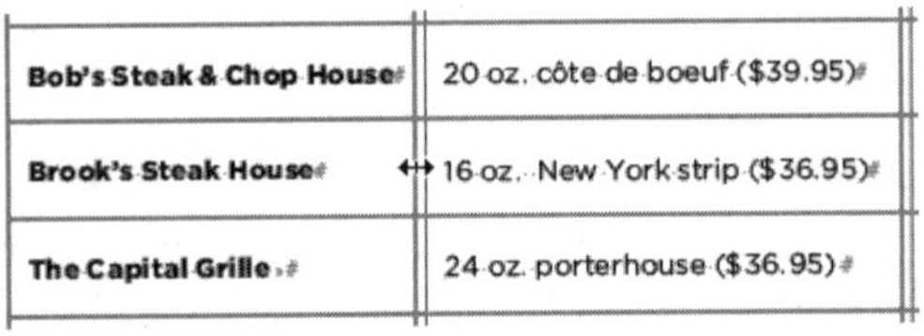

Bob's Steak & Chop House	20 oz. côte de boeuf ($39.95)
Brook's Steak House	16 oz. New York strip ($36.95)
The Capital Grille	24 oz. porterhouse ($36.95)

Figure 46c Using the Type tool, drag the gridlines to adjust column widths and row heights.

Tip

When specifying the height of rows in the Table panel or the Rows and Columns panel (Table > Cell Options), the Row Height menu lets you specify whether selected rows increase in height when you add content to cells. If you choose At Least, you specify the minimum height for the row, and the row height will expand as necessary to fit the content. (You can specify a maximum height in the Rows and Columns panel.) If you choose Exactly, the row height is fixed and text will be overset if it doesn't fit in its cell.

Merging and Splitting Cells

You may need to merge and split cells for various reasons such as creating a single-cell row for a table's title, adding a column that contains a vertical graphic, or dividing a cell into two to contain a note along with data.

To merge cells, first select the cells to merge with the Type tool. You can select any number of adjacent cells, including selecting cells across rows and columns to create a large rectangular cell. When the cells are selected, choose Table > Merge Cells (**Figure 46d**). If you change your mind about the merged cells, select the cell and choose Table > Unmerge Cells.

To split a cell, click in it to select it. Then, choose Table > Split Cell Horizontally or Table > Split Cell Vertically.

Tip

The commands for merging and splitting cells are also available in the Table panel menu.

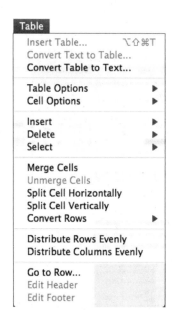

Figure 46d The Table menu lets you merge and split cells.

CHAPTER FIVE

Drawing Lines and Shapes

Although InDesign is not a dedicated illustration program like its close cousin, Illustrator, it includes several drawing tools and illustration features that you can use to create virtually any kind of line or shape you can imagine. You can use the lines and shapes you create as graphic elements, as containers for text and graphics, and as paths along which text flows.

In this chapter, you'll start by learning how to use the Line and Pencil tools to draw relatively simple lines. Next, you'll learn how to use the Pen tool to create complex lines and shapes. Then you'll move on to drawing basic shapes with the Rectangle, Ellipse, and Polygon tools. And finally we'll show you how to create more complex shapes using the Pathfinder panel and other InDesign drawing features.

#**47** Drawing Simple Lines

Before taking a look at InDesign's drawing tools, it's worth noting that InDesign doesn't distinguish between open and closed shapes, which are collectively referred to as *paths*. You can use any path as a graphic element or as a frame to hold text or a graphic, and you can flow text along any path. For example, you can draw a wavy line with the Pen tool and then:

- Add a stroke and a fill

- Use it as a container for text or a graphic

- Flow text along it

If a layout requires a straight line of any kind, the Line tool offers the easiest way to create it. Select the Line tool, and then click and drag on a page or on the pasteboard (**Figure 47a**). The point where you click is one end of the line; the point where you release the mouse button is the other end. As you drag, InDesign displays a line between the start point and endpoint and also indicates the line's midpoint. A live length value is also displayed as you drag. If you hold down the Shift key as you drag, the angle of the line is restricted to increments of 45°. New in InDesign CS4, the Show Transformation Values preference option in the Interface pane of the Preferences dialog box lets you show or hide the live values displayed next to the pointer as you drag.

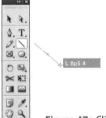

Figure 47a Click and drag with the Line tool to create a straight line. If Show Transformation Values—a new preference option in the Interface pane of the Preferences dialog box in InDesign CS4—is checked, InDesign displays the length of a line as you drag.

Drawing Lines and Shapes

Creating straight lines is a cinch. Creating curvy lines is another matter. One option is to use the Pencil tool, which lets you use the mouse as a pencil; the other option is the Pen tool, which lets you create complex paths but is not particularly easy to use. (See #49 for more about using the Pen tool.) To use the Pencil tool, select it, and then click and drag the mouse as if it were a pencil (**Figure 47b**). You'll quickly learn that a mouse is not a very good pencil. If you need more control than the mouse offers, you might want to consider purchasing a graphics tablet.

If you want to create a closed path with the Pencil tool, begin dragging and then hold down Option (Mac OS) or Alt (Windows) as you drag. To close the path, make sure you release the mouse button before you release the Alt or Option key.

Figure 47b The Pencil tool lets you draw freeform lines. This example was created using a graphics tablet, which is easier to use than a mouse for creating freeform shapes.

After you create a line, use the Selection tool to select and move it or to resize it by dragging a bounding box handle. Use the Direct Selection tool to move either of the endpoints of a straight line or any of the anchor points of a line created with the Pencil tool or the Pen tool.

You can modify lines in many ways. For example, you can assign a stroke weight and line style, and apply a color and tint. You can rotate, shear, and flip lines, and so on. (For more about modifying lines and other objects, see Chapter 7, "Working with Objects.")

Setting Defaults for the Drawing Tools

By default, the Basic Graphics Frame object style is applied to objects you create with the Line, Pencil, and Pen tools, as well as the Rectangle, Ellipse, and Polygon tools (but not the Rectangle Frame, Ellipse Frame, and Polygon Frame tools and the Type tool). Unless you modify it, the Basic Graphics Frame object style produces objects with a 1-point stroke and no fill. The Rectangle Frame, Ellipse Frame, and Polygon Frame tools always create objects with no fill and no stroke.

To change the default settings used by the Line, Pencil, Pen, Rectangle, Ellipse, and Polygon tools, make sure no objects are selected, and then modify the Basic Graphics Frame style, assign a different object style to the tools, or change any object-related settings (such as stroke, fill, drop shadow, or blending mode). (For more about using object styles, see #66.)

By default, the Basic Text Frame object style is applied to text frames you create with the Type tool. The easiest way to change the appearance of text frames created with this tool is to modify the Basic Text Frame object style when nothing is selected.

#48 Drawing Complex Lines

Most page-layout and graphics programs have a drawing tool that's similar to the Pen tool in InDesign. These tools let you create Bézier curves (also known as vector shapes), which are mathematically defined line segments. Bézier curves can be formed into complex paths that have straight edges, curved edges, or both.

If you're an Illustrator user or you've used Bézier tools in other programs, you'll be immediately comfortable with InDesign's Pen tool. If you've never used a tool like the Pen tool, it will probably take a little time for you to get the hang of it.

Here's an easy way to get started with the Pen tool:

1. Select the Pen tool in the Tools panel.

2. Click an empty area of a page or the pasteboard and release the mouse button to establish the first endpoint.

3. Move the Pen pointer, and then click and release the mouse button again to make a segment and another endpoint.

4. To draw additional straight segments, continue moving the pointer, and then clicking and releasing the mouse (**Figure 48a**).

5. To create an open path with two endpoints, select another tool when you're done adding segments. To create a closed path, move the pointer back to the first point you made, and then click the mouse when a small white circle is displayed next to the Pen pointer.

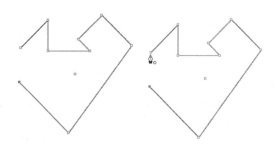

Figure 48a Click and release the mouse button to create straight-edged paths with the Pen tool (left). Click the starting point to create a closed path (right).

Drawing a path that's made up of curved lines is a little different than drawing straight-edged paths. Instead of clicking and releasing the mouse button when using the Pen tool, click and drag about one-third of the distance to the next anchor point before releasing the mouse.

When you click and drag with the Pen tool, InDesign creates an anchor point and a pair of opposing direction lines that form a straight line and meet at the anchor point. A curved segment is drawn to the preceding anchor point (**Figure 48b**). Continue clicking and dragging to set additional points and form curved segments. Choose a different tool or click the starting point to complete the object.

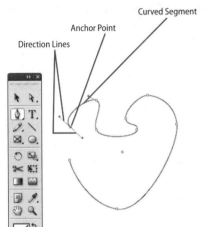

Figure 48b Click and drag the mouse in the direction of the next anchor point to create curved lines and shapes. This example shows the anchor points along a curved path. The anchor point that ends the path is selected, and you can see the direction lines that are displayed each time you click and drag to create an anchor point and a curved segment.

By combining the click-and-release method for creating straight segments and the click-and-drag method for drawing curved segments, you can use the Pen tool to draw paths that have both straight edges and curved edges.

If you're not satisfied with the results after using the Pen tool, it's easy to modify your creation. Use the Direct Selection tool to select and move anchor points and the endpoints of their accompanying direction lines. You can also use the Direct Selection tool to click and drag a segment (a portion of a path between anchor points) of a path. Use the Selection tool to move the object or to resize its bounding box.

The tools grouped with the Pen tool in the Tools panel also let you modify paths:

 Add Anchor Point tool: Click a path with the Add Anchor Point tool to add an anchor point.

 Delete Anchor Point tool: Click an anchor point with the Delete Anchor Point tool to remove an anchor point.

 Convert Direction Point tool: Click a corner anchor point with the Convert Direction Point tool, and then drag to convert it to a smooth anchor point. Or, click a smooth point to collapse its direction lines and convert it to a corner point.

By default, the Pen tool adds a 1-point stroke and no fill to the paths you create with it. To change the default settings for the Pen tool, modify the settings of the Basic Graphics Frame object style, choose a different object style from the Object Style menu in the Control panel when no objects are selected, or change object attributes such as fill color and tint, stroke weight and style, and so on, when no objects are selected.

#49 Drawing Basic Shapes

The Rectangle, Ellipse, and Polygon tools, and their next-door neighbors, the Rectangle Frame, Ellipse Frame, and Polygon Frame tools, let you create closed shapes that you can use as graphic elements, containers for text and graphics, and paths along which text flows.

The Rectangle, Ellipse, and Polygon tools let you create "unassigned" frames—that is, frames whose content is undefined (neither text nor graphics)—whereas the three frame tools let you create graphics frames into which you can import graphics. (You can tell the difference between an unassigned frame and an empty graphics frame by the X that's displayed within the graphics frame.) Because it's easy to change the content of an empty frame, it doesn't matter whether you use the Rectangle, Ellipse, or Polygon tools or the corresponding frame tools (Rectangle Frame, Ellipse Frame, or Polygon Frame) to create basic shapes.

To create a basic shape, select the appropriate tool, and then click and drag (**Figure 49**).

Figure 49 Click and drag the mouse to create a basic shape. In this example, the Polygon tool was configured to create six-sided shapes with no star inset. Holding down the Shift key while dragging creates a polygon with equal sides and angles.

- The Rectangle and Rectangle Frame tools let you create rectangles and squares. Hold down the Shift key when dragging to create a square.

- The Ellipse and Ellipse Frame tools let you create ellipses and circles. Hold down the Shift key when dragging to create a circle.

Setting Defaults for the Polygon Tool

To set defaults for the Polygon tool and the Polygon Frame tool, double-click either tool in the Tools panel. The Polygon Settings dialog box lets you specify the number of sides and, optionally, a star inset, which creates a starburst shape. The settings you specify are used for new polygons until you change settings again.

Changing the Content Type of an Empty Frame

InDesign lets you create three types of frames: text frames (with the Type tool), graphics frames (with the Rectangle Frame, Ellipse Frame, and Polygon Frame tools), and unassigned frames (with the Rectangle, Ellipse, and Polygon tools). You can change the content type for an empty frame by selecting it, choosing Object > Content, and then making a selection from the submenu (Graphic, Text, or Unassigned).

Using the Type Tool to Create Text Frames

Click and drag with the Type tool to create a new rectangular text frame. You can also use the Rectangle or Rectangle Frame tool, and then click within the frame with the Type tool. Hold down the Shift key as you drag to create a square frame. If you need to create a text frame within a text frame, use the Rectangle or Rectangle Frame tool to create the inner frame, and then select Object > Content > Text.

- The Polygon and Polygon Frame tools let you create equal-sided polygons and starburst shapes. Hold down the Shift key to create a polygon with equal sides and angles. Press the up arrow key as you drag to add sides to the polygon you're creating; press the down arrow key to subtract sides. Press the right arrow key as you drag to increase the star inset in 10% increments; press the left arrow key as you drag to decrease the star inset in 10% increments. Press the up and down arrow keys while dragging to continually add or delete points. (Note: When a star inset is specified in the Polygon Settings dialog box, the Polygon and Polygon Frame tools create a starburst shape instead of a regular polygon. Double-click the Polygon tool or Polygon Frame tool to display the Polygon Setting dialog box.)

In addition to the click-and-drag method of drawing basic shapes, you can also click once on a page or on the pasteboard when any of the shape-drawing tools is selected (not the Pen, Pencil, or Line tools). When you click, a dialog box lets you specify the height and width of the shape.

#50 Creating Complex Shapes

While the Pen tool is the only tool that lets you *draw* complex shapes, InDesign offers a handy panel that lets you *create* complex shapes from two or more basic shapes. When multiple objects are selected, the Pathfinder panel (Window > Object & Layout > Pathfinder) provides five options for creating a single shape that's generated from the selected objects. The results you get from the Pathfinder options depend on the stacking order of the selected objects. If you don't get the results you want, use the Arrange commands (Object > Arrange) to adjust the stacking order.

Here's a brief explanation of the Pathfinder options:

 Add: Combines the selected objects to form a single, all-encompassing shape (**Figure 50a**).

 Subtract: All objects in front of the backmost object are removed from (that is, punched out of) the backmost object (**Figure 50b**).

 Intersect: Creates a shape from overlapping areas and excludes areas that don't overlap (**Figure 50c**).

 Exclude Overlap: The opposite of Intersect. This option creates a shape from areas that do not overlap (**Figure 50d**).

 Minus Back: Somewhat like Subtract. All objects in back of the frontmost object are removed from (punched out of) the frontmost object (**Figure 50e**).

The five Pathfinder options are also available as commands in the Object menu (Object > Pathfinder).

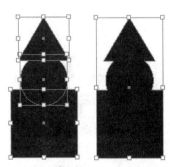 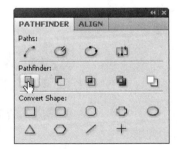

Figure 50a The Add button combines multiple objects into a single object.

If You Can't Draw It Easily with InDesign …

InDesign's drawing features are capable of handling many illustration tasks, but if your drawing requirements exceed InDesign's capabilities, your best bet is to use a dedicated illustration program, like Adobe Illustrator. You can even begin work on an illustration in Illustrator, and then copy and paste it into InDesign and use InDesign's drawing features to further modify the illustration.

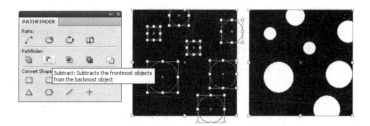

Figure 50b In this example, the Subtract option in the Pathfinder panel generated the shape on the right by "punching out" several circles from a square black background frame (center).

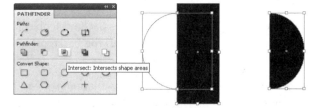

Figure 50c The Intersect button creates an object from overlapping areas.

Figure 50d The Exclude Overlap button creates an object from areas that don't overlap.

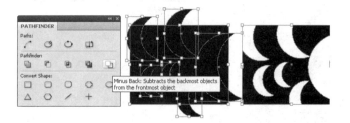

Figure 50e The Minus Back button removes the background objects (the crescent moon shapes) from the frontmost object (the rectangle).

#51 Converting Shapes

If you need to make minor modifications to an object's shape, select it with the Direct Selection tool, and then move anchor points, direction points, and segments. For bigger modifications, use the Add Anchor Point, Delete Anchor Point, and Convert Direction Point tools, which are grouped with the Pen tool in the Tools panel. To convert an object into one of nine predefined shapes, use the Pathfinder panel (Window > Object & Layout > Pathfinder).

To change an object's shape with the Pathfinder panel, select the object, and then click one of the nine Convert Shape buttons in the panel (**Figure 51**):

Rectangle

Rounded Corner Rectangle

Beveled Corner Rectangle

Inverse Rounded Corner Rectangle

Ellipse

Triangle

Polygon

Line

Vertical/Horizontal Line

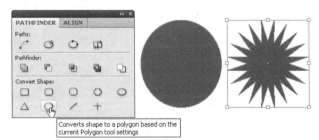

Figure 51 Click one of the Convert Shape buttons in the Pathfinder panel to change the shape of the selected object. In this example, the circle was converted to a polygon. When you convert a shape to a polygon, the current settings of the Polygon and Polygon Frame tool are used.

Using the Scissors Tool

You can use the Scissors tool to convert a closed path into an open path and to cut an open path into two separate open paths. To use the Scissors tool, select it in the Tools panel, and then move the crosshair pointer over the edge of an object. When a circle is displayed in the middle of the crosshairs—indicating that the pointer is over the edge of the object—click the mouse button. An anchor point is added where you click. If you select this anchor point with the Direct Selection tool and move it, you'll find another anchor point in the same place. This anchor point is the other endpoint if you cut a closed path. It's an endpoint on a separate path if you cut an open path.

You'll find four additional buttons for changing the shape of objects at the top of the Pathfinder panel. The same four options are also available in the Object menu (Object > Paths):

 Join Path button: When an open path is selected, clicking the Join Path button connects the two endpoints of the path to create a closed shape. When two open paths are selected, clicking the Join Path button connects an endpoint from each path to create a single open path.

 Open Path button: The Open Path button creates an open shape from a closed shape, much like using the Scissors tool on a closed path. InDesign chooses an anchor point at which the path is opened. You may need to select the object with the Direct Selection tool to determine where the object has been split.

 Close Path button: The Close Path button creates a closed path from an open path by connecting the two endpoints.

 Reverse Path button: If you've created a shape with one or more "holes" in it—for example, a doughnut shape created by using the Subtract button on a pair of concentric circles—selecting the inner path and then clicking the Reverse Path button in the Pathfinder panel will eliminate the hole while keeping the path. Clicking the Reverse Path button again will show the hole.

CHAPTER SIX

Working with Graphics

In addition to using InDesign's drawing tools to create graphic elements within InDesign, you can also import graphics created with other programs, such as Adobe Photoshop and Adobe Illustrator. After you import a graphic into an InDesign layout, you can modify it in many ways, including cropping, scaling, rotating, and flipping it horizontally or vertically. You can also use InDesign to apply see-through effects to imported graphics that make them appear translucent.

In this chapter we begin by explaining how to import graphics into InDesign layouts, and then tell you how to use some of InDesign's most powerful features to modify imported graphics and manage graphic files.

#52 Placing Graphics

InDesign lets you import a broad range of common graphic formats, including TIFF, JPEG, PDF, and EPS, as well as several lesser-known formats like DCS, PNG, and Scitex CT. You can also import native Photoshop and Illustrator files. Once you import a graphic into a layout, InDesign lets you modify it in several ways, as explained in #54, #55, #56, and #57.

To place a graphic into an InDesign document, simply choose File > Place. InDesign doesn't require you to create a frame before you import a graphic, although you can work this way in InDesign if you want to. The Place dialog box (**Figure 52**) lets you locate and choose the graphic. What happens after you click Open depends on what object, if any, is selected.

Importing InDesign Files

The ability to use the Place command (File menu) to import InDesign files into an InDesign layout was introduced in InDesign CS3. When you import an InDesign file into a layout, the placed file is treated the same as any other graphic. If you change and then resave the original InDesign file, the status of the placed file is updated in the Links panel in InDesign.

Changing Your Mind After Importing a Graphic

If you click the Open button in the Place dialog box and then discover that you've mistakenly placed a graphic into the wrong frame, press Command+Z (Mac OS) or Ctrl+Z (Windows). The loaded graphics icon is displayed, and you can click within an empty frame, click an empty area on the page or pasteboard to create a new graphics frame that's the same size as the graphic, or click and drag to create a new custom-size graphics frame.

Figure 52 The Place dialog box lets you select the graphic you want to place into an InDesign layout. If you select Show Import Options, another dialog box is displayed after you click Open and offers several options for controlling the display of the graphic.

- If nothing is selected, the loaded graphics icon 📷 is displayed in the upper-left corner of a thumbnail proxy of the graphic, and you can click once or click and drag to place the graphic into a new graphics frame. If you click once, the resulting frame is the same size as the full-size graphic. If you click and drag, the rectangle you create becomes the frame that contains the graphic. As you drag, the rectangle that's displayed automatically matches the proportions of the graphic. When you release the mouse after clicking and dragging, the graphic is scaled up or down to fit within the frame while the graphic's original proportions are maintained. You can also click the loaded graphics icon within an empty frame to place the graphic within it.

- If a graphics or unassigned frame is selected, the graphic is placed within the frame.

- If the text insertion cursor is flashing, the graphic is placed within the text frame as an anchored graphic. (See #36 for more about anchored objects.) An anchored graphic is treated like a text character and moves when editing causes text to reflow.

Importing Multiple Graphics

If you want, you can import multiple graphics at once into a layout. To do this, choose File > Place, and then select the files you want to import. (All files must be in a single folder, and you can select any combination of graphics files and text files.) When you click Open in the Place dialog box, a number indicating the number of loaded files is displayed in parentheses next to the loaded graphics icon. Ctrl+click (Windows) or Command+click (Mac OS) to cascade all of the loaded files onto a single page, or click once with the mouse to place only the next loaded graphic. The number of remaining files is displayed along with a thumbnail proxy of the next graphic.

After you import a graphic into an InDesign layout, InDesign maintains a link between the graphic file and the InDesign document. InDesign uses the original graphic file to display it at high resolution, and the original graphic files are also used when you print or export an InDesign document that contains imported graphics. The Links panel (Window > Links) displays a list of all placed graphics. For information about managing links to graphic files, see #58.

Dragging and Dropping Graphics

In addition to using the Place command (File menu) to import graphics, you can drag and drop graphic files into InDesign layouts. To drag and drop a graphic, click a graphic file in the Mac OS Finder, Windows Explorer, the desktop, or Adobe Bridge, drag the file icon into an InDesign document window, and then release the mouse button.

#53 Cropping and Resizing Graphics

After you import a graphic, chances are you'll want to resize it, crop it, or both. InDesign offers several ways to scale and crop imported graphics. But before you begin working with graphics, it's important to understand some basics about how InDesign handles them.

Every imported graphic is contained within a graphics frame. Most graphics frames are rectangular; however, you can use any object (except a text frame) as a graphics frame regardless of its shape.

Use the Selection tool to select a graphic and its frame, or use the Direct Selection tool or the Position tool, which is paired with the Direct Selection tool in the Tools panel, to select only the graphic (**Figure 53a**). If you look closely, you'll notice that the bounding box of a selected graphics frame is displayed in a different color than the border around a selected graphic. Once you select a graphics frame or graphic, you're ready to modify the selection.

Selected graphics frame   Selected graphic

Figure 53a This graphic is larger than the frame that contains it and is cropped on all four sides by the frame. Clicking the graphic with the Selection tool selects the graphics frame (left). Clicking the graphic with the Direct Selection tool selects the graphic itself (right). The color of the bounding box of a selected graphics frame is different from that of a selected graphic.

Crop a Graphic

You can show and hide different portions of a graphic by adjusting the size and shape of its frame or by adjusting the size of the graphic. The Selection tool is the best tool for cropping graphics. To crop a graphic by resizing its frame:

1. Choose the Selection tool, and then click on or within a graphics frame.

2. Drag any of the eight resizing handles to control what portion of the graphic is visible. If the frame is an irregular shape, use the Selection tool to resize its bounding box or use the Direct Selection tool to drag anchor points or segments and change the shape of the frame.

Resize a Graphic and Its Frame

You can resize a graphic and its frame at the same time manually or by specifying scale percentages. To resize a graphic and its frame manually:

1. Select the frame with the Selection tool.

2. Hold down the Shift and Ctrl keys (Windows) or the Shift and Command keys (Mac OS), and drag a handle. If you hold down only the Ctrl key or the Command key as you drag, the frame and graphic are scaled disproportionately. If you hold down only the Shift key, the frame is scaled proportionally and the scale of the graphic does not change.

To resize a graphic and its frame by specifying scale percentages:

1. Select the frame with the Selection tool.

2. Enter values in the Scale X Percentage or Scale Y Percentage fields in the Transform panel or the Control panel. If you click the Constrain Proportions for Scaling button next to the scale fields in either panel, horizontal scale (Scale X) is automatically adjusted when you change vertical scale (Scale Y) and vice versa.

Resize a Graphic

To manually resize a graphic but not its frame:

1. Choose the Direct Selection tool or the Position tool, and then click a graphic.

2. Drag any of the eight resizing handles. To maintain the graphic's proportions, hold down the Shift key when dragging.

Direct Selection Tool versus the Position Tool

The Direct Selection tool and the Position tool are paired in the Tools panel because they work similarly. Use the Position tool if you want to move a graphic within its frame or resize the frame. Use the Direct Selection tool if you want to move a graphic within its frame or change the shape of a frame by dragging an anchor point or segment.

You can also change the scale of a selected graphic by modifying the Scale X Percentage or Scale Y Percentage values in the Control panel or the Transform panel (**Figure 53b**). If the Constrain Proportions for Scaling button next to the scale fields in either panel is enabled, horizontal scale (Scale X) is automatically adjusted when you change vertical scale (Scale Y) and vice versa.

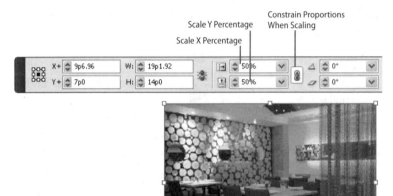

Figure 53b The Scale X Percentage and Scale Y Percentage fields in the Control panel show that the selected graphic is scaled to 50% of its original size. (The graphic was selected by clicking it with the Direct Selection tool.) The Constrain Proportions When Scaling button to the right of the fields is selected, which means the graphic's proportions will be maintained if you change either of the scale values.

Fit Options

InDesign includes a set of fitting options that lets you resize a graphic to fit within its frame or resize a frame to fit the graphic. To use the fitting options, first select a graphic or a graphics frame. Next, click any of the five fitting buttons at the right end of the Control panel. The options are

 Fit content to frame: Resizes the graphic to fill the frame. The graphic's proportions are not maintained if the frame is not proportional to the graphic.

Fit content proportionally: Resizes the graphic so that it fits within the frame while maintaining the graphic's proportions. If the frame is not proportional to the graphic, part of the frame background is visible below or to the right of the graphic.

Center content: Aligns the center point of the graphic with the center point of the frame.

Fit frame to content: Adjusts the size of the frame so that it matches the size of the graphic.

Fill frame proportionally: Resizes the graphic so that it fills the frame while maintaining the graphic's proportions. If the frame is not proportional to the graphic, part of the graphic is cropped from the bottom or the right edge of the graphic.

Note
The Fitting buttons in the Control panel let you resize a graphic to fit its frame and vice versa. The same options are available in the Object menu (Object > Fitting).

The Info Panel

When a graphic or frame that contains a graphic is selected, the Info panel (Window > Info) provides useful information about the graphic, including its file type (EPS, TIFF, Photoshop, and so on), actual and effective resolution (for pixel-based graphics), color space (RGB, CMYK, and so on), and ICC profile (if the graphic includes one).

#54 Modifying Graphics and Graphics Frames

Cropping and scaling are only the beginning of what you can do to imported graphics with InDesign. You can also modify a graphic, its frame, or both by rotating, shearing (slanting), or flipping horizontally or vertically or both—not to mention applying any of several special effects that are explained in #55. In InDesign the controls for making basic modifications to graphics are available in the Control panel and the Transform panel (Window > Object & Layout > Transform).

As is the case with cropping and scaling, it's important that you make the correct selection before you modify a graphic. To modify a graphic and its frame, select the frame with the Selection tool. To modify only the graphic, select the graphic with the Direct Selection or Position tool. If you look carefully, you'll notice that the border displayed around a selected graphics frame is a different color than the border that's displayed around a selected graphic.

Use the Control or Transform panel to make the following modifications (**Figure 54a**):

- **To change the position of the selection:** Change the X Location or Y Location value. If a graphics frame is selected, the values are measured from the ruler origin to the selected reference point, which is highlighted in the Reference Point button at the left of the Control and Transform panels. (By default, an object's center point is its reference point; however, you can change the reference point of a selected object by clicking a different handle in the Reference Point button.) If a graphic is selected, the values are measured from the reference point of the frame to the reference point of the graphic.

- **To change the size of the selection:** Change the Width or Height values. By default, the accompanying Constrain Proportions for Width and Height button is selected, which means that changing either the Width or Height value will automatically change the other value to maintain the object's proportions.

- **To change the scale of the selection:** Change the values in the Scale X Percentage (horizontal scale) or Scale Y Percentage (vertical scale) fields or choose a value from the accompanying menu. By default, the Constrain Proportions When Scaling button (to the right of the two fields) is selected, which means that changing either the horizontal or vertical scale value will automatically change the other value to maintain the graphic's proportions.

- **To rotate the selection:** Enter a value other than 0 in the Rotation Angle field or choose a value from the accompanying menu.

- **To shear the selection:** Enter a value other than 0 in the Shear X Angle field or choose a value from the accompanying menu. Positive values slant the selection to the right; negative values slant it to the left.

The Control and Transform panel menus include additional commands for modifying objects, including Flip Horizontal, Flip Vertical, Flip Both, Rotate 180°, Rotate 90° CW (clockwise), and Rotate 90° CCW (counterclockwise).

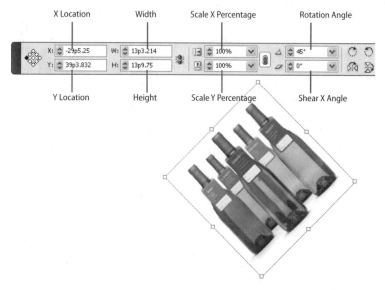

Figure 54a The Control panel (shown here) and Transform panels include controls for modifying graphics and graphics frames, as well as other objects. In this example, the selected graphics frame—and the graphic within—are rotated 45°.

Other Ways to Modify Graphics

In addition to the object modification controls in the Control and Transform panels, similar functionality is available in the Tools panel and the Object menu. Use any of the four transform tools— Rotate, Scale, Shear, and Free Transform—to modify a graphic by clicking and dragging. Double-click the Rotate, Scale, or Shear tool to display a dialog box that lets you specify various settings. Choosing Object > Transform displays four options for modifying objects: Move, Scale, Rotate, and Shear. Choose any of these options to display a dialog box that lets you specify settings.

You can also modify a graphics frame by adding a stroke (border) or a background fill or both. To add a stroke to a graphics frame:

1. Choose Window > Stroke to open the Stroke panel (**Figure 54b**).

2. Specify a stroke width in the Weight field and choose a stroke style from the Type menu in the Stroke panel. The Stroke panel includes other options that let you control the appearance of a stroke.

3. To apply a color to the stroke, open the Swatches panel (Window > Swatches), click the Stroke button in the upper-left corner of the panel, and then choose a color. If you want, you can apply a tint (shade) of the selected color swatch by specifying a value in the Tint field at the top of the Swatches panel.

Figure 54b Use the Stroke panel to add a border around a graphics frame. In this example, the graphics frame has a 10-point double-striped stroke.

To add a background fill to a graphics frame, click the Fill button in the Tools panel or the Swatches panel, and then choose a color in the Swatches panel (**Figure 54c**). Optionally, specify a Tint value. A background fill is visible only outside the rectangle that contains the graphic—unless the graphic was saved with a transparent background or it is displayed using a clipping path.

Fill button
Stroke button

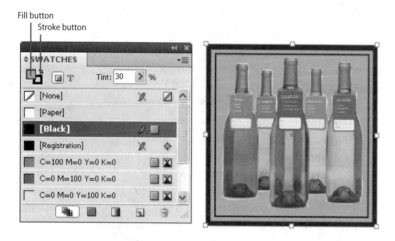

Figure 54c Use the Swatches panel to add a fill color to a graphics frame. In this example, the graphic is masked using a clipping path, and the graphics frame has a black background with a 30% tint.

#55 Special Effects for Graphics

If you're looking for more exotic graphics modifications than simple rotation, scale, and shear, InDesign offers several special effects for creating see-through objects through which underlying objects are visible. For example, you can apply a basic feather to a graphic so that it fades to transparent near its edge. You can apply Photoshop effects—collectively referred to as *transparency* effects in InDesign—independently to an object or its fill, stroke, or content (text or graphic).

Before you apply a transparency effect, make sure you use the correct tool to select a graphics frame or a graphic. Use the Selection tool to select the frame; use the Direct Selection or Position tool to select the graphic within. Generally, you'll apply these special effects to graphics frames; however, you can achieve different results by applying them to graphics—or both. Do whatever achieves the results you want.

To apply an effect to the selection, choose Object > Effects, and then select Transparency or an effect from the submenu. The same options are available if you choose Effects from the Effects panel menu (Window > Effects), or if you click the *fx* button at the bottom of the Effects panel. When you choose a command, the Effects dialog box is displayed. The Settings For menu at the top of the dialog box lets you apply effects independently to the object, stroke, or fill if a graphic frame is selected or to the graphic if a graphic is selected. InDesign includes the following transparency effects:

- **Drop Shadow** adds a soft- or hard-edged shadow behind graphics and graphics frames (**Figure 55a**). The controls in the Effects dialog box let you specify the placement and appearance of the shadow.

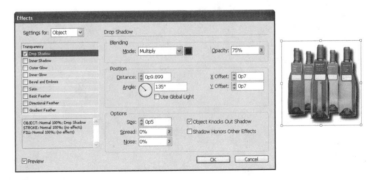

Figure 55a A drop shadow adds a three-dimensional look to a page.

- **Inner Shadow** adds a shadow inside the edge of an object's content to create a recessed appearance.

- **Outer Glow** and **Inner Glow** add glows to the outer or inner edges of an object's content.

- **Bevel and Emboss** add highlights and shadows to create a raised appearance.

- **Satin** applies shading that creates a smooth, satin-like appearance.

- **Basic Feather** fades the edge of a graphic or a graphics frame from opaque to transparent.

- **Directional Feather** is similar to a basic feather but includes separate controls for the top, bottom, left, and right edges of the selection.

- **Gradient Feather** lets you fade an object from opaque to transparent with controls for specifying the type of gradient (linear or radial), the length of the gradient, and its angle (**Figure 55b**).

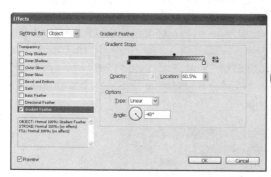

Figure 55b Gradient Feather fades an object from opaque to transparent. A gradient feather is applied to the wine bottle graphic (bottom-right) to slowly reveal the gray shape behind. The original, unmodified wine bottle graphic (top) is opaque.

- **Blending Mode** blends the colors where objects overlap. Use the Blending Mode menu in the Effects panel to apply a blending mode. You can also specify a blending mode in the Effects dialog box by selecting Transparency in the list of effects.

Removing Effects

To remove a transparency effect from an object, select the object, and then uncheck the effect in the Transparency dialog box (Object > Effects > Transparency). To remove all transparency effects from an object, select the object and then choose Object > Effects > Clear All Transparency. This command is also available in the Effects panel menu and in the fx menu at the bottom of the Effects panel.

Applying Effects to Other Objects

You can apply InDesign's transparency effects to any object. For example, you can apply a drop shadow to a text frame or the text within a text frame, and you can apply a blending mode and opacity and also feather the edges of shapes and lines you create with the drawing tools. When you apply a drop shadow to a text frame, a shadow is created for all the text within the selected frame. You cannot apply a drop shadow to a range of text.

Converting a Clipping Path to a Frame

The Clipping Path command (Object menu) lets you mask portions of an imported graphic using built-in clipping paths or alpha channels or an InDesign-generated clipping path based on the graphic's contrast. While it's not possible to stroke a clipping path, you can convert a clipping path to a frame, and then apply a stroke to the frame. To change a clipping path into a frame:

1. Choose Object > Clipping Path > Options, and then use the controls in the Clipping Path dialog box to apply a clipping path to a selected graphic. Click OK to close the dialog box.

2. Choose Object > Clipping Path > Convert Clipping Path to Frame. After you convert a clipping path to a frame, you can apply a stroke to the frame, assign a frame style and color, and so on.

- **Opacity** makes a graphic appear to be translucent. The Opacity controls are in the Effects panel (**Figure 55c**). You can also specify opacity in the Effects dialog box by selecting Transparency in the list of effects. Lower the opacity value to make the selection increasingly lighter and more translucent.

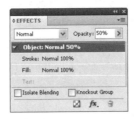

Figure 55c The Opacity field in the Effects panel lets you make an object translucent. In this example, the graphic on the right has an opacity of 50%, which reveals the shape beneath it. The original, unmodified graphic (left) is opaque.

To mask portions of a graphic so they're not visible, you can use a clipping path. The Clipping Path dialog box (Object > Clipping Path > Options) lets you choose a clipping path or an alpha channel that's built into a graphic, or you can choose Detect Edges in the Clipping Path dialog box's Type menu to have InDesign create a clipping path based on light and dark areas (**Figure 55d**). Detect Edges works best when the portion of the image you want to keep is silhouetted against a background that's uniformly lighter or darker.

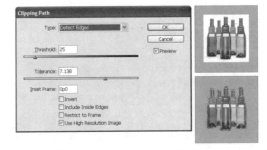

Figure 55d In this example, the Detect Edges option was used to create a clipping path for the graphic. The original graphic without a clipping path is on the top. The clipping path removes the white background from the picture.

#56 Working with Illustrator Graphics

InDesign and Illustrator are close cousins and very much alike. They're both vector-based programs, they're both from Adobe, and they share many of the same features. One benefit of the similarity between Illustrator and InDesign is that you can copy objects between the two programs. This lets you take advantage of the features in both programs to create graphic elements.

The easiest way to add an Illustrator file to an InDesign layout is to use the Place command (File menu). When you place a graphic into a layout, InDesign maintains a link to the graphic file and uses the original file when displaying at high resolution, printing, and exporting the graphic. (When you place an Illustrator graphic into an InDesign layout, you cannot modify any of the objects within the graphic. If you need to modify the graphic, you must open it in Illustrator and then make the changes.) Subsequent changes you make to the graphic file in Illustrator are reflected in the InDesign layout. Not only does InDesign support native Illustrator (.ai) files, but it also supports illustrations saved as EPS or PDF.

In addition to importing Illustrator graphics into InDesign layouts, you can also copy and paste or drag and drop objects between the two programs. The benefit of being able to use these methods is that they let you use InDesign to modify objects you've created in Illustrator, and vice versa. Before you copy and paste or drag and drop Illustrator objects into InDesign, make sure to check AICB (Adobe Illustrator Clipboard) in the File Handling & Clipboard pane of Illustrator's Preferences dialog box (Illustrator > Preferences > File Handling & Clipboard [Mac OS]; Edit > Preferences > File Handling & Clipboard [Windows]).

To use the copy-and-paste method:

1. Select one or more objects in Illustrator.

2. Choose Edit > Copy.

3. Switch to InDesign and choose Edit > Paste. The copied elements are pasted into InDesign as a group of editable objects.

To use the drag-and-drop method:

1. Arrange an Illustrator document window and an InDesign document window so you can see both onscreen.

2. Select one or more Illustrator objects, drag them into the InDesign window, and then release the mouse button.

When you copy and paste or drag and drop Illustrator objects into an InDesign layout, the objects behave as though you created them in InDesign, and InDesign does not maintain a link to the Illustrator file (that is, they're not listed in the Links panel).

Yet another option for working with Illustrator is to copy and paste or drag and drop InDesign objects into Illustrator, modify them in Illustrator, and then copy and paste or drag and drop the modified objects back into InDesign. This is called "round tripping." See **Figure 56** for an example.

Figure 56 The original checkerboard graphic (left) was created in InDesign, and then copied and pasted into an Illustrator document. Illustrator's Twirl tool was used to create the variation on the right, which was copied and pasted into the InDesign layout to complete the round trip.

#57 Working with Photoshop Graphics

While the InDesign interface has more in common with Illustrator than with Photoshop, InDesign and Photoshop are also tightly integrated. You can import native Photoshop (.psd) files into InDesign layouts, and you can import other Photoshop-generated bitmap graphics such as TIFF, JPEG, and DCS. InDesign's support of native Photoshop files also includes several features that let you control how images are displayed and printed.

Show/Hide Layers and Layer Comps

When you import a Photoshop file that includes layers or layer comps, you can control the visibility of both within InDesign.

1. Choose File > Place.

2. Check Show Import Options in the Place dialog box, and then click Open.

3. Display the Layers pane and make sure Show Preview is checked.

4. To achieve the result you want, do one of the following:

   • Choose a layer comp from the Layer Comp menu (**Figure 57a**).

   • Click the eye to the left of a layer name to alternately show or hide the layer.

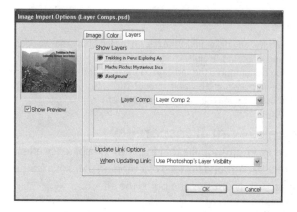

Figure 57a When you import a Photoshop file that includes layers or layer comps, you can use the controls in the Layers pane of the Image Import Options dialog box to adjust the visibility of the layers and layer comps in the InDesign layout.

Masking Portions of a Graphic

If you import a Photoshop file that contains clipping paths or alpha channels into an InDesign layout, you can use them to mask parts of a graphic or wrap text around them. To apply a clipping path or an alpha channel to a graphic:

1. Select the graphic or its frame, and then choose Object > Clipping Path.

2. In the Clipping Path dialog box, choose Alpha Channel or Clipping Path from the Type menu (**Figure 57b**). (If these options are not available, the graphic has no alpha channels or clipping paths.) If you choose Detect Edges in the Type menu, InDesign will generate a clipping path based on the light and dark areas of the image.

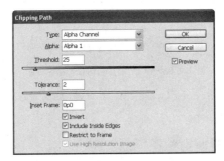 

Figure 57b The original graphic (the one on the left above) has an opaque white background. Choosing an alpha channel and adjusting the settings in the Clipping Path dialog box produced the variation on the right. Notice how the circular shape behind the graphics frame is visible through the background of the graphic on the right that uses an alpha channel as a clipping path.

Display and Print Transparency

If you import a Photoshop file that includes transparency effects, such as a transparent background (instead of a clipping path) or a feathered edge, InDesign accurately displays and prints the effects.

#58 Managing Graphic Links

Each time you place a graphic into an InDesign layout, InDesign collects and stores information about the graphic file, including its size, file type, link status (Up to Date, Modified, Missing, or Embedded), and location. InDesign uses the original graphic files when printing and exporting documents that contain imported graphics, as well as when displaying graphics at high resolution.

The Links panel (Window > Links) has been completely redesigned for InDesign CS4 and displays a list of all graphic files that have been placed in an InDesign layout and provides information about the files (**Figure 58**). It also includes commands and controls for managing the links between the document and the imported graphic files.

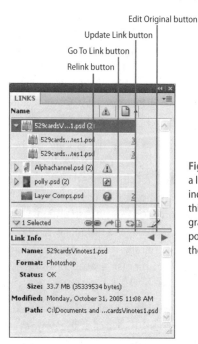

Edit Original button
Update Link button
Go To Link button
Relink button

Figure 58 The Links panel displays a list of all imported graphics and indicates the status of each one. In this example, the Alphachannel.psd graphic is listed as modified, the polly.psd graphic is embedded, and the Layer Comps.psd file is missing.

Displaying Graphics at High Resolution

To display a selected graphic at high resolution, choose Object > Display Performance > High Quality Display. To enable high-resolution display for all imported graphics, open the Display Performance panel in InDesign's Preferences dialog box (InDesign > Preferences > Display Performance [Mac OS]; Edit > Preferences > Display Performance [Windows]), and then choose Default View > High Quality. InDesign uses the original graphic files to create high-resolution previews. If your graphic links aren't up to date, InDesign can't display them at high resolution. (Note: Displaying graphics at high resolution on older computers can noticeably slow down screen display.)

For each graphic file listed in the Links panel, InDesign displays a thumbnail of the graphic, an icon that indicates the status of the source file (Modified, Missing, or Embedded; no icon is displayed for graphics whose status is OK), and the number of the page that contains the graphic. A triangle is displayed to the left of graphics that have been placed more than once. Click this triangle to display each instance.

Customizing the Links Panel

If you choose Panel Options from the Links panel menu, you can use the controls in the Panel Options dialog box to customize the panel. For example, you can specify small, regular, or large rows; you can display or hide thumbnails in the Name column and the Link Info area; and you can choose the information that's displayed in the panel list and the Link Info area. You can also drag the column headings to reorder the columns.

Modifying Linked Graphics

As you work on a layout, you may need to modify an imported graphic. To quickly open the source file of an imported graphic, select the graphic or its frame, and then choose Edit With in the Links panel menu. This displays a list of applications that can open the file. Choose the one you want to use to modify the graphic. Make and save your changes to the graphic, and then return to InDesign to continue working on the layout.

- **OK:** If only the page number is displayed to the right of a graphic file, it means that the link is up-to-date (that is, the original file is not missing and has not been modified since it was imported).

- **Missing:** The red missing link icon indicates that the graphic file has been moved or renamed since it was imported. To fix a missing link, select it in the Links panel, click the Relink button at the bottom of the panel or choose Relink from the panel menu, and then locate and open the graphic file. If the graphic file has been modified since you imported it, the status indicator will change from Missing to Modified. If the selected file has been placed more than once, the Relink button changes to Relink All Instances.

- **Modified:** The yellow modified link icon indicates that the current version of the graphic file is more recent than the version used when the file was imported. To update the link, click the Update Link button at the bottom of the panel or choose Update Link from the panel menu. Update Link changes to Update All Instances if you select a file that's been imported more than once.

- **Embedded:** The embedded icon indicates that the graphic file has been embedded within the InDesign file. You can embed a graphic by selecting it in the Links panel and then choosing Embed File from the Links panel menu. When you embed a graphic file, a copy of the file is stored within the InDesign file, and InDesign does not maintain a link to the original file. Any changes you make to the original file are not reflected in the InDesign document. Generally, it's not a good idea to embed graphic files within InDesign documents because InDesign file sizes can become prohibitively large.

To view all information available for a particular graphic, double-click its name in the Links panel. This expands the Link Info area at the bottom of the panel. Double-click the filename again to collapse the Link Info area.

Although it's possible to display, export, and print documents that have modified or missing graphics, you should make sure all links are up to date before you perform any of these functions. If you try to export or print a document with missing or modified links, InDesign will warn you and let you update the links, or you can continue, in which case InDesign will use low-resolution graphics.

CHAPTER SEVEN

Working
with Objects

No matter how comfortable you get with InDesign's drawing tools (see
Chapter 5, "Drawing Lines and Shapes"), you'll want to modify nearly every
object you create by applying a fill color or a stroke; by scaling, rotating, or
flipping horizontally or vertically; by moving or resizing, and so on. One
of the most enjoyable benefits of using InDesign is that it allows you to
change your mind as often as you want and modify objects in many ways.
But before you can modify an object, you must first select it.

In this chapter you'll learn how to use two tools to select objects. This
chapter also explains how you can use many of InDesign's most powerful
features to modify objects and create eye-catching graphic elements.

#59 Selecting and Deleting Objects

InDesign's Tools panel has two tools for selecting objects: the Selection tool and the Direct Selection tool. Understanding the difference between these tools is critical if you want to work efficiently.

In most cases, you'll use the Selection tool ![cursor] to select objects. When you click an object with the Selection tool, the rectangular shape that encloses the object—its *bounding box*—is displayed with eight resizing handles around the perimeter and a center point in the middle. For rectangular objects, the bounding box and the shape of the object are identical. When you select a nonrectangular object with the Selection tool, you're actually selecting the bounding box rectangle that surrounds the object within (**Figure 59a**). You can drag a handle to resize a bounding box and the object within, and you can click within the object and drag to move it.

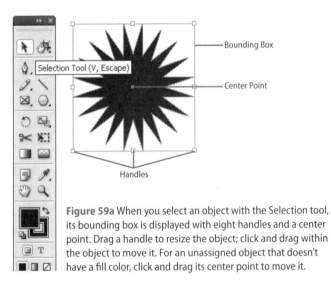

Figure 59a When you select an object with the Selection tool, its bounding box is displayed with eight handles and a center point. Drag a handle to resize the object; click and drag within the object to move it. For an unassigned object that doesn't have a fill color, click and drag its center point to move it.

When you click an object with the Direct Selection tool ![cursor], the object's anchor points and segments are displayed, and you can drag them to change the object's shape (**Figure 59b**). You can also use the Direct Selection tool to click and drag a graphic within a graphics frame.

For rectangular objects—most text and graphics frames are rectangles—it's hard to tell the difference between an object and its bounding box. However, if you look closely at a rectangular frame selected with the Direct Selection tool, you'll see that anchor points are displayed only at the four corners, in contrast to the eight handles that are displayed if you use the Selection tool.

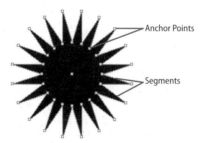

Anchor Points

Segments

Figure 59b When you select an object with the Direct Selection tool, its anchor points and segments are displayed. Drag an anchor point or segment to reshape the object; click and drag within the object to move it. For an unassigned object that doesn't have a fill color, click and drag its center point to move it.

Once you understand the difference between the Selection tool and the Direct Selection tool, you'll choose and use the right tool without a second thought. Here are a few more details you should know about selecting objects:

- Several commands for selecting objects and their contents are available in the Object menu. Choose Object > Select to display a list of commands for selecting objects above and below the currently selected object. If a graphic or graphics frame is selected, the Content and Container commands let you choose the graphic or its frame. If a group is selected, the Next Object in Group and Previous Object in Group commands let you select other objects in the group. Four of these options—Select Content, Select Container, Select Next Object,

Selecting an Empty Unassigned Frame

You can click anywhere within an empty graphics frame or text frame to select it, but if you click within an empty unassigned frame (for example, a frame created with the Rectangle, Ellipse, or Polygon tool), nothing happens—that is, the object is not selected. That's because you're actually clicking through the object and onto whatever is below (probably the page background). To select an empty unassigned frame, click its edge. You can then drag its center point to move it, resize its bounding box (if the Selection tool is selected), or reshape it by dragging anchor points and segments (if the Direct Selection tool is selected).

and Select Previous Object—are available as buttons in the Control panel when an object is selected.

- You have two options for manually selecting multiple objects. Hold down the Shift key as you click objects with the Selection or Direct Selection tool, or click an empty area of the pasteboard or page and then drag a rectangle that includes any portion of the objects you want to select.

- If the text insertion cursor is not flashing, choose Edit > Select All to select all objects on the page or spread.

- To temporarily switch to the Selection tool or Direct Selection tool when you're using another tool, press and hold the Command key (Mac OS) or the Ctrl key (Windows). When you use this shortcut, InDesign switches to the tool (Selection or Direct Selection) that you most recently used.

- Use the Direct Selection tool to select an object that's part of a group. After you select a grouped object, click within the object and drag to move it (click and drag the center point of an unassigned frame with no fill color); drag an anchor point or a segment to reshape the object. Switch to the Selection tool to select the object's bounding box.

The easiest way to delete an object is to select it with the Selection tool, and then press the Backspace or Delete key. You can also choose Edit > Clear. Choose Edit > Cut if you want to delete the object from its current location and paste it elsewhere (Edit > Paste). A cut or copied object is saved to the clipboard until you cut or copy something else or quit InDesign.

#60 Moving and Locking Objects

One of the most common tasks you'll perform when laying out pages is moving objects, which involves selecting text frames, graphics frames, or other graphic elements and then repositioning them within a page or moving them to another page.

You have two options for moving objects:

- Use the Selection tool to manually move objects by clicking and dragging. If you hold down the Shift key when dragging an object, its movement is restricted to vertical, horizontal, and 45° angles.

- To move objects more precisely, you can change the X and Y values that specify an object's position relative to the zero point (the upper-left corner of the page by default). When an object is selected, the X Location and Y Location fields in the Control panel and Transform panel display the object's coordinates (**Figure 60**). By default, the X value represents the horizontal distance from the zero point to the object's center; the Y value represents the vertical distance from the zero point to the object's center. If you don't want to use an object's center point as the reference point, click one of the nine handles in the Reference Point icon at the left of the Control and Transform panels.

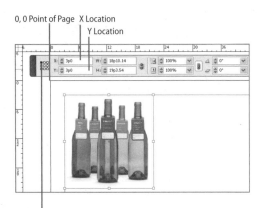

0, 0 Point of Page   X Location
Y Location

Reference Point

Figure 60 In this example, the upper-left corner of the selected object is its reference point. The X Location and Y Location values in the Control panel show that the upper-left corner of the object is one-half inch (3 picas) inside the left edge of the page and one-half inch below the top edge.

Snapping Objects to Guides and Grids

If Snap to Guides is checked in the View menu (View > Grids & Guides > Snap to Guides) when you drag an object, any edge of the object's bounding box will snap to a guide line (margin guide, column guide, or ruler guide) when the edge comes within four pixels of the guide. This makes it easy to align object edges with guidelines.

Smart Guides

Four new Smart Guide options in the Guides & Pasteboard pane of the Preferences dialog box expand the options for aligning, sizing, and positioning objects as you create and move them. The options are: Align to Object Center, Align to Object Edges, Smart Dimensions, and Smart Spacing. You can enable or disable each option. The Smart Guides command in the View menu (View > Grids & Guides > Smart Guides) lets you enable and disable the Smart Guides feature.

You can use the up/down, left/right arrow keys on your keyboard to nudge objects vertically and horizontally in small increments. By default, each press of an arrow key will move the selected object one point. To change the increment, open the Units & Increments pane of the Preferences dialog box and specify a different value for Cursor Key.

While it's possible to drag objects between pages, dragging objects to distant pages can get cumbersome. If you need to move an object to a different page, the Cut/Paste option is easiest.

1. Select the object.

2. Choose Edit > Cut.

3. Navigate to the page where you want to place the object, and then choose Edit > Paste. If you want to place the object in the same position on the new page as it was on the original page, choose Edit > Paste in Place.

If you want to prevent an object from being moved, select the object and then choose Object > Lock Position. When an object is locked, it can't be moved, either manually or by changing the X Location or Y Location value in the Control panel or Transform panel. You can, however, select and modify a locked object—for example, you can apply a stroke or a fill color. To unlock a locked object, select it, and then choose Object > Unlock Position.

#61 Filling Objects with Color

If you use InDesign to create color publications, adding color to objects and changing the color of objects are common tasks. You can apply a background color—or in InDesign terminology, a *fill*—to any object. For example, you can apply a fill color to a text frame to provide a nonwhite background for the text within it. You can apply a fill color to objects you've created using InDesign's drawing tools. And in some cases, you can even apply a fill color to imported graphics.

You have two options for applying fill color to a selected object: the Swatches panel and the Color panel.

Using the Swatches Panel

The Swatches panel (Window > Swatches) lists a document's colors and gradients (**Figure 61a**). (See Chapter 8, "Working with Color," for information about creating colors and gradients.)

Click the Fill box in the upper-left corner of the Swatches panel, and then click a color in the list. The Swatches panel also includes Tint controls that let you create color tints from 0% to 100%.

Fill Box   Tint Field

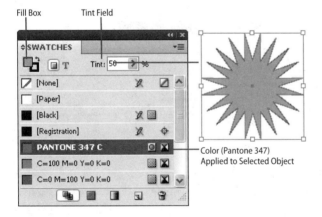

Color (Pantone 347) Applied to Selected Object

Figure 61a The Swatches panel lists a document's colors and lets you apply a color and a tint to selected objects. In this example, the object is filled with a 50% tint of Pantone 347.

Applying Color to Pictures

You can apply color to imported black-and-white and grayscale images. Use the Direct Selection tool to select the image, click the Fill box in the Tools, Swatches, or Color panel, and then click a color in the Swatches panel or create a color with the Color panel.

Drag-and-Drop Color

In addition to the other ways mentioned to apply color, you can apply a fill or a stroke color to any object by dragging a swatch from a panel and dropping it onto the object or stroke you want to color.

Using the Color Panel

The Color panel (Window > Color; **Figure 61b**) lets you create colors on the fly—that is, without having to choose New Color Swatch from the Swatches panel menu. The downside is that these colors are not added to the document's color list, which means they don't show up in the Swatches panel, and you can't apply them to other objects unless you save or re-create them. (To save a color you've created with the Color panel, choose Add to Swatches from the panel menu or drag the swatch from the Color panel to the Swatches panel.)

To create a color to use as a fill color, click the Fill box in the upper-left corner of the Swatches panel, and then choose a color model—RGB, CMYK, or Lab—from the Color panel menu. Use the slider controls or the fields to specify a color. The controls vary depending on the color model you select. If an object is selected when you create a fill color with the Color panel, the color is applied to the selected object. If nothing is selected, the color is used as the fill color for new objects created with the Rectangle, Ellipse, and Polygon tools.

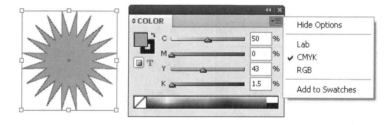

Figure 61b The Color panel provides controls for creating CMYK, RGB, and Lab colors.

In addition to the Fill boxes in the Swatches and Color panels, there's a Fill box in the Tools panel. Clicking any of these Fill boxes selects all three.

To remove an object's fill color, select the object and then click None or Paper in the Swatches panel. If you click None, the object is transparent. If you click Paper, the object is opaque white (unless you've modified the Paper swatch).

#62 Adding a Stroke to Objects

Adding a stroke to an object can mean the difference between a mere graphic element and a graphic element that stands out on a page. For example, a stroke around a sidebar can set it apart from the surrounding elements and draw the reader's attention. Similarly, a stroke around a graphic can both contain the image within and isolate it from other graphic elements.

The Stroke box is paired with the Fill box in the Swatches panel, Color panel, and Tools panel, and the two work similarly. To add a stroke to a selected object, first click any Stroke box. (Note: By default, the Rectangle, Ellipse, and Polygon tools create objects with a one-point black stroke.)

When you apply a stroke to an object, you may not be able to see it if the stroke has no width or no color. The easiest way to specify a stroke's width is to choose a weight from the Weight menu in the Control panel or enter a weight value in the accompanying field (**Figure 62a**). The Stroke Type menu in the Control panel lets you choose a stroke style. (See #63 for information about adding custom stroke styles.)

Use the Swatches panel or the Color panel to assign a color to the stroke. (See #61 for information about the Swatches and Color panels.)

Adding Corner Styles to Stroked Objects

The Corner Options command (Object menu) lets you apply any of five corner styles to stroked objects: Fancy, Bevel, Inset, Inverse Rounded, and Rounded. The Size field lets you control the size of the corner effect.

Stroke Type Menu

Stroke Weight Field

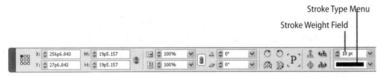

Figure 62a The Weight field in the Control panel specifies a 10-point-wide stroke. Below the Weight field, the Solid style is selected in the (Stroke) Type menu.

Stroking Text

You can add a stroke to text and modify the appearance of the stroke the same as you do with objects. See #33 for more about stroking text.

Switching an Object's Stroke and Fill

When applying fills and strokes to objects, it's easy to accidentally switch the stroke and fill colors. If you find yourself in this situation, click the Swap Fill and Stroke button ↰ in the Swatches panel, Color panel, or Tools panel. This will switch the fill and stroke colors.

In addition to specifying a stroke's weight, type, and color, you can use the Stroke panel (Window > Stroke) to modify several other stroke characteristics (**Figure 62b**). The Stroke panel includes controls for specifying how segments connect and where the stroke is placed relative to the edge of the object (Align Stroke to Center, Align Stroke to Inside, or Align Stroke to Outside). You can also specify a Gap Color and Gap Tint for dashed, striped, and dotted stroke styles. The Start and End menus are available only for open paths and let you choose among several graphic endpoints, including arrowheads, squares, and circles.

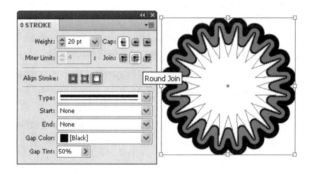

Figure 62b The Stroke panel includes several controls for modifying the appearance of a stroke. In this example, a 20-point black stroke with a round join is applied to a 20-sided polygon with a 50% star inset. A Thick-Thin (Stroke) Type is also applied, and the gap between the thick and thin strokes is a 50% tint of black.

To remove a stroke from an object, select the object, and then set the stroke weight to 0. You can do this using the Weight field in the Control panel or the Stroke panel. You can also set the stroke color to None to remove a stroke from an object.

#63 Creating Custom Stroke Styles

InDesign has 18 built-in stroke styles, ranging from stripes to dots, dashes, and hash marks. If these aren't enough for you, you can also create your own custom stroke styles.

To create a custom stroke style:

1. Choose Stroke Styles from the Stroke panel menu.

2. Click New in the Stroke Styles dialog box.

3. In the New Stroke Style dialog box (**Figure 63a**), enter a name for the style and choose a Type: Stripe, Dotted, or Dash. The choice you make determines the controls displayed below. Each stroke type offers a different set of controls.

4. Use the controls in the New Stroke Style dialog box to specify the appearance of the style, and then click OK to close the dialog box and save the style, or click Add to save the style and continue creating new styles.

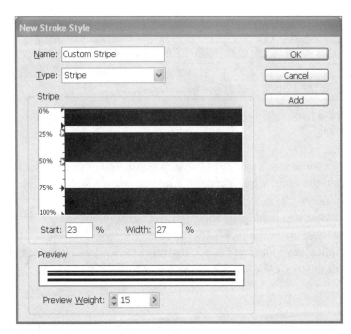

Figure 63a The controls for creating a custom stripe. The controls are slightly different for Dash and Dotted strokes.

Sharing Stroke Styles

Use the Save button in the Stroke Styles dialog box to share stroke styles with other InDesign users. When you save stroke styles, InDesign creates a separate file and assigns it an .inst extension. Other InDesign users can click the Load button in the Stroke Styles panel, select an .inst file, and click Open to add the stroke styles to a document. If no documents are open when you load stroke styles, they are added to the list of default styles and are automatically included in all new documents.

There are too many controls in the New Stroke Style dialog box (**Figure 63b**) to explain each one in this book. Fortunately, they're intuitive and easy to use. A few minutes of creative fiddling and you'll be comfortable.

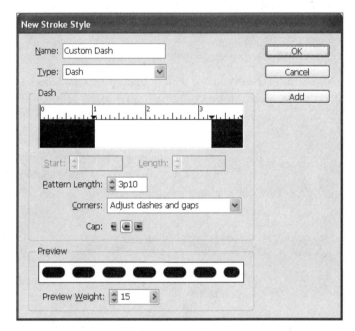

Figure 63b The controls for creating a custom dash. In this example, the dashes have round caps.

After you create a new stroke style, it's displayed in the (Stroke) Type menu in the Control panel and the Stroke panel, and you can choose it when applying a stroke to an object or text.

If you want to modify the appearance of a custom stroke style, choose Stroke Styles in the Stroke panel menu, select the style in the list, and then click Edit. Make your changes, and then click OK to close the Edit Stroke Style dialog box. Click OK to close the Stroke Styles dialog box.

#64 Transforming Objects

InDesign provides many features that let you modify the appearance of an object. Four of these features are grouped together and referred to collectively as *transformations*:

- **Rotate:** Rotate objects to any angle.

- **Scale X Percentage:** Lengthen or shorten objects horizontally as a percentage of the current width.

- **Scale Y Percentage:** Lengthen or shorten objects vertically as a percentage of the current height.

- **Shear:** Specify a shear angle between –90° and 90° to slant an object along its horizontal axis.

As is true for many features, InDesign offers several methods for applying these transformations to selected objects:

- **Transform controls in the Control panel:** In addition to the four basic transformation controls—Rotate, Scale X Percentage, Scale Y Percentage, and Shear—the Control panel also includes controls for changing the location of an object (X and Y fields), as well as its height and width (H and W fields), for applying a stroke weight and style, and more (**Figure 64a**). The Control panel menu offers several additional commands for modifying objects, including Flip Horizontal, Flip Vertical, and Flip Both. The Control panel is the most versatile option for applying basic transformations and making other common changes to objects.

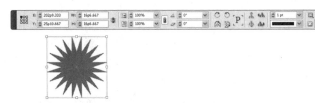

Figure 64a When an object is selected, the context-sensitive Control panel offers controls for modifying the position, size, and appearance of the object.

- **Transform panel:** The controls in the Transform panel (Window > Transform; **Figure 64b**) are a subset of the controls in the Control

Scaling Objects Manually

You can scale objects manually using the Selection tool. Select an object with the Selection tool, and then drag a bounding box handle. Hold down the Shift key as you drag to maintain proportion. To scale a graphics frame and the graphic within, hold down the Command key (Mac OS) or Ctrl key (Windows) as you drag a bounding box handle. Add the Shift key to maintain the proportion of the graphic and frame.

Scaling Objects versus Scaling Graphics

To scale a graphic but not its frame, select the graphic with the Direct Selection tool, and then specify a Scale X Percentage or Scale Y Percentage value in the Control or Transform panel, or drag one of the eight resizing handles on the graphic's border. Hold down the Shift key to maintain proportion. To determine how much a graphic has been scaled, select it with the Direct Selection tool, then check the Scale X Percentage and Scale Y Percentage values.

Repeating Transformations

If you make one or more transformations to an object, InDesign remembers what you've done and lets you apply the transformations to other objects. To repeat transformations, select one or more objects, choose Object > Transform Again, and then choose one of the four options:

1. Transform Again applies the most recent change to the selected object. If multiple objects are selected, they're treated as a group.

2. Transform Again Individually applies the most recent change to each object separately if multiple objects are selected.

3. Transform Sequence Again applies the most recent series of changes to the selected object. If multiple objects are selected, they're treated as a group.

4. Transform Sequence Again Individually applies the most recent series of changes to each object separately if multiple objects are selected.

panel, which is a good reason to use the Control panel unless you have a particular affinity for the Transform panel.

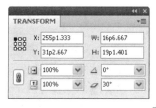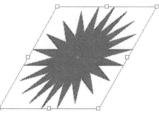

Figure 64b The Transform panel contains a subset of the controls available in the Control panel, including the four basic transformations: Rotate, Scale X Percentage, Scale Y Percentage, and Shear. In this example, a 30° shear angle is applied to the object.

- **Tools panel transformation tools:** The Tools panel contains four transformation tools: Rotate tool ( ), Scale tool ( ), Shear tool ( ), and Free Transform tool ( ). (Note: the Scale tool and Shear tool are paired together in the Tools panel.) There are two ways to use the Rotate tool, Scale tool, and Shear tool: 1) Select one of the tools, click an object to select it, and then click and drag; or 2) Select an object, and then double-click one of the tools. A dialog box is displayed with controls for specifying transformations. To use the Free Transform tool, select it, and then click an object. Drag a bounding-box handle to scale the object. To rotate the object, move the pointer just outside a corner handle to display a rotation pointer , and then click and drag.

- **Transform commands:** The Transform commands in the Object menu provide yet another option for making basic transformations. Choose Object > Move, Scale, Rotate, or Shear to display a dialog box with controls for transforming the selected object.

To maintain an object's proportions when scaling it horizontally or vertically, make sure the linked chain icon (not the broken chain icon) is displayed for the Constrain Proportions button in the Control and Transform panels. The Constrain Proportions button has two states represented by two icons: 1) When the feature is enabled, the icon is a linked chain. 2) When the feature is disabled, the icon is a broken chain. Clicking the button toggles between the two states.

#65 Special Effects for Objects

If you're a Photoshop user, you've probably modified images by applying special effects such as blending modes, opacity, shadows, glows, and feathered edges. InDesign includes several Photoshop-like creative effects, and you can apply them to any object. You even have the option to apply these special effects independently to a frame, or to its fill, stroke, or content (text or graphic).

Collectively, these features are called *transparency effects* because they produce see-through effects for objects that would otherwise be opaque, and they let you create eye-catching special effects without having to switch to Photoshop.

To apply a blending mode or change opacity:

1. Select an object.

2. Choose Window > Effects to open the Effects panel (**Figure 65a**).

3. Choose a blending mode from the Blending Mode menu or change the Opacity value. If you select Stroke, Fill, Text, or Graphic (rather than Object) in the Effects panel, you can apply a blending mode and specify opacity for that component of the selection. (Note: As you decrease the opacity percentage, an object becomes lighter and more transparent. An object with 0% opacity is invisible.)

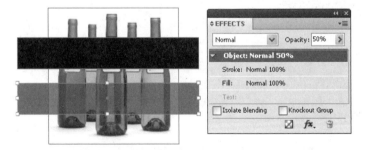

Figure 65a In this example, the two rectangles have a 100% black fill. An opacity value of 50% is applied to the one on the bottom, making it both lighter and translucent.

Drag-and-Drop Effects

When you apply an effect to an object, a stroke, a fill, text, or graphic, an "fx" is displayed in the Effects panel to the right of the affected component. You can transfer effects from one object to another by selecting the source object and then clicking and dragging an fx from the Effects panel list onto the target object.

The rest of the creative effects—Drop Shadow, Inner Shadow, Inner and Outer Glow, Bevel and Emboss, Satin, Basic Feather, Directional Feather, and Gradient Feather—are available in the Object menu (Object > Effects) and the Effects panel. To apply an effect:

1. Select an object.

2. Choose Object > Effects, and then choose Transparency or any of the effects. (You can also display a list of effects by clicking the fx button at the bottom of the Effects panel.)

3. In the Effects dialog box, check Preview, and then adjust the controls for the selected effect until you achieve the desired result (**Figure 65b**).

By default, a creative effect is applied to an entire object (its stroke, fill, and content). If you don't want to apply an effect to an entire object, choose an option other than Object from the Settings For menu (Stroke, Fill, Text, or Graphic) in the Effects dialog box.

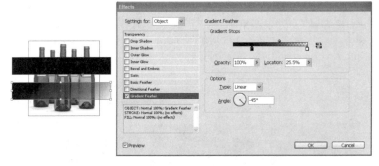

Figure 65b In this example, a gradient feather is applied to the lower of the two black rectangles to create a gradient that fades from opaque black to transparent at a 45° angle.

To remove an effect from an object, uncheck the effect in the Effects dialog box (Object > Effects > Transparency). To remove all effects from an object, select the object, and then choose Object > Effects > Clear Effects. To remove all effects, as well as any applied blending mode and opacity value, choose Object > Effects > Clear All Transparency. These commands are also available in the Effects panel menu.

#66 Using Object Styles

The ability to format text using character and paragraph styles is one of InDesign's most useful and powerful features. Object styles let you quickly format objects in much the same way character and paragraph styles let you format text. For example, if you create a newsletter that regularly uses sidebar text frames that include strokes, fills, and text insets, you can create an object style with these settings, and then use the object style to quickly format new sidebar frames.

The easiest way to create an object style is to first modify an object manually so that it includes all the settings you want to include in the object style—fill color and tint, stroke weight and style, drop shadow, and so on. After the object is correctly formatted:

1. Open the Object Styles panel (Window > Object Styles) and choose New Object Style from the panel menu.

2. The New Object Style dialog box (**Figure 66a**) displays the settings applied to the selected object. Name the object style, if you want, assign a keyboard shortcut (in the General pane), and then click OK. The new object style is displayed in the Object Styles panel.

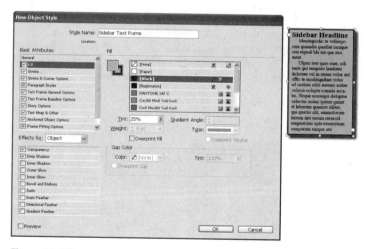

Figure 66a When you create a new object style, the settings applied to the selected object are used. In this example, the text frame has a tinted fill, a stroke, a drop shadow, and text insets.

Setting the Default Object Style for Frames

The Object Styles panel includes two default object styles: Basic Graphics Frame and Basic Text Frame. A small, square icon is displayed to the right of Basic Graphics Frame, indicating that this object style is used for new objects created with the Rectangle, Ellipse, and Polygon tools. A small, square icon with a T is displayed to the right of Basic Text Frame, indicating that this object style is used for new text frames created with the Type tool. You can drag either of these icons to other object styles to change the default style used for the Rectangle, Ellipse, Polygon, and Type tools.

You don't have to modify an object before you can create an object style. If you choose New Object Style from the Object Styles panel when nothing is selected, you can create the new object style from scratch by changing the settings in the Object Style Options dialog box.

To apply an object style, select an object, and then click the name of the object style in the Object Styles panel (**Figure 66b**) or use the keyboard shortcut, if you assigned one.

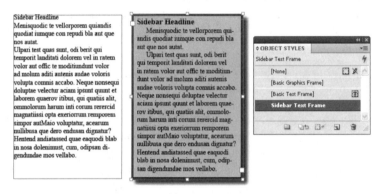

Figure 66b In this example, the Sidebar Text Frame object style was used to format the text frame on the right. The other text frame on the left is the original, unstyled frame. Notice how the object style formatted both the frame—by adding a fill color and tint, a frame, and a drop shadow—and the text within. Because an object style can include a paragraph style, you can use object styles to format both text frames and the text within.

#67 Grouping Objects

There are times when you'll want to handle multiple objects as if they were a single object. For example, if you've placed a caption next to a photograph, you'll want to keep them together if you decide to move the photo. Or if you've created an illustration or a logo using several objects created with InDesign's drawing tools, you'll want to treat them as a single object when scaling, rotating, or shearing. The most efficient way to work with multiple objects at once is to create a group. In general, a group of objects behaves like a single object; however, you can still select and modify individual objects within a group.

To create a group, select two or more objects, and then choose Object > Group. (See #59 for more about selecting objects.) That's it.

To select a group, click any object in the group with the Selection tool (**Figure 67**). A selected group is contained within a bounding box that has eight resizing handles and a center point. Click and drag any object to move the entire group. If you apply transformations, such as rotate, scale, shear, or flip horizontal/vertical, they're applied to the group as a whole rather than to each object individually.

Figure 67 When you select a group, a rectangular bounding box with eight resizing handles is displayed around the perimeter of the grouped objects. This group contains three objects: a graphics frame with a placed graphic, a straight line, and a text frame.

Groups within Groups

A group can contain one or more subgroups, or *nested* groups. For example, if you create two groups, select both groups, and then choose Object > Group, the resulting group contains two nested groups. To ungroup nested groups, you must first ungroup (Object > Ungroup) the parent group.

Groups and Layers

When you create a group, all selected objects are stacked in succession beneath the frontmost object. If you create a group from objects that are on different layers, all of the objects move to the layer of the frontmost object and are stacked in succession beneath it. For more about layers see #81.

Nesting Objects

The Paste Into command (Edit menu) lets you place a copied object (that is, the last object you copied to the clipboard by choosing Edit > Copy or Edit > Cut) within a frame. The pasted object is said to be *nested* within the containing frame, which acts as a cropping shape for the pasted object. Selecting a nested object is like selecting an object in a group—click it with the Direct Selection tool.

Selecting an object within a group can be a little tricky. You can't simply click it with the Selection tool because that selects the entire group. To select an object that's part of a group, click the object using the Direct Selection tool. If you want, you can then switch to the Selection tool, in which case the object behaves as though you selected it with the Selection tool in the first place.

If you click within a graphics frame using the Direct Selection tool, you select the graphic, not the frame. The easiest way to select a graphics frame within a group is to click the edge of the frame using the Direct Selection tool. If necessary, you can then switch to the Selection tool.

When an object that's part of a group is selected, the Select command (Object menu) displays two choices for selecting other objects within the group: Select Previous Object and Select Next Object. When a graphic or graphics frame is selected, you can choose Object > Select > Content and Object > Select > Container to select the graphic or the frame (whichever isn't selected).

To ungroup a group, select it, and then choose Object > Ungroup.

#68 Aligning Objects

You're probably already familiar with the concept of text alignment. InDesign provides several paragraph alignment options, including left-aligned, center-aligned, right-aligned, and justified. In much the same way as you control the alignment of lines in a paragraph, you can control the alignment of objects.

If you like icon-based user interfaces, you'll love the Align panel (Window > Object & Layout > Align). When two or more objects are selected, the 12 buttons in the Align panel let you control the placement of the objects relative to each other (**Figure 68**). Each button icon indicates graphically what will happen to the selected objects when you click the button.

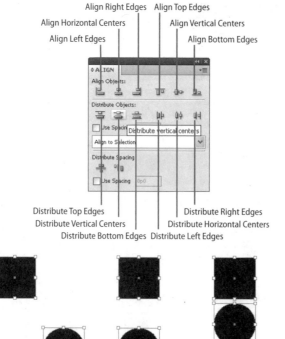

Figure 68 The original, unaligned objects are on the left. Clicking Align Horizontal Centers in the Align panel produced the middle set. Clicking Distribute Vertical Centers produced the aligned and evenly spaced result on the right.

Aligning Objects with Smart Guides

Four new Smart Guide options in the Guides & Pasteboard pane of the Preferences dialog box expand the options for aligning, sizing, and positioning objects as you create and move them. The options are: Align to Object Center, Align to Object Edges, Smart Dimensions, and Smart Spacing. You can enable or disable each option.

When Align to Object Center is enabled, the center point of an object snaps to guidelines (margin, column, and ruler guides), as well as to the center points and edges of other objects, as you drag the object.

When Align to Object Edge is enabled, the edges and the center point of an object snap to guidelines, as well as to the edges of other objects, as you drag the object.

In addition to snapping, Smart Guides are dynamically displayed to provide feedback about which objects and which edges and center points are snapping to each other.

Adding Space between Objects

If you choose Show Options in the Align panel menu, the panel displays additional controls for specifying the vertical or horizontal space between selected objects. Check Use Spacing, and in the accompanying field, enter the amount of space you want to place between the selected objects. Then click the Distribute Vertical Space or Distribute Horizontal Space button.

The six Align Objects buttons let you align objects along a vertical or horizontal axis. The six Distribute Objects buttons let you place a specified amount of space between objects along a horizontal or vertical axis. The Align Objects buttons in the Align panel are also available in the Control panel when multiple objects are selected.

The menu below the Align and Distribute buttons contains four options for aligning objects—Align to Selection, Align to Margins, Align to Page, and Align to Spread. You should make your choice from this menu before clicking one of the Align or Distribute buttons.

Getting the results you want using the Align panel takes a little practice. If you click one of the Align/Distribute buttons and don't like the results, you can always undo the action (Edit > Undo).

#69 Duplicating Objects

Sometimes in life, you have to do the same job more than once. Mowing your lawn and washing your clothes, for example. Fortunately, as an InDesign user, you never have to create the same object twice.

InDesign provides several options for making copies of objects. The method you choose depends on the number of copies you need and where you want to place them.

- **The Duplicate command** in the Edit menu creates a single copy of whatever's selected. The copy is placed 1 pica below and to the right of the original unless you've used the Step and Repeat command (see the last bullet item in this list).

- **Hold down Option (Mac OS) or Alt (Windows)** when you drag an object with the Selection tool or Direct Selection tool to create a duplicate of the object (**Figure 69a**). The copied object is placed where you release the mouse button; the original object is unchanged. If you hold down the Shift key when you Alt/Option+drag an object, you can drag only in directions that are multiples of 45°.

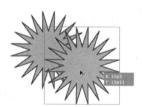

Figure 69a If you hold down the Option key (Mac OS) or the Alt key (Windows) when dragging an object with the Selection tool or Direct Selection tool, a pair of arrow pointers is displayed as you drag. The white one indicates that you're dragging a copy of the original object. If you pause briefly before Alt/Option+dragging an object, the duplicate is displayed as you drag. As you drag, live X (horizontal location) and Y (vertical location) values of the new object are displayed.

Creating a Copy When You Modify an Object

You can modify objects by changing settings in panels. For example, you can rotate an object by entering a value in the Rotation Angle field in the Control panel. Or you can scale an object by entering a value in the Scale X Percentage or Scale Y Percentage field in the Transform panel. If you hold down the Option key (Mac OS) or the Alt key (Windows) when you press Return or Enter to exit a panel field after changing a value, the new setting is applied to a copy of the selected object, and the copy is placed in front of the original.

Storing Objects in Libraries and as Snippets

If you want to save a copy of an object for use in other documents, you can save the object in an InDesign library or you can create a *snippet* file. You can share both libraries and snippet files with colleagues and clients. See #71 for more about libraries; see #72 for more about snippets.

- **The Copy and Paste commands** in the Edit menu provide another option for duplicating an object. Whatever you copy with the Copy command is saved to the clipboard until you copy or cut something else. The Edit menu also provides three choices for pasting copied objects: 1) Choose Paste to place copied objects in the middle of the currently displayed page; 2) choose Paste Into to place the copied object into a selected frame and create a nested object; or 3) choose Paste in Place to place the selected objects using the X and Y offsets of the original objects. The latter option comes in handy if you want to cut and paste or copy and paste something onto a new page while retaining the position of the original.

- **The Step and Repeat command** in the Edit menu lets you create multiple copies of an object and specify the placement of the copies relative to the original (**Figure 69b**). (Note: the Horizontal Offset and Vertical Offset values used most recently in the Step and Repeat dialog box are used when you choose Edit > Duplicate.)

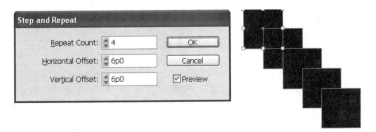

Figure 69b The Step and Repeat command (Edit menu) lets you create multiple duplicates in a single operation. In this example, the settings in the Step and Repeat dialog box produced the final result at the right from a single frame.

#70 Changing the Stacking Order

Every object on a page occupies a specific place in the page's *stacking order*. The first object you create on a page is placed at the bottom of the stack of objects. Each new object is placed successively higher in the stack.

If objects don't overlap, their stacking order is not important; however, if objects overlap, the stacking order determines which object is visible in the overlapping areas. You may find that you need to move objects forward or backward in the stacking order to create the desired result (**Figure 70**).

The Arrange command (Object menu) displays four options for changing the position of the selected object in the stacking order:

- **Bring to Front:** Moves an object to the top of the stack.

- **Bring Forward:** Moves an object one level higher in the stack.

- **Send Backward:** Moves an object one level lower in the stack.

- **Send to Back:** Moves an object to the bottom of the stack.

Figure 70 Four objects are stacked upon each other (left). The text frame is at the top of the stack; the empty circular frame is at the bottom. Selecting the circular frame and choosing Object > Arrange > Bring to Front produced the result on the right.

Moving an Object to a Different Layer

By default InDesign layouts have one layer (named Layer 1). The objects on each layer have a stacking order, and the layers have a stacking order. The layer listed first in the Layers panel is the topmost layer. If your InDesign layout contains multiple layers, you can use the Layers panel to move an object to a different layer. Select the object, and then open the Layers panel. Drag the small, colored square that's displayed to the right of the name of the selected layer to another layer. The object is placed at the top of the stacking order on its new layer. Then use the Arrange options to change the object's placement within the layer's stacking order. (For more about layers, see #81.)

Selecting an Object That's Behind Another Object

If you need to select an object that's behind another object, one option is to select the frontmost object, and then send it backward so that you can see and then select the object that was behind it. If you hold down the Command key (Mac OS) or the Ctrl key (Windows) and click an area where multiple objects overlap, each click selects the next lowest object in the stacking order. Once you reach the bottom object, the next Command/Ctrl-click selects the topmost object.

Layers have their own stacking order just like objects. (For more about layers, see #81.) When you choose any of the four Arrange commands (Bring to Front, Bring Forward, Send to Back, and Send Backward), the selected object moves forward or backward only within its own layer. This means, for example, that if you choose Object > Arrange > Bring to Front, the selected object may not be the frontmost object if it's on a layer that's below another layer. To place an object in front of all other objects, move it to the front of the frontmost layer.

When you create a new object on a master page, it's placed at the top of the stacking order of the currently selected layer. These master objects are placed behind objects that you create on the same layer on document pages based on that master page. If you want to place master objects in front of objects on document pages, create a layer for the master objects and place that layer on top of the layer you use for objects on document pages.

#71 Using Libraries

InDesign libraries provide quick access to objects you use repeatedly—such as logos, boilerplate text, house ads, frequently used graphics, and so on. A library file is essentially a collection of objects, and an open library file is displayed as a panel with thumbnail previews of the objects it contains. It's easy to place objects into libraries, and it's just as easy to place copies of library objects onto pages.

Using libraries requires three steps:

1. **Create a library.** Choose File > New > Library. Name and save the library. Library files are automatically assigned an .indl extension to differentiate them from InDesign layouts, which are assigned an .indd extension. After you click Save, an empty library window is displayed with the name you assigned in the tab. You can create as many different library files as you want. For example, you might have one library named "Frequently Used Corporate Logos" that contains nothing but logos and another named "Disclaimer Text" that contains nothing but text frames with different kinds of legal copy.

2. **Add objects to the library.** Select one or more objects, and then drag them into the library panel (**Figure 71a**). Generally, you'll want to add objects that you're likely to use repeatedly. You can add any object or multiple-selected objects to an open library, and there's virtually no limit to the number of objects a library can contain.

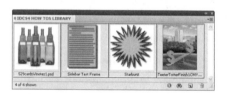

Figure 71a A library panel displays thumbnails of the objects it contains. Click and drag a thumbnail onto a page or the pasteboard to add a library object to a document.

3. **Place library objects into documents.** Click and drag a thumbnail from the library panel onto a page or the pasteboard. You can navigate to a different page, open a new document, or switch to a different document window if multiple documents are open. In each case, simply drag a thumbnail from the library panel to the document window to add the object to the document.

Sharing Libraries

Although it's possible to share libraries stored on a server or a shared computer, only one InDesign user at a time can open a library file unless the file is locked. If you lock a library file, multiple users can open it simultaneously, but none of them can add objects to or delete objects from the library.

Closing Libraries

To close a library window, click the close button in the upper-left corner. Library panels behave like other panels, which means you can dock them to the edge of your monitor, expand and collapse them, group them with other panels, and so on. Choose File > Open to open an existing library.

Graphics in Libraries

It's worth noting that if you add a graphics frame containing a graphic to a library, InDesign does not save the original graphic file in the library file—it saves only the path to the original file and a low-resolution preview. If you intend to share the library, you'll also have to provide the graphics file for users of the library to display and print the graphic at the highest possible resolution.

Double-click a thumbnail in a library panel to display the Item Information dialog box, where you can assign a name to the object, add a comment, and assign any of seven object types (**Figure 71b**). You can sort and search for library objects based on their name and other information.

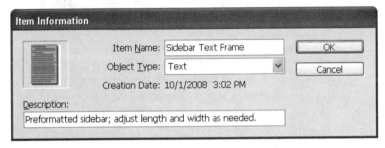

Figure 71b You can assign a name to a library object, add a description, and choose an object type, and you can use this information to sort and locate objects within a library.

The library panel menu includes several other useful commands for working with libraries:

- **Add Item:** Adds the selected object to the library.

- **Add Items on Page:** Adds all objects on the currently displayed page to the library as a single object.

- **Add Items on Page as Separate Objects:** Adds all objects on the currently displayed page to the library as separate objects.

- **Update Library Item:** If you drag a thumbnail from a library panel to a document and then change the object in the document, click Update Library Item to apply the changes you made to the library object.

- **Place Item(s):** Places the objects selected in the library panel into the active document.

- **Delete Item(s):** Removes the objects selected in the library panel from the library.

- **Sort Items:** Lets you sort library objects based on Name, Oldest, Newest, and Type.

#72 Using Snippets

Snippets are similar to libraries in that you can use them to save and share InDesign objects. A snippet is a file that contains one or more InDesign objects. Snippet files are much like graphic files—for example, you can import snippet files using the Place command (File menu) or drag and drop them into InDesign layouts; however, you create snippets with InDesign rather than a graphic program, such as Photoshop or Illustrator. A snippet stores not only InDesign objects—text frames, graphics frames, lines, and so on—but their page location and other information as well. This means that when you place a snippet into a layout, you can choose whether the objects it contains retain their original positions.

As with libraries, you must create a snippet before you can use it in other InDesign documents or share it with other InDesign users. To begin, select one or more objects that you want to save and reuse. You can then use any of three methods to create a snippet:

- Choose File > Export to display the Export dialog box and then choose InDesign Snippet from the Format menu (Mac OS) or the Save as type menu (Windows). Name the file and choose a storage folder. Snippet files are automatically assigned the extension ".idms."

- Drag the selected objects into the Bridge window and drop them onto a volume or folder icon or into the open volume or folder (**Figure 72**). The snippet file is automatically given a name that begins with "Snippet." You can change the name of the file, but you should keep the .idms filename extension.

More About Snippets

Snippet files are eXtensible Markup Language (XML) files. The XML file format allows snippets to contain not only information about InDesign objects, but also information about the file in the form of metadata. You can use Adobe Bridge to view a snippet's metadata, such as filename, creation date, and modification date, and to view, add, and remove keywords. You can use the Find feature in Bridge to perform metadata-based file searches.

Graphics in Snippets

If you create a snippet that includes a graphics frame that contains an imported graphic, only the path to the graphic file is saved in the snippet. If you want to share the snippet, you should include a copy of the graphic file along with the snippet file or provide users with access to the graphic file.

Snippet Preferences

The File Handling panel in the Preferences dialog box includes Snippet Import controls. If you choose Position At Original Location, the snippet is placed in the same position as the original object when you place a snippet. If you choose Position At Cursor Location, the snippet is placed where you click. Press Option (Mac OS) or Alt (Windows) when placing a snippet to temporarily switch the preference setting.

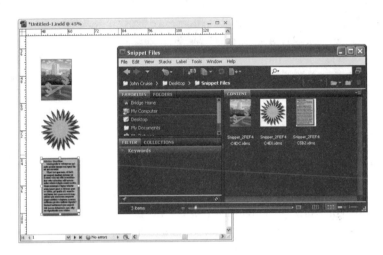

Figure 72 The graphics frame in the InDesign document window on the left was dragged into the Bridge window on the right to create a snippet.

- Drag and drop the selected objects onto the desktop or onto a volume or folder icon on the desktop. The snippet file is given a name beginning with "Snippet_." You can change the name of the file, but you should keep the .idms extension.

After you create a snippet, you can use it repeatedly in your InDesign layouts or share it with other InDesign users. You have two options for placing a snippet into a layout:

- Use the Place command (File menu) to import a snippet the same way you import a graphic. (See #52 for information about placing graphics.) If you press Option (Mac OS) or Alt (Windows) when the loaded graphics icon is displayed, the objects in the snippet are placed at the same location as the original objects used to create the snippet (that is, their original X Location and Y Location values are used) when you click. If you don't press Option or Alt when the loaded graphics icon is displayed, the objects in the snippet are placed relative to the point where you click.

- Drag a snippet file from the Bridge window, the Mac OS Finder, or Windows Explorer and drop it into an InDesign document window.

CHAPTER EIGHT

Working with Color

Adding color to a publication can make the difference between drab and dazzling. InDesign provides many features for creating several different kinds of colors and applying them to text and objects.

In this chapter you'll learn how to use commands in the Swatches panel to add process and spot colors, tints, multicolor gradients, and mixed ink colors and how to use the Gradient and Color panels to quickly build and apply gradients and colors on the fly. In addition, we'll take a brief look at InDesign's color management capabilities and show you how to specify color settings.

#73 Using Spot Colors, Process Colors, and Tints

If you intend to create a color publication, you'll probably want to add some colors to your InDesign layout, after which you can apply the colors to text, object backgrounds, and strokes. The Swatches panel (Windows > Swatches) displays a list of available colors, including spot colors, process colors (CMYK), tints, gradients, and mixed ink colors, as well as controls for creating new colors and managing colors.

The method for adding a spot color or a process color is much the same. To add a spot color:

1. Choose New Color Swatch from the Swatches panel menu.

2. In the New Color Swatch dialog box (**Figure 73a**), choose Spot in the Color Type menu, and then choose a spot color library in the Color Mode menu.

3. Select a color from the scroll list or enter a number in the field above the scroll list.

4. Click OK to add the color to the Swatches panel and close the dialog box, or click Add to add the color to the Swatches panel and keep the dialog box open so you can add more swatches.

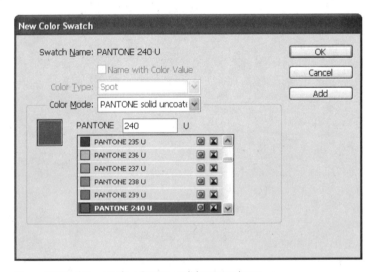

Figure 73a In this example, a Pantone solid uncoated spot color—Pantone 240 U—is defined in the New Color Swatch dialog box.

To add a process color:

1. Choose New Color Swatch from the Swatches panel.

2. In the New Color Swatch dialog box (**Figure 73b**), choose Process in the Color Type menu, and then choose CMYK or a process color library, such as FOCOLTONE or TRUMATCH, in the Color Mode menu. If you choose CMYK, use the Cyan, Magenta, Yellow, and Black controls to define the color. If you check Name with Color Value, a process CMYK color is automatically assigned a name that includes its CMYK percentages (for example, C=30 M=100 Y=50 K=0). If you uncheck Name with Color Value, you can assign a name of your choice.

3. Click OK to add the color to the Swatches panel and close the dialog box, or click Add to add the color to the Swatches panel and keep the dialog box open so you can add more swatches.

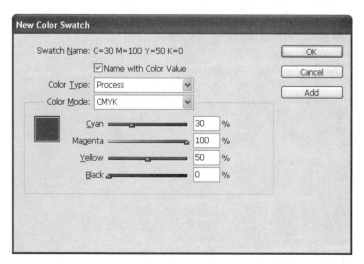

Figure 73b When you define a process CMYK color, use the Cyan, Magenta, Yellow, and Black controls to specify the percentage of each process color.

After you create a color, it is added to the list of swatches in the Swatches panel, and you can apply it to text, fills, and strokes. (See #61 and #62 for information about applying color to fills and strokes.) The spot color icon is displayed to the right of the names of spot colors in the Swatches panel; the process color icon is displayed next to process colors.

#73: Using Spot Colors, Process Colors, and Tints

Using the Eyedropper Tool to Add Colors from Graphics

You can use the Eyedropper tool to "pick up" colors from imported graphics, and you can save these colors and apply them to other objects. To add a color from an imported graphic to the Swatches panel list, select the Eyedropper tool, and then click within an imported graphic. The single pixel you click on is used, so you might want to zoom in before you click. After you click, the color of the pixel you clicked on is displayed in the Fill box or Stroke box (whichever is currently selected) in the Tools panel, the Swatches panel, and the Color panel. Drag any of these Fill or Stroke boxes to the Swatches panel list to add the color to the document. Clicking an RGB image creates an RGB color; clicking a CMYK image creates a CMYK color.

Applying and Saving Tints

If you want to apply a tint (that is, a percentage) of a color to an object instead of applying the color at full intensity, use the Swatches panel to first apply the color, and then use the Tint controls in the Swatches panel to assign a tint value between 0% and 100%. The lower the Tint value, the lighter the color.

You can also add tints to the list of swatches in the Swatches panel, and then apply them to objects in the same way as you apply other swatches. To add a tint of a color, select the color in the Swatches panel list, and then choose New Tint Swatch from the panel menu. Use the Tint controls in the New Tint Swatch dialog box to specify a tint value.

If an object is selected when you create a new color, the color is applied to the object's stroke or fill, depending on whether the Stroke box or the Fill box is selected in the Tools panel. If nothing is selected when you create a new color, the color becomes the default stroke or fill for new objects created with the drawing tools (with the exception of the three frame tools).

The Swatches panel and its menu (**Figure 73c**) contain many controls and commands for working with colors. In addition to commands for creating new spot and process colors, tints, gradients, and mixed ink colors, the Swatches panel menu includes commands for:

- Deleting (Delete Swatch) and modifying swatches (Swatch Options).

- Exporting (Save Swatches) and importing (Load Swatches) swatches.

- Displaying swatches in the panel (Name, Small Name, Small Swatch, Large Swatch).

Figure 73c The Swatches panel displays a list of available colors and includes many controls and commands for creating and managing colors.

#74 Using Gradients

A gradient is a smooth transition from one color or tint to another color or tint. A well-designed and well-placed gradient adds movement and contrast to a page—both of which add visual appeal. InDesign lets you create multicolor gradients and apply them as fills and strokes to text and objects.

Creating Gradients Using the Swatches Panel

The most efficient way to use a gradient is to first add it to the Swatches panel list, after which you can apply it to text and objects.

To create a gradient:

1. Open the Swatches panel (Window > Swatches) and choose New Gradient Swatch from the Swatches panel menu.

2. In the New Gradient Swatch dialog box (**Figure 74a**), enter a name for the gradient in the Swatch Name field and choose Linear or Radial from the Type menu.

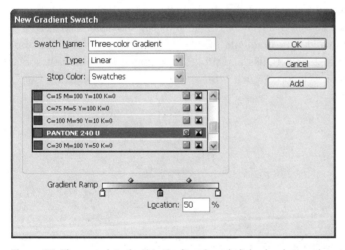

Figure 74a The controls in the New Gradient Swatch dialog box let you choose a gradient's colors.

3. The Gradient Ramp displays the gradient. Below the ramp, color stops—the small, colored squares—show the colors in the gradient. Above the ramp, small diamonds indicate the midpoints between pairs of colors. To specify the start color, click the white square at the

Creating See-Through Gradients

Although you cannot choose None (transparent) as a color in a gradient, there are a couple of ways to create a gradient that goes from opaque to transparent:

1. Select an object with a Fill color other than None, and then choose Object > Effects > Gradient Feather. Click Preview, and then adjust the settings in the Gradient Feather area to control the appearance of the gradient.

2. Create a gradient that includes white (Paper color)—for example, a simple black-to-white gradient. Fill a frame with the gradient, and then apply the Multiply blending mode to the frame (Window > Effects; Blending Mode menu > Multiply). Place the frame in front of another object. White areas in the gradient are transparent, and as the gradient gets darker, it becomes less transparent.

left end of the Gradient Ramp, and then use the controls in the Stop Color area to assign a color. Click the black square at the right end of the Gradient Ramp to specify the end color. The controls in the Stop Color area vary, depending on the choice you make in the Stop Color menu. If you choose Lab, CMYK, or RGB, the controls let you create new colors. If you choose Swatches, the document's swatches (spot and process colors, gradients, tints, and mixed ink colors) are listed.

4. To add a color to a gradient, click just below the ramp. A color stop is added where you click. Use the controls in the Stop Color area to change the color.

5. To delete a color from a gradient, click its color stop and drag downward. You can also modify a gradient by dragging color stops and midpoints or by selecting a color stop or midpoint and changing the Location value.

6. When you're ready to save a gradient, click OK to add the gradient to the Swatches panel and close the dialog box. Or, click Add to add the gradient to the Swatches panel and keep the dialog box open so you can add more gradients. After you create a gradient, you can apply it to text, objects, fills, and strokes in the same way you apply spot and process colors (**Figure 74b**).

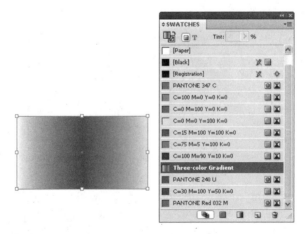

Figure 74b In this example, a linear gradient—named "Three-color Gradient"—is used to fill an empty frame.

Creating Gradients Using the Gradient Panel

In addition to creating gradient swatches that are displayed in the Swatches panel list, you can use the Gradient panel (Window > Gradient) to create gradients on the fly (that is, without having to open the New Gradient Swatch dialog box). If you create a gradient using the Gradient panel, the gradient is applied to the fill or stroke of selected text or objects, depending on whether the Fill box or the Stroke box is selected in the Tools panel. If nothing is selected when you create a gradient, it becomes the default stroke or fill for new objects created with the drawing tools (with the exception of the three frame tools).

The controls in the Gradient panel are similar to the controls in the New Gradient Swatch dialog box. The gradient ramp works the same as the gradient ramp in the New Gradient Swatch dialog box with one exception: To add a color stop, drag a swatch from the Swatches panel and release it on the ramp. Release the swatch on an existing color stop to replace it. The Type menu and Location fields are the same as those in the New Gradient Swatch dialog box. The Reverse button lets you flip a gradient, and the Angle field lets you rotate a linear gradient.

Using the Gradient Tool

The Gradient tool provides another option for applying a blend. To use the Gradient tool, first apply a gradient to the fill or stroke of an object or text. With the object or text still selected, select the Gradient tool, and then click and drag on the page. The spot where you click is the start point of the blend; the spot where you release the mouse is the endpoint of the blend (**Figure 74c**).

Figure 74c In this example, clicking and dragging with the Gradient tool produces a slightly off-center radial blend. The white/highlight spot is the start point; the crosshair pointer indicates the endpoint.

Saving Gradients from the Gradient Panel

Gradients you create with the Gradient panel are not automatically added to the Swatches panel list. If you want to save a gradient you create with the Gradient panel, drag the Fill box from the Gradient panel to the Swatches panel.

#75 Using Mixed Ink Colors

In addition to creating and applying spot and process colors, tints, and gradients, you can create mixed ink colors that combine a spot color with one or more spot or process colors. For example, if you're working on a publication that uses black and one Pantone color, you can create a mixed ink color that combines a tint of black and the Pantone color.

To create a mixed ink color:

1. Open the Swatches panel (Window > Swatches) and choose New Mixed Ink Swatch from the Swatches panel menu.

2. In the New Mixed Ink Swatch dialog box (**Figure 75a**), enter a name for the mixed ink. (It's a good idea to include the names and percentages of the component colors.)

3. Click the empty square to the left of each color you want to include.

4. For each color you choose, enter a tint value from 0% to 100% by adjusting the slider or entering a value in the % field.

5. When you're done choosing colors and specifying tints, click OK to add the mixed ink color to the Swatches panel and close the dialog box, or click Add to add the mixed ink color to the Swatches panel and keep the dialog box open so you can add more mixed ink colors. After you create a mixed ink color, you can apply it to text, fills, and strokes in the same way as you apply spot and process colors.

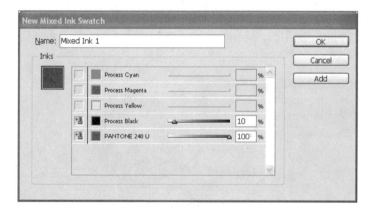

Figure 75a The New Mixed Ink Swatch dialog box lets you create a swatch that combines two or more colors. In this example, a spot color—Pantone 240 U—is mixed with a 10% tint of black.

You can create mixed ink color swatches one at a time by choosing New Mixed Ink Swatch from the Swatches panel menu, or you can create several variations of a particular combination of colors at once by choosing New Mixed Ink Group. In the New Mixed Ink Group dialog box (**Figure 75b**), select the colors you want to include by clicking the empty box next to them. For each color, specify:

- The percentage of the starting tint in the Initial field.

- The number of times you want to repeat the increment in the Repeat field.

- The amount of change between tints in the Increment field.

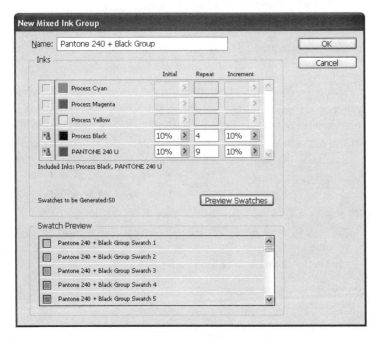

Figure 75b The New Mixed Ink Group dialog box lets you mix several combinations of tints and colors at once. In this example, a Pantone spot color—Pantone 240 U—is combined with black. 10% tint increments of Pantone 240 U (starting at 10% and repeating nine times) are mixed with 10% tint increments of black (starting at 10% and repeating four times). These settings produce a group with 50 mixed ink colors. You can see the first five colors in the Swatch Preview area.

Can't Create a Mixed Ink Color?

The Create New Mixed Ink command is available in the Swatches panel menu only if the Swatches panel list includes at least one spot color. A mixed ink color must have at least one spot color.

#76 Using the Color Panel

Like the Gradient panel, the Color panel (Window > Color) lets you create colors on the fly—that is, without having to open the New Color Swatch dialog box. Generally, it's a good idea to choose New Color Swatch from the Swatches panel menu when you need a new color because the color is added to the Swatches panel list and you can apply it whenever you want. That said, the Color panel (**Figure 76**) provides a quick alternative for creating colors.

The controls in the Color panel are similar to the controls in the New Color Swatch dialog box. To create a color:

1. Choose Lab, CMYK, or RGB from the Color panel menu to specify the kind of color you want to create. The color controls displayed depend on the selected color model. A color spectrum is displayed below the tint percentage fields and sliders.

2. Click the spectrum or use the fields and sliders to specify color settings.

To add the color in the Color panel to the Swatches panel list, choose Add to Swatches from the Color panel menu, drag the Fill box from the Color panel to the Swatches panel, or click the New Swatch button at the bottom of the Swatches panel. To add all colors you've applied using the Color panel to the Swatches panel list, choose Add Unnamed Colors from the Swatches panel menu.

When you create a color using the Color panel, it's applied to the current selection. If nothing is selected, the color is the default color for the fill or stroke of new objects (except for frames created with any of the three frame tools), depending on whether the Fill box or the Stroke box is selected in the Color panel or Tools panel.

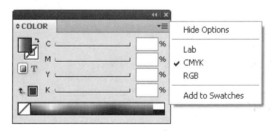

Figure 76 Use the Color panel to quickly create new colors without having to open the New Color Swatch dialog box.

#77 Setting Up Color Management

Color management is the process of transforming colors to compensate for the different capabilities of devices such as monitors and printers so that colors look as consistent as possible throughout your workflow. Providing a brief how-to about color management is a little like providing a brief how-to about nuclear physics. Thick books by smart people have been written about the physics, physiology, and psychology of color and managing color in a publishing workflow. It's hard to reduce the topic of color management to a single bit of advice. That said, it's easy to enable InDesign's color management feature, and with minimal effort you can set up a simple color-managed workflow.

By default, color management is turned on in InDesign. If you use InDesign as part of Adobe Creative Suite, you can use Adobe Bridge to synchronize color settings across all applications so that colors look the same throughout the suite.

To set up color management in InDesign, choose Edit > Color Settings. The Settings menu in the Color Settings dialog box (**Figure 77**) offers several options. Choose the option that is most appropriate for the kinds of publications you create with InDesign:

- Choose Monitor Color only if you create designs for video or onscreen presentation.

- Choose North America General Purpose 2 to use typical settings for publications that will be printed with desktop printers (laser and inkjet) and for onscreen publications in North America.

- Choose North America Prepress 2 to use typical settings for publications that will be printed on a printing press in North America.

- Choose North America Web/Internet to use typical settings for onscreen presentation in North America.

Synchronizing Color Settings Across Adobe Creative Suite

If you own Adobe CS4, you can specify custom color settings within each component application, but you'll probably want to synchronize color settings across all applications. To do this, open Adobe Bridge, and then choose Edit > Creative Suite Color Settings. In the Suite Color Settings dialog box, select a color setting and click Apply.

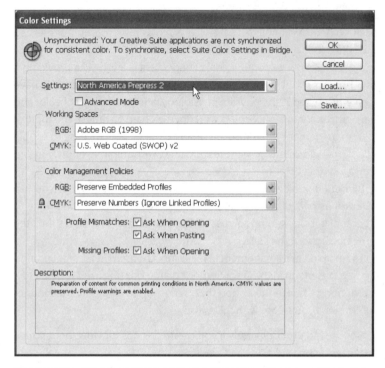

Figure 77 One option for managing color in InDesign is to choose one of the built-in settings available in the Settings menu of the Color Settings (Edit > Color Settings) dialog box.

If you're knowledgeable about color management and aren't satisfied with the default settings in the Color Settings dialog box, you can specify custom settings. Click Save to save custom settings in a file you can share with colleagues and clients.

If you use InDesign as part of Adobe Creative Suite, InDesign's color management settings are automatically synchronized with the other applications. When you first open the Color Settings dialog box, "Synchronized" is displayed in the upper-left corner to let you know that the settings are in synch with the other Creative Suite applications. If you change any of the settings in the Color Settings dialog box, "Synchronized" changes to "Unsynchronized."

CHAPTER NINE

Laying Out Pages and Creating Long Documents

If text frames, graphics frames, lines, and shapes are the building blocks of layouts, then your InDesign documents are the architectural masterpieces you create with the building blocks. By setting up a solid framework using master pages, guidelines, and layers, and by taking advantage of several long-document features, you can quickly build a wide range of design-intensive multipage documents—from newsletters and newspapers to catalogs, magazines, and books.

In this chapter, you'll learn how to use master pages as backgrounds for document pages and how to use several different kinds of guidelines to place and align objects on pages. You'll also learn how to use layers to organize objects within documents. Additionally, we explain how to add, move, and delete pages in a multipage document and how to take advantage of features for working with and organizing long documents.

#78 Working with Master Pages

If you use InDesign to create long documents, such as books, catalogs, magazines, and newspapers, understanding and using master pages is critical to working efficiently. A master page serves as the background for document pages and contains elements that appear on all pages, such as page numbers, page headers, and page footers. A master page can also contain placeholder frames for text and graphics. Placing objects on master pages, and then basing document pages on master pages saves you the time and effort required to manually place repeated elements on multiple document pages.

When you create a new document, it contains a single blank master page called A-Master. For facing-page documents, A-Master has a left (verso) page and a right (recto) page. By default, all document pages are based on A-Master. Objects that you place on A-Master are automatically placed on document pages based on A-Master.

The Pages panel (Window > Pages; **Figure 78a**) displays thumbnails of master pages (top) and document pages (below). To display a master page in the document window, double-click a master page thumbnail. Use InDesign's drawing tools to add objects to master pages the same way you do for document pages. Objects you place on a left-side master page in a facing-page document are placed on even-numbered pages; objects you place on a right-side master page are placed on odd-numbered pages. Master objects are placed at the bottom of the layer they're on—that is, at the bottom of the stacking order (see #81 for more information about layers). If you want to place master objects in front of objects on document pages, create a layer for them and make it the topmost layer.

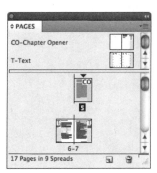

Figure 78a By default, master page thumbnails are displayed at the top of the Pages panel. Document page thumbnails display below.

You can create and use as many master pages as a project requires. For example, a newsletter might have a master page that's based on a three-column format and another that's based on a two-column format. When laying out the newsletter, you can base its pages on either the three-column or two-column master page.

To create a new master page, choose New Master from the Pages panel menu. In the New Master dialog box (**Figure 78b**) assign a prefix and a name. The Based on Master menu lets you base a new master page on an existing master page to create a parent-child relationship between the two. Changes you make to the parent master page are automatically applied to the child master page. For a facing-page document, the Number of Pages should be 2 (left side and right side).

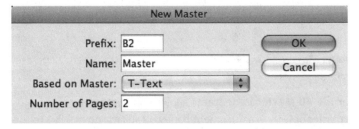

Figure 78b When you create a new master page, you can assign a prefix and a name, and choose another master page as its "parent."

You can apply a master page to a document page in several ways:

- Drag a master page thumbnail onto a document page thumbnail. If you drag a master page thumbnail onto the corner of a facing-page document page, a black border is displayed around the spread. Release the mouse to apply the master page to both pages of the spread.

- Select one or more document page thumbnails, choose Apply Master to Pages from the Pages panel menu, and then choose a master page from the Apply Master menu.

- If you choose Insert Pages from the Pages panel menu to add pages to a document, you can assign a master page for the new pages by choosing one from the Master menu in the Insert Pages dialog box.

The "None" Master Page

In addition to the A-Master master page, all documents include a master page called None. The None master page is completely blank—no margins, columns, or objects—and you can't modify it. You can use the None master page for blank document pages. For example, if you're laying out a magazine, you could use the None master page as a placeholder for document pages that will contain full-page ads.

Selecting and Modifying Master Objects on Document Pages

The objects you place on a master page are referred to as *master objects* or *master items*. You can't select a master object on a document page by simply clicking it with a selection tool as you do with nonmaster objects. To select a master object on a document page, press Command+Shift (Mac OS) or Ctrl+Shift (Windows) and click the object with a selection tool.

If you are unable to select a master object on a document page, it means that Allow Master Item Overrides On Selection (see description at right) was not selected for the object on the master page. Master objects that can be selected on document pages are indicated by an additional blue line on their frame edges.

When you change a document page's master page, the margins, columns, and objects from the old master page are removed from the document page, and the margins, columns, and objects on the new master page are added. When you change an object on a master page, the change is reflected on all pages based on that master page.

If you make a change to a master object on a document page, it remains a master object, and subsequent changes you make to the object on the master page are applied to the master object you modified on the document page. To break a link between a master object on a document page and its master page, select the object on the document page (see sidebar), and then choose Detach Selection From Master from the Pages panel menu. The Pages panel menu includes several commands for working with master pages. Here's a brief description of a few that are particularly useful:

- **Save As Master** allows you to save the current document page as a master page.

- **Override All Master Page Items** allows you to make local changes to a master object on a document page and still maintain a link to the object on the master page.

- **Remove All Local Overrides** allows you to undo any changes you've made to master objects on a document page. Note that this means text and graphics you've added to master frames will be deleted.

- **Detach All Objects From Master** allows you to break the link between master objects on the current page and its master page.

- **Allow Master Item Overrides On Selection.** If you check this option, for a selected object on a master page, you can select the object on document pages (Command+Shift-click on Mac OS or Ctrl+Shift-click on Windows) and then modify the object. (This is the default behavior of InDesign—you *can* modify master items.) If you don't check this option for an object on a master page, you cannot select the object on a document page.

#79 Setting Margins and Columns

When you create a new document, you can specify the number of columns, the gutter width between columns, and a margin for each page edge. Column and margin settings are used to display guidelines that help you position text frames, graphic frames, and other elements on pages. The settings you specify in the New Document dialog box are used for all document pages unless you change the column and margin settings for the document's master pages, or you change the settings for individual document pages.

Before you can change column and margin settings for a master page or specific document pages, you must first select—or *target*—the pages you want to change in the Pages panel. To target both pages of a facing-page master page, click the name of the master page. To target only the verso or recto page of a facing-page master page, click the left or right master page thumbnail. To target a document page, click its thumbnail. To target a range of document or master pages, click the thumbnail of the first page, and then Shift-click the thumbnail of the last page. Command-click (Mac OS) or Ctrl-click (Windows) to select multiple, nonsequential master or document pages.

After you've targeted the pages whose column and margin settings you want to change, choose Layout > Margins and Columns. In the Margins and Columns dialog box (**Figure 79**), change the margin and column settings.

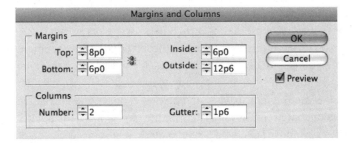

Figure 79 The settings you apply in the Margins and Columns dialog box are applied to the pages targeted in the Pages panel.

If you change the settings in the Margins and Columns dialog box when no documents are open, the modified settings become the default settings used in the New Document dialog box.

Showing and Hiding Margin and Column Guides

To turn off the display of margin and column guides, choose View > Grids & Guides > Hide Guides or choose Preview mode from the view mode buttons on the Tools panel.

Margins, Bleeds, and Printing

It's easy to confuse the margin guides with the outside edge of a page or spread. Margin guides are displayed in color, whereas page edges are black. You'll probably place most elements within the margin guides, but there's no restriction on placing objects between the margin guides and the edge of the page. Objects that extend beyond the edge of the page are referred to as *bleed objects*. Most desktop printers cannot print to the edge of the page, which means that bleed objects get clipped.

#80 Using Guides and Grids

If you like to use guidelines when you lay out pages, you may need more than margin and column guides. If that's the case, you can use ruler guides, a document-wide grid, or a combination of both. For example, you can quickly divide a page into quadrants by adding a vertical ruler guide and a horizontal ruler guide that intersect at the center of the page. Or you can use a document-wide baseline grid for aligning text and objects across columns. While it's nice to have so many options when it comes to adding guidelines, you probably won't use them all.

Ruler guides and grids are similar in that they don't print (unless you want to print them), and they help you align objects. They're also different in some ways:

- **Ruler guides** are much like objects. You can select them with the selection tools to move and delete them, and they're layer specific. Ruler guides can be vertical or horizontal only.

- **Gridlines** are document-wide and cannot be selected or modified.

Working with Guides

You can create ruler guides in two ways: manually by clicking and dragging from a ruler or automatically using the Create Guides command (Layout menu).

- **To create a ruler guide manually,** click the ruler along the left or top edge of the document window and drag the pointer onto a page or the pasteboard. (Choose View > Show Rulers if the rulers are not showing.) If you click the vertical ruler along the left edge of the document window, you create a vertical ruler guide. If you click the horizontal ruler at the top of the document window, you create a horizontal ruler guide. Release the mouse when the pointer is on a page to create a page guide that spans the page. Release the mouse when the pointer is on the pasteboard to create a spread guide that spans the page or spread and pasteboard.

Snapping Objects to Guides and Grids

If the Snap to Guides and Snap to Document Grid commands (View > Grids & Guides) are checked, object edges and center points will snap to ruler guides and gridlines, respectively, when you drag objects near them. The Snap to Zone value in the Guides & Pasteboard pane in the Preferences dialog box determines the distance at which an object will snap to a ruler guide or gridline.

- **To create ruler guides automatically,** select the document or master pages to which you want to add guides in the Pages panel, and then choose Layout > Create Guides. The controls in the Create Guides dialog box (**Figure 80a**) let you create horizontal guides (Rows), vertical ruler guides (Columns), or both. If you don't specify a Gutter value, a single guide is placed for each row/column. If you specify a Gutter value, it's used as the space between a pair of ruler guides. Other options let you fit the guides within the margins or the page and remove existing ruler guides.

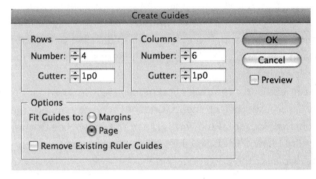

Figure 80a Use the controls in the Create Guides dialog box to divide a page into rows and columns using ruler guides.

Regardless of the method you use to create ruler guides, you can select, move, and delete them just like objects. You can also copy ruler guides into a Library and between pages.

Tip

In addition to the guides you create, InDesign has "smart guides" that appear temporarily as you work. Smart guides make it easy to align objects with each other and with the page. You may find the smart guides so handy that you end up creating fewer guides. However, you may find that they inhibit your creativity by forcing objects to align. If you want to turn off smart guides, choose View > Grids & Guides > Smart Guides. You can customize how smart guides work in the Guides & Pasteboard pane of the Preferences dialog box.

Guides and Layers

When you create ruler guides, they're placed on the layer that's currently selected in the Layers panel. You can hide a layer's ruler guides by double-clicking the layer in the Layers panel and unchecking Show Guides in the Layer Options dialog box.

Working with Grids

If you like to use a grid to lay out pages, InDesign offers two options:

- **A baseline grid** is a set of evenly spaced horizontal lines that help align text and objects across multiple columns.

- **A document grid** is a set of evenly spaced horizontal and vertical lines that resembles graph paper.

The Baseline Grid controls in the Grids pane in the Preferences dialog box (**Figure 80b**) let you modify a document's baseline grid. You can specify the Color, Start point, Increment, and View Threshold. The Show/Hide Baseline Grid command (View > Grids & Guides) lets you control the display of the baseline grid. (Note: The Align to Baseline Grid button in the Paragraph panel lets you align the baselines of selected paragraphs to the baseline grid.)

The Document Grid controls let you modify the document grid. You can specify Color as well as increments (Gridline Every) and subincrements (Subdivisions) for Horizontal and Vertical lines. The Show/Hide Document Grid command (View > Grids & Guides > Show Document Grid) lets you control the display of the document grid.

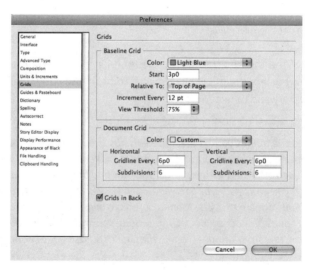

Figure 80b Use the controls in the Grids pane in the Preferences dialog box to modify a document's baseline grid and document grid.

#81 Working with Layers

By default, every time you create a new document, it contains a single layer named "Layer 1." Each new object you create occupies a successively higher position in the layer's stacking order. If you want, you can create additional layers and then use them for organizing objects. For example, you could create one layer called "Text" for all of the text frames in a document and another layer called "Graphics" that holds all graphic elements. You could then show, hide, or print each layer individually or together.

To create a new layer, open the Layers panel (Window > Layers), and then choose New Layer from the panel menu. In the New Layer dialog box (**Figure 81a**), enter a Name for the layer and use the controls to specify layer attributes.

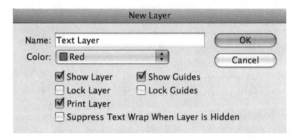

Figure 81a Use the controls in the New Layer dialog box to specify attributes of a new layer.

After you create a new layer, it's displayed in the Layers panel as the topmost layer in the list, which means it's the topmost layer in the layer stacking order. The selected layer is indicated by the Pen icon (**Figure 81b**). The small, square icon to the right of the Pen icon shows that the layer contains a selected object. New objects you create with the drawing tools are placed on the selected layer. If you want to add new objects to a different layer, select the layer in the panel, and then add the objects.

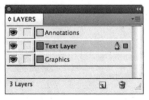

Figure 81b The Layers panel displays a list of a document's layers and includes controls and commands for working with layers. Here, the second layer in the stacking order, the Text Layer, is selected and contains a selected object.

Paste Remembers Layers

If you check Paste Remembers Layers in the Layers panel menu, objects you cut or copy retain their layer when you choose Edit > Paste. If you paste objects into a different document, layer names are also copied and added to the Layers panel if they don't exist in the target document. If Paste Remembers Layers is unchecked, all cut or copied objects are pasted onto the selected layer.

Two buttons are displayed to the left of each layer's name:

- Click the button on the left to show and hide a layer.

- Click the button on the right to lock or unlock a layer. You can't select objects on locked layers.

You can also use the controls in the Layers panel to:

- **Delete layers** by selecting them and then clicking the Delete (Trash) button.

- **Rearrange layers** by dragging selected layers up or down within the list. The layer at the bottom of the list is the lowest layer in the stacking order.

- **Move a selected object to a different layer** by dragging the small square on the right side of the panel to a new layer.

The Layers panel menu contains additional commands for working with layers, including Delete, Hide Others, Lock Others, Merge, and Delete Unused Layers.

Some other details you should know about layers include:

- If you create a group that contains objects on different layers, all objects are moved to the layer of the topmost object and placed consecutively in the stacking order.

- If you place an object on a master page, it's placed at the bottom of the stacking order of the selected layer. If you want a master object to be placed in front of other objects, put it on a layer that's higher in the stacking order than the other objects.

#82 Working with Pages

When you create a new document, the value you enter in the Number of Pages field in the New Document dialog box determines how many pages the document has; however, you're free to change your mind later and add or delete pages as needed. You can also move pages within a document.

The Pages panel (Window > Pages; **Figure 82a**) provides the easiest method for working with the pages in a multipage document. By default, the thumbnails at the top of the panel represent a document's master pages; the thumbnails at the bottom of the panel represent document pages. (For more information about master pages, see #78.)

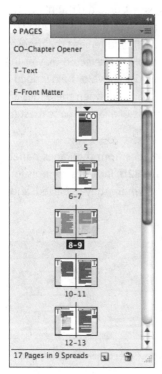

Figure 82a The Pages panel displays thumbnails of master pages (top) and document pages (bottom), and includes controls and commands for working with pages.

Keeping a Facing-Page Spread Together

If you design a facing-page spread and you want to make sure that the two pages are not separated if pages are added, deleted, or moved, select both thumbnails in the Pages panel and then uncheck Allow Selected Spread to Shuffle from the panel menu.

Creating a Gatefold

Some publications contain fold-out pages that open into three-page spreads called *gatefolds*. To create a three-page spread in a facing-page layout, select a spread in the Pages panel. Uncheck Allow Document Pages to Shuffle and Allow Selected Spread to Shuffle in the Pages panel menu. Then drag a master page icon to the edge of the page you want to fold out. Generally, you create a gatefold by adding an extra page on the right side of a facing-page spread, and then adding an extra page on the left side of the next facing-page spread.

Adding Pages

You can add pages to a document in several ways:

- **To add a single blank page,** click the Create New Page button at the bottom of the Pages panel. The new page is placed after the page that's currently displayed in the document window—or at the end of the document if a master page is currently displayed—and uses the master page of the preceding page.

- **To add a single page based on a particular master page,** drag a master page thumbnail from the top of the panel to the bottom of the panel. To control where the new page is placed, drag the thumbnail to the left or the right edge of a document page. A vertical bar is displayed to indicate where the page will be placed. (If you release the mouse when a page icon is highlighted, you'll apply the selected master to the document page.) Drag the thumbnail just above or below document page thumbnails to place the new page between the pages. If you select both the left and right thumbnails of a facing-page master page before dragging, two pages are inserted.

- **To add multiple pages,** choose Insert Pages from the Pages panel menu. The Insert Pages dialog box (**Figure 82b**) includes controls for specifying the number of pages to insert, where they're placed, and which master page they're based on.

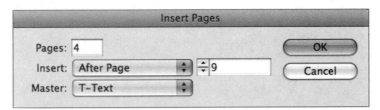

Figure 82b When you choose Insert Pages from the Pages panel menu, the Insert pages dialog box lets you specify the number of pages to add, where to place them, and which master page they're based on.

A document can contain as many as 9,999 pages, although you wouldn't want to create such a large document. If you need to create a long document, it's often a good idea to use InDesign's book feature to organize it as several smaller documents. For more about creating books, see #84.

Moving Pages

Although it's easy to move pages within a document, you should do so with great care. If a document contains facing-page spreads that were designed as a pair, moving a single page can split them. To move a page, select its thumbnail in the Pages panel and drag it elsewhere. As you drag the thumbnail, a vertical bar is displayed when it's next to a page edge to indicate where the page will be placed. If you drag the thumbnail between page icons, an arrow indicates how the pages will be pushed apart to accommodate the moved page. To move a spread, select the page numbers below the page icons and drag the spread to a new location.

Deleting Pages

To delete a page, click its thumbnail in the Pages panel, and then click the Delete (Trash) button. Command-click (Mac OS) or Ctrl-click (Windows) to select multiple, nonsequential pages. Click a thumbnail, and then Shift-click another thumbnail to select a range of pages.

Manipulating Pages

The Pages panel menu includes several more commands for working with documents, master pages, and spreads. Before you choose a command in the Pages panel, you should select the thumbnails of the pages you want to work with. The commands vary depending on whether a single page, a single spread, multiple pages, or multiple spreads are selected in the panel. For example, you can select a page and choose Save As Master to quickly create a master page based on a document page.

The Layout > Pages menu also includes several commands for working with pages, including Add Page, Insert Pages, Move Pages, Duplicate Spread, Delete Pages, and Apply Master to Pages.

Copying Pages Between Documents

You can copy pages between two open documents by displaying the document windows side by side (choose Window > Arrange > Tile to arrange document windows), selecting the thumbnails of the pages you want to copy in the Pages panel, and then dragging and dropping the page icons within the other document window. Copied pages are placed at the end of the target document. When you copy pages between documents, character and paragraph styles, colors, layers, and master pages are also copied.

#83 Numbering Pages and Creating Sections

Since publications are not always numbered from page 1 to the end—and since each InDesign document doesn't necessarily contain an entire publication—you have complete control over the format, placement, and starting number for automatic page numbering. A book, for example, might start out with Roman numerals (i–xvi) for the front matter and then use standard numerals (1–64) for the chapters. A textbook might preface each page number with a letter and start each chapter on page one (A.1–A.24, B.1–B.36, and so on). A range of pages in a document with different page numbering—the front matter, for example—is referred to as a *section*.

To get started with page numbers, you first need to insert the Auto Page Number character in text. Then you can use the Section options to customize it.

Inserting the Auto Page Number Character

Generally, you will place the Auto Page Number character on a master page. That way, all pages based on that page will have a page number. However, you can insert the Auto Page Number Character on any page, in any location, and it will display the appropriate page number. If you reorder pages, the page numbers update as well. To insert the Auto Page Number character:

1. Select the Type tool.

2. Click in a text frame or on a type path (usually on a master page).

3. Choose Type > Insert Special Character > Markers > Current Page Number.

4. If you're on a master page, a placeholder displays. The placeholder is the same as the letter prefacing the master page name (that is, A-Master's Auto Page Number placeholder is a "A"). If you're on a document page, the appropriate page number displays.

5. Select the page number or placeholder and use the character options in the Control panel or the Character panel (Type menu) to format it (**Figure 83a**).

Figure 83a Adding the Current Page Number character to master page B-Master results in the placeholder character "B." Formatting the selected "B" indicates the character formatting you want for the page numbers.

Creating Sections

While the look of page numbers depends on character formats you apply to the Auto Page Number character, all other attributes of page numbers come from the New Section or Numbering & Section Options dialog box. You need to create a section to use Roman numerals rather than Arabic numerals, begin a document on a different page number, include a preface with page numbers, and more. A section of automatic page numbering will continue through a document until you create a new section (**Figure 83b**).

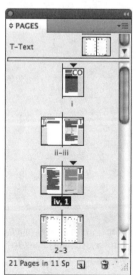

Figure 83b In this document, the first four pages have Roman numerals, i–iv. A new section begins on the fifth page of the document, but starts the numbering at 1 with Arabic numerals.

Facing Pages and Page Numbers

When working in documents with facing pages, the right-facing pages must have odd page numbers and the left-facing pages must have even page numbers. If you select a right-facing page as a section start and then give it an even page number, it will become a left-facing page, reordering all the subsequent pages automatically. You can prevent this by unchecking Allow Document Pages to Shuffle in the Pages panel menu.

In addition to having specific page numbers, sections can have *section marker* text that you can insert on any page. For example, if you have a section for each chapter in a book, the marker for each section might be the chapter name. If you then put the section marker at the top of the master page, the pages in each section will always show the correct chapter name—even if you pick up pages and move them to a different chapter.

To use a section marker, enter the text for it in the Section Marker field in the New Section or Numbering & Section Options dialog box. Then, on a page or master page, choose Type > Insert Special Character > Markers > Section Marker.

To create a section:

1. In the Pages panel, click the page you want to be the first page in the section.

2. Choose Numbering & Section Options from the Layout menu or the Pages panel menu. The New Section dialog box displays (**Figure 83c**); if a section already starts on the selected page, the Numbering & Section Options dialog box displays.

3. Check Start Section. (This is unavailable if you've selected the first page of the document.)

4. To pick up the page numbering where the last section left off, click Automatic Page Numbering. To specify a starting page number, click Start Page Numbering At and enter the page number in the field.

5. If you want to include a prefix for page numbers—such as "Chapter 1-" or "Index"—enter that text in the Section Prefix field. To separate the prefix text from the page number, be sure to include a space or other separation character after the text in the Section Prefix field.

6. By default, the prefix text shows with the page number at the bottom of the document window. To actually add the prefix text to the page numbers on the page, check Include Prefix When Numbering Pages.

For information about the Section Marker field, see the sidebar.

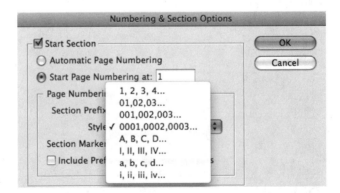

Figure 83c The New Section dialog box lets you specify the starting page number, the type of numerals to use, and the page number prefix for a section of pages. The lower portion of the dialog box, not shown here, gives you control over the page numbering of chapters within books.

#84 Creating a Book

When working on longer publications such as magazines and books, it's common to separate the content into multiple documents such as one document per article or one document per chapter. This allows multiple people to work on different parts of the publication, and it keeps the file sizes small, which results in files that open and save faster. To manage multiple documents for the same publication—including updating page numbers across documents and making sure styles remain consistent—InDesign provides *book* files. A book actually displays as a panel, which serves as a container for the documents that make up the publication.

Creating a Book File

A book is another type of InDesign file, recognized by the file extension of .indb. Before you create a book file, however, it's helpful to get your project organized. Create a folder for the project and place all the documents for the book in it. (You do not need to have all the documents ready—you can add documents to a book at any time.) The project folder is also a good place to store any templates, libraries, graphics, and fonts for the project. To create a book:

1. Choose File > New > Book.

2. In the New Book dialog box, enter a name for the book in the Save As field.

3. Navigate to the folder containing the documents for the book. You can save the book in another location, but it's easiest to keep track of the files if you store the book and its documents in the same folder.

4. Click Save. The book panel opens with the name of the book.

Opening and Closing a Book

You can open the book like you open any other file—choose File > Open or double-click a book file icon on the desktop. If multiple books are open, each book displays on a separate tab in the Book panel. You can tear off tabs to create individual panels for each book.

To close a book, click the panel's close button or choose Close Book from the Book panel menu. You will be prompted to save changes to the book (such as adding or rearranging documents) before you close the book. A book does not have to remain open while you work on its documents.

Saving Books

Adding Documents

When you first create a book, it is empty and waiting for you to add documents. You can add up to 1,000 documents to a book, and a single document can be included in multiple books. To add documents to a book:

1. Click the Add Documents button ⊞ at the bottom of the Book panel or choose Add Document from the Book panel menu.

2. Select the document you want to add to the book. If multiple documents are in the same folder, you can add them all at once. Command-click (Mac OS) or Ctrl-click (Windows) to select multiple documents, or Shift-click to select a continuous range of documents.

3. Click Open to add the documents.

4. You may see alerts regarding missing fonts, but you can click OK to bypass these for the purposes of adding the documents to the book. (Later, for accurate page numbering and output, you need to be sure no fonts are missing.)

   You can also add documents to a book by dragging InDesign files from the desktop into the book.

Working with Books

Once documents are in a book, you can open them through the book for editing, rearrange documents in a book, replace documents with different ones, and remove documents from a book.

- **To open a document for editing,** open its book. Then double-click the document name in the Book panel.

- **To replace a document in a book,** select the document in the book and choose Replace Document from the Book panel menu.

- **To remove a document from a book,** select it and click the Remove Documents button ⊟ at the bottom of the Book panel or choose Remove Document from the panel menu.

- **To rearrange the documents in a book,** click a document name and drag it up or down within the list (**Figure 84**). If you're using automatic page numbering within the book, the page numbers update when you reorder chapters.

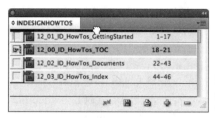

Figure 84 You can drag a document to a new location within a book.

Synchronizing Book Styles

To make sure that all the documents that make up a book remain consistent, you can synchronize styles, including master pages, object styles, paragraph styles, character styles, and color swatches. This way, if you modify or add a style, the change can be implemented automatically throughout the entire book. You can synchronize all the documents in a book or selected documents. To synchronize:

1. Determine which document has the "right" styles that you want in all the documents. (For example, if you want to make a global change in a paragraph style, be sure the document in which you make the change has all the appropriate styles.)

2. Click in the box to the left of a document name in the Book panel. The Style Source icon indicates the styles in that document will be copied to other documents when the book is synchronized.

3. Select the documents in the book that you want to synchronize. To synchronize the entire book, click in the blank area at the bottom of the panel to make sure no documents are selected.

4. Click Synchronize at the bottom of the Book panel or choose Synchronize Selected Documents from the panel menu.

5. An alert regarding missing fonts may display, but you can click OK to bypass this alert for synchronization purposes.

6. InDesign opens each document, makes the changes, saves it, and closes it. Therefore, you *cannot* undo synchronization.

To customize this feature, you can specify which styles synchronize by choosing Synchronize Options from the Book panel menu. Check the styles you want to synchronize, then click the Synchronize button to synchronize all the documents in the book.

#85 Paginating a Book

One advantage of using a book to manage multiple documents is the ability to use automatic pagination. As you work on documents in a book, adding and removing pages, InDesign can update page numbers throughout all the documents. In addition, if you want all the documents to start on a left-facing (even-numbered) or right-facing (odd-numbered) page, InDesign can automatically insert pages at the end of one document to ensure the next document starts on the correct odd or even page.

By default, books are paginated the same way the documents are. If all the documents that comprise a book use automatic page numbering, and each begins on page 1, the book is paginated sequentially from the first page of the first document to the last page of the last document. If there are any sections of page numbers created within a document, those are reflected in the book. At the start of a new section, the pagination of that section continues to the start of the next section.

For example, the first document in this book (**Figure 85a**) is the Table of Contents, and it spans pages i–iv. The second document, which is Chapter 1: Getting Started, has a section start and starts on page 1. The next document follows the previous document's page numbering, so you see pages 18–39 followed by pages 40–42.

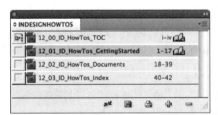

Figure 85a Books can have many sections of page numbers.

To specify how page numbering works for a book, choose Book Page Numbering Options from the Book panel menu. In the Page Order area (**Figure 85b**), specify how each document should start:

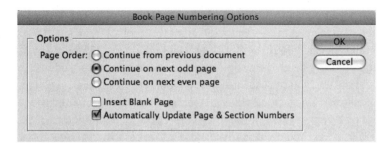

Figure 85b The Book Page Numbering Options dialog box helps you ensure that pages are numbered correctly from document to document.

- **Continue From Previous Document** starts the page numbering according to the last page of the previous document. If the previous document ends on page 10, the next document starts on page 11. If the previous document ends on page 11, the next document starts on page 12. This setting is appropriate for single-sided documents.

- **Continue on Next Odd Page** always starts the page numbering of a document on an odd (right-facing) page. If a document ends on page 11, the next document starts on page 13. This setting might be appropriate for chapters of a book, which usually start on a right-facing page.

- **Continue on Next Even Page** always starts the page numbering of a document on an even (left-facing) page. If a document ends on page 12, the next document starts on page 14. This setting might be appropriate for a magazine in which each document is a feature that starts on a left-facing page.

- **To insert blank pages at the ends of chapters,** click Continue on Next Odd Page or Continue on Next Even Page, and InDesign will insert the blank pages. So, if a document ends on page 12 but the next document must start on page 14, InDesign will automatically insert a blank page 13 at the end of the document. To do this, check Insert Blank Page.

- **Check Automatically Update Page & Section Numbers** to continually repaginate the book as you work on chapters. If you prefer to wait until the book is more final, you can uncheck this option and choose Update Numbering from the Book panel menu any time you want to update the pagination.

Controlling Page Numbering for Book Chapters

To change the page numbering of an individual document in a book, select the document and choose Document Numbering Options from the Book panel menu. (As a shortcut, you can double-click the document's page numbers shown in the Book panel.) Use the Document Chapter Numbering controls in the New Section dialog box. If you create a section for a document, that page numbering is followed through the documents in the book until another section start is encountered.

#86 Inserting Cross-references

Updating Cross-references

The page numbers in cross-references continually update as you work. However, you may need to update cross-references if referenced text changes. You will be alerted to outdated cross-references when you output the document.

To update cross-references in a document, make sure nothing is selected and choose Type > Hyperlinks & Cross-References > Update Cross-Reference.

Long documents such as reports and technical books often contain cross-references to point the reader to a different section. If the cross-references contain specific information, such as "see #9 on page 20," the text and page numbers need to stay up-to-date as the documents are edited. To automate this, you can use InDesign's cross-reference features.

You can create a cross-reference that references text formatted with a specific paragraph style within the current document or another document in a book. You can also create cross-references to hyperlink anchors.

To create a cross-reference:

1. Using the Type tool, click in text where you want to place the cross-reference. Include any text that will surround the cross-reference such as "see" (**Figure 86a**).

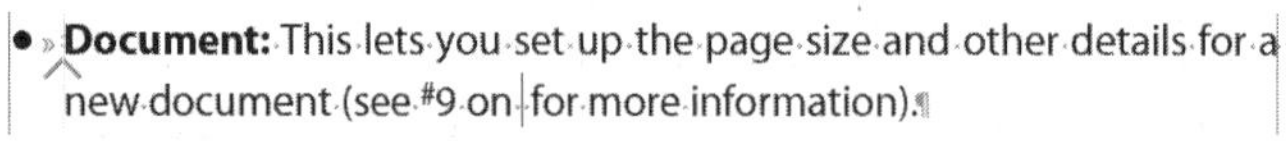

   • **Document:** This lets you set up the page size and other details for a new document (see #9 on for more information).

   Figure 86a Click in text to indicate where to place the cross-reference; in this case, the page number will be filled in after "see #9 on."

2. With the text insertion bar in the correct location, choose Type > Hyperlinks & Cross-References > Insert Cross-Reference. You can also choose Insert Cross-Reference from the Hyperlinks panel menu.

3. To link to text in a specific paragraph style (such as a head), choose Paragraph from the Link To menu. To link to a hyperlink anchor, choose Text Anchor. (See #90 for information about creating hyperlinks.)

4. Choose the document that contains the text you are referencing from the Destination menu. The menu should list all the documents in the current book; if not, choose Browse and locate the document.

5. In the scroll list at left, click the paragraph style applied to the text you wish to reference. At right, all the text formatted with that paragraph style displays.

6. Click the text you want to reference at right.

7. To specify what you want the cross-reference to say, choose an option from the Format menu under Cross-Reference Format. For example, you can include the Paragraph Text & Page Number or only the Page Number (**Figure 86b**). (Note that InDesign will insert "page" before a page number automatically.)

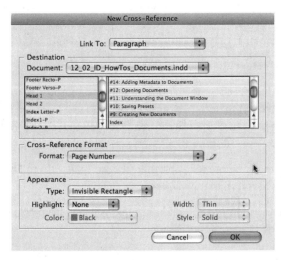

Figure 86b In this example, the cross-reference is to "#9 Creating New Documents," which is formatted with Head 1. The cross-reference will show only the word "page" and the page number.

8. To apply a character style to the cross-reference text, click the pencil icon next to the Format menu. In the Cross-Reference Formats dialog box, select a character style.

9. To specify how the cross-reference text looks, change options in the Appearance area. When you click OK, InDesign inserts the desired cross-reference information (**Figure 86c**).

• › **Document:** This lets you set up the page size and other details for a new document (see #9 on page 20 for more information).

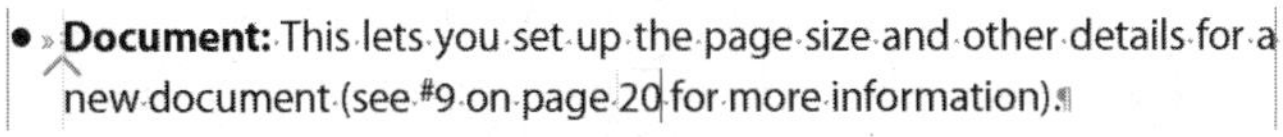

Figure 86c The cross-reference inserts the word "page" along with the correct page number.

#87 Inserting Footnotes

Importing Footnotes from Word

When you import text from Microsoft Word that has footnotes, you can import and place the footnotes automatically. To do this, click Show Import Options in the Place dialog box, and then check Footnotes. The footnote reference numbers and text are imported from Word but formatted and placed according to settings in the InDesign Footnote Options dialog box.

If you need to insert footnotes, InDesign can automatically format the footnote reference numbers, place and format the footnote text, and update the footnotes as text changes and footnotes are added. You have complete control over the text formatting and layout, so you decide precisely how every aspect of footnotes look. This takes working with footnotes from being a potentially tedious and time-consuming task to an almost effortless process.

To insert a footnote:

1. Click anywhere in text using the Type tool.

2. Choose Type > Insert Footnote. A footnote reference number is automatically inserted in the body text, and the flashing text insertion bar is placed at the bottom of the column, ready for you to type the footnote's explanatory text (**Figure 87a**).

3. Enter or paste the footnote text, and then choose Type > Go to Footnote Reference to return to the main text.

If text reflows, the footnote and reference text will flow from column to column and page to page as necessary.

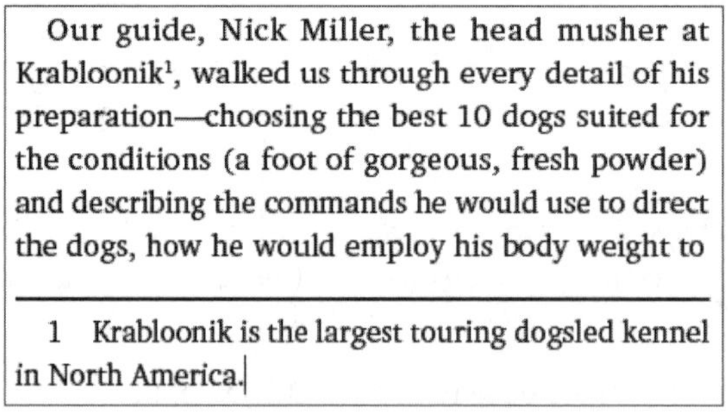

Our guide, Nick Miller, the head musher at Krabloonik[1], walked us through every detail of his preparation—choosing the best 10 dogs suited for the conditions (a foot of gorgeous, fresh powder) and describing the commands he would use to direct the dogs, how he would employ his body weight to

1   Krabloonik is the largest touring dogsled kennel in North America.

Figure 87a A footnote is inserted next to "Krabloonik" in the second line of the paragraph. Then, for the footnote text, a definition of "Krabloonik" was typed in.

Footnotes generally look the same throughout an entire document. Therefore, the controls for specifying the text formatting and placement of footnotes work for all the footnotes in a document, not for individual footnotes. You can change the formatting at any time, but to prevent a lot of text reflow, you may want to set up the footnote formatting before you start inserting footnotes. To format footnotes, choose Type > Document Footnote Options.

Use the Numbering and Formatting tab (**Figure 87b**) to specify how footnotes are numbered, the formatting of the footnote reference in text, and the formatting of the actual footnote text.

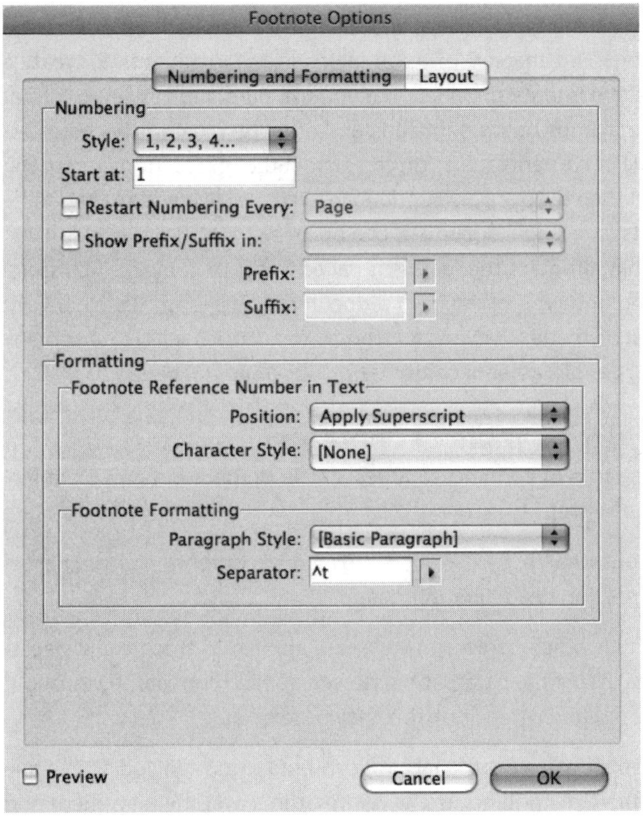

Figure 87b In the Numbering and Formatting tab, you can select a character style for footnote reference numbers and a paragraph style for footnote text, among many other formatting options.

Use the Layout tab to control how footnotes are placed on the page, including the amount of space before and between footnotes, and how footnotes are handled if the text is too long to fit on the page. If you want to place a rule above footnotes, you can specify its usage and formatting.

#**88** Creating Tables of Contents

Creating and updating a table of contents, especially for a long book, can be a chore. Often, the names of heads and subheads change, page numbers change, and chapter order changes—so you're constantly modifying what's supposed to be the "final" table of contents. Then there's the proofreading, to ensure that all the text and page numbers actually match the final content. Fortunately, InDesign offers an automatic way to create a final table of contents, provided that you use paragraph styles to format the chapter names, heads, subheads, and other text that will become part of the table of contents. InDesign can extract the text in those paragraph styles, and then produce and update an accurate, richly formatted table of contents for a single document or a book.

Note that although the feature is called "table of contents," it's useful for creating any type of list from a document. For example, you might create a list of images or charts for a book. You can, in fact, create as many different types of "tables of contents" for a book as you need.

Planning for a Table of Contents

Creating a table of contents requires a little preparation and planning. Here are a few steps to start with:

1. Figure out what text you want in the table of contents, such as chapter heads, section heads, and subheads.

2. Determine which paragraph styles are applied to that text. (If necessary, make sure the paragraph styles are applied consistently throughout the documents—if not, text may be left out.)

3. Decide how you want the table of contents to look, including the title of the table of contents, the text formatting, and the placement and look of page numbers.

4. Create paragraph and character styles for the table of contents, including its title, each level of text (chapter names, section heads, and so on), and page numbers. If you use a tab to separate each table of contents entry from its page number, be sure to set that tab and specify any leader characters—such as an ellipsis—in the paragraph style.

5. Create a placeholder for the table of contents—either blank pages in a document or a blank document in a book. If the table of contents will have a special design, create a master page for it as well.

As an example, this craft book has a main table of contents for the entire book and a mini-table of contents for each chapter (**Figure 88a**). Some of the formatting, such as the bullets and the bracket under the chapter name, are on the master page. The text consists of the chapter name, "Backyard Botanicals," and the craft names followed by a tab, a bracket, and the page number. In the formatted table of contents, the chapter name is centered in 27-point Baskerville Old Face font; the craft names are deeply indented, 12-point Syntax; and the page numbers are 11-point Helvetica Neue Medium Italic.

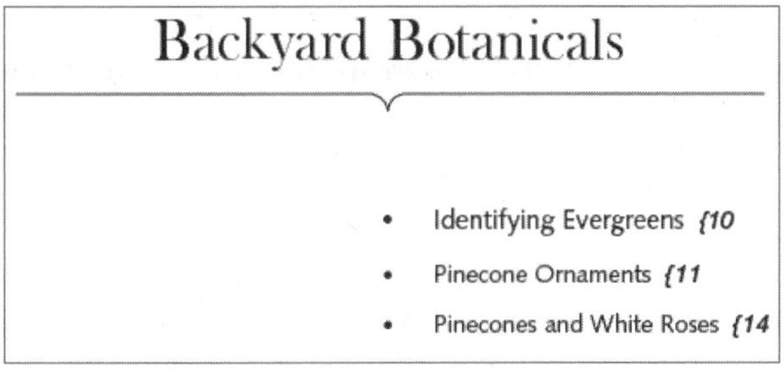

Backyard Botanicals

- Identifying Evergreens {10
- Pinecone Ornaments {11
- Pinecones and White Roses {14

Figure 88a InDesign can create richly formatted tables of contents such as this one.

Generating a Table of Contents

Once you've prepared by identifying the text you want to include in the table of contents and creating paragraph and character styles for it, choose Layout > Table of Contents. In the Table of Contents dialog box (**Figure 88b**), you can specify the styles used to create the table of contents or list, how it should be formatted, and more.

- **Title area:** If you want to place a heading on the table of contents (such as "Contents" or "Figures List"), enter the text in the Title field. To specify the formatting of the title, choose an option from the Style menu at right.

Importing Tables of Contents from Word

If you import text from Microsoft Word that contains an automatic table of contents, the entries and page numbers can be imported as well. However, the page numbers may not be accurate after the text is flowed into the InDesign document, and there is no way to update them. You may be better off not importing the table of contents. To do this, click Show Import Options in the Place dialog box, and then uncheck Table of Contents Text in the Include area.

- **Styles in Table of Contents area:** This is where you specify what text goes into the table of contents. In the Other Styles list at right, locate the paragraph style applied to the first level of head that will go in the table of contents—such as Chapter Head. Select it in the list and click Add. Then select the paragraph style applied to the second level of head and click Add. Continue adding paragraph styles in hierarchical order until you've added all the styles that should appear in the table of contents. Be sure to add the styles according to the hierarchy of information, such as Chapter Heads, Section Heads, Subheads, and so on.

- **Style area:** To specify the formatting for the table of contents, click the first paragraph style in the Include Paragraph Styles list. Then choose a paragraph style from the Entry Style menu below. For example, you might map the Chapter Head paragraph style to the TOC Level 1 paragraph style.

- **More Options button:** To further fine-tune the formatting for each table of contents entry, click More Options. In the Style area, you can specify where page numbers are placed (such as before or after the text) and how they are separated from the entries (such as with an em space or tab). You can also choose character styles for the page numbers and separation characters. In this same area, you can specify that the entries be alphabetized and change the level of information. All the controls in the Style area are specific to the paragraph style selected in the Include Paragraph Styles area; therefore, you may need to set these options for each included style.

- **Options area:** To produce a table of contents for an entire book, check Include Book Documents. Other options in this area let you automatically create PDF bookmarks for table-of-contents entries, replace an existing table of contents, create a "run-in" table of contents (with semicolons rather than paragraph returns separating entries), and specify whether to include text on hidden layers.

Once you're finished setting up the table of contents, click OK in the Table of Contents dialog box. InDesign looks through the document or book, finds all the text, formats it, and then loads the cursor with the fully formatted table of contents. Flow the text into a text frame as you usually would.

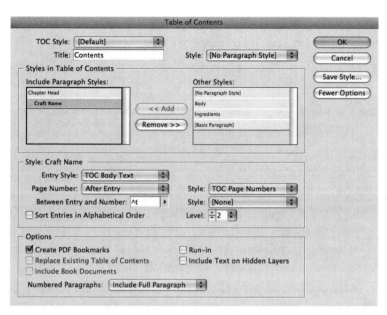

Figure 88b The Table of Contents dialog box lets you specify what text goes into a table of contents and precisely how it should look. To make the table of contents shown in Figure 88a, the paragraph style "Craft Name" is mapped to "TOC Level 2" and separated from its page number with a tab and a left-facing bracket. Both the page number and bracket are formatted with a character style called "TOC Page Numbers."

Don't be surprised if your table of contents is not perfect the first time. With all the detailed settings, you might miss a paragraph style or forget to select the character style for the page numbers. But don't be tempted to manually touch up the table of contents. For one thing, manual changes will not be reflected if you create PDF bookmarks. Furthermore, you will inevitably end up making those manual changes more than once. No matter how "final" you think the document or book is, you usually end up generating the table of contents several times. Generating the table of contents is fairly quick, even for a long book, so you can whip one up just to see how many pages you need or to see if you got all the settings right. Then update it as often as needed.

Saving Tables of Contents as Styles

If you have multiple "tables of contents" in a document or book—for example, an actual table of contents and a figures list—you can save those as styles. You can then select a style from the TOC Style menu at the top of the Table of Contents dialog box.

To save table of contents settings as a style, click Save Style in the Table of Contents dialog box. You can also choose Layout > Table of Contents Styles to create, edit, and delete table of contents styles.

Creating a Table of Contents for a Book

If you're creating a table of contents for a book, follow these steps:

1. Be sure all the documents in the book are available (not missing or open by another user).

2. Make sure all the fonts are active. If text is reflowing due to missing fonts, the page numbers may not be accurate.

3. Choose Update Numbering from the Book panel menu before you create the table of contents.

4. Open the document in the book that will contain the table of contents. The document must contain all the necessary paragraph and character styles for creating and formatting the table of contents. If necessary, synchronize the book to make sure all the necessary styles are in that document. See #84 for more information.

5. If the table of contents is flowed into the first document in the book, you may want to run a "draft" version first to see how many pages it takes up. Then update the page numbering for the book and update the table of contents. If, for example, you save one page for a table of contents and end up using 10 pages, all the page numbers listed in the table of contents will be wrong (unless the table of contents is in its own section of page numbers).

6. Check Include Book Documents in the Table of Contents dialog box when setting up the table of contents.

7. Click OK in the Table of Contents dialog box to load the cursor with the fully formatted table of contents.

Updating a Table of Contents

As you work on a document or book, the table of contents *does not* update automatically. You need to update it manually to reflect changes to text, page numbers, and so on by choosing Layout > Update Table of Contents. If Replace Existing Table of Contents is checked in the Table of Contents dialog box, an alert displays indicating a successful update. If the option is not checked, the loaded text icon displays, and you can flow the table of contents wherever you want.

#89 Exporting a Book for PDF or Print

An advantage to working with books rather than juggling multiple documents is that you can output all the documents in a book at once. This includes preflighting, collecting files for output, exporting to PDF, and printing. Before working with output options, be sure all the documents are available (not open by other users or missing), all the linked graphic files are available, and all the necessary fonts are active.

You can output selected documents in a book or all the documents in a book. To work with all the documents, click in the blank area at the bottom of the Book panel to deselect all the documents. To select individual documents, Command-click (Mac OS) or Ctrl-click the document names; to select a continuous range of documents, use Shift-click. To access the output options for books, click the Book panel menu (**Figure 89**):

- **Preflight Book** checks each document's fonts, images, colors, and more to make sure they're ready for output. See #94 for information about preflighting.

- **Package Book** lets you choose Book For Print or Book For GoLive, and collects all the necessary files, including documents, fonts, and linked images. See #96 for information about packaging.

- **Export Book to Digital Editions** exports the book as an XHTML-based eBook intended for the Adobe Digital Editions reader. See the Adobe Web site (www.adobe.com) for more information.

- **Export Book to PDF** lets you output all the selected documents in the book as a single PDF. If you checked Create PDF Bookmarks in the Table of Contents dialog box, the PDF will already have links in it. See #97 for more information.

- **Print Book** opens the Print dialog box so you can print a hard copy of the book. See #98 for more information about printing. In addition to choosing Print Book, you can click the Print Book button 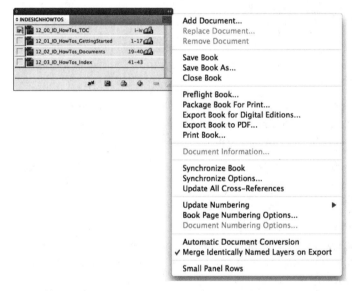 at the bottom of the Book panel.

Note
When documents are selected in the Book panel, the output commands in the Book panel menu change from "Book" to "Selected Documents." For example, Preflight Book becomes Preflight Selected Documents.

Figure 89 The Book panel menu provides options for outputting all the documents in the book with the same settings. These include preflighting, collecting files for output, exporting the book to PDF, and printing the book.

CHAPTER TEN

Creating Rich Interactive Documents

InDesign is generally thought of as page layout software for print publishers, and rightly so. It has many typographic, page design, and long document features that print publishers use to create design-intensive publications. InDesign also has several features that let you create visually rich, interactive *online* publications.

The ability to export InDesign layouts as dynamic SWF files is new in InDesign CS4 and allows publication designers and interactive design professionals to collaborate on interactive documents. The SWF files you export can include interactive buttons, hyperlinks, and page transitions and can be viewed using the free Adobe Flash Player. If you want to take things even further, InDesign CS4 lets you export XFL files, which you can open in Flash CS4 Professional to add more sophisticated interactivity, movies, animation, sound, and navigation.

You can also create media-rich interactive documents for online distribution and viewing by exporting InDesign layouts as Adobe PDF files. Over the past decade, PDF has become an important technology for both print and Web publishing. InDesign lets print publishers export documents and books as PDF documents that can be used for a variety of purposes, from electronic distribution and onscreen review to high-resolution output. Web publishers can create InDesign layouts that include hyperlinks, bookmarks, buttons, movies, and sounds. Viewers can use the free Adobe Reader to view the interactive, media-rich PDF documents that you export from InDesign.

In this chapter you'll learn how to add hyperlinks, buttons, and page transitions to InDesign layouts that you will export as SWF and PDF.

#90 Creating Hyperlinks

If you want to export a layout that was created for onscreen display as a SWF file or PDF document, you have the option to include hyperlinks that viewers of the exported files can click to jump to other places within the document, to other documents, or to Web sites.

To create a hyperlink, you have to specify two components: the *source*, which is the object or text that will act as the jumping-off point, and the *destination* to which the source points and where the user is taken after clicking. A hyperlink destination can be a page or a range of text within the document, another document, or a Web site.

To create a hyperlink destination on the Internet:

1. Choose Window > Interactive > Hyperlinks to open the Hyperlinks panel.

2. Choose New Hyperlink Destination from the panel menu.

3. In the New Hyperlink Destination dialog box (**Figure 90a**), choose URL from the Type menu. Specify a name for the destination and enter a valid Internet address in the URL field. Click OK.

Figure 90a When you create a hyperlink destination, you can choose Page, Text Anchor, or URL from the Type menu. The controls displayed depend on the choice you make. Here you see the controls available for a URL destination.

To create a hyperlink that jumps to a range of text within a layout, you must first create a text anchor to use as the hyperlink destination. To create a text anchor, click within text or select a range of text, and then choose New Hyperlink Destination from the Hyperlinks panel menu. You can use the default name in the Name field or assign a different name.

After you create hyperlink destinations, you're ready to create the source hyperlinks that jump to them. To create a new hyperlink:

1. Select an object or highlight a range of text, and then choose New Hyperlink from the Hyperlinks panel menu.

2. In the New Hyperlink dialog box (**Figure 90b**), choose Shared Destination in the Link To menu so that you can select the hyperlink destination you created earlier. The choice you make in this menu determines the controls displayed in the Destination section.

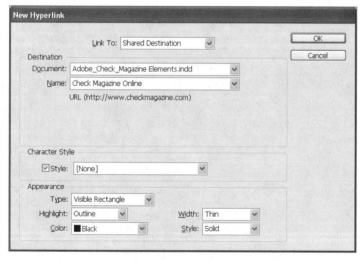

Figure 90b When you create a hyperlink, the New Hyperlink dialog box lets you choose the destination and control the appearance of the hyperlink in the exported PDF document.

3. Choose the hyperlink destination you created earlier (see previous page) from the Name menu in the Destination section (or choose a different name if you've created more destinations).

Creating Bookmarks

In addition to adding hyperlinks to InDesign documents that you intend to export as PDF, you can also include bookmarks. Bookmarks are links that help Acrobat and Reader viewers navigate PDF documents. The bookmarks you create in InDesign are displayed in the Bookmarks tab of Acrobat and Reader, and each bookmark jumps to a page, text, or object in the document, much like a hyperlink. (For information about exporting a table of contents as bookmarks, see #88.)

4. Use the controls in the Appearance area to specify how the hyperlink is displayed in the exported SWF or PDF document.

You can test a hyperlink by selecting it in the Hyperlinks panel and then choosing Go To Destination from the panel menu.

If you've included hyperlinks in an InDesign document, make sure you check Include Hyperlinks in the Export SWF dialog box or the General tab of the Export Adobe PDF dialog box when you export the document. For information about exporting InDesign documents as SWF and PDF, see #93.

#91 Creating Buttons

Creating hyperlinks is one way to add interactivity to InDesign documents that you export as SWF or PDF. Adding buttons is another. Buttons are similar to hyperlinks in that you can configure them to jump to other pages within a document, to other documents, and to URLs; however, buttons can also perform other actions, such as opening a file, changing the view magnification, or—in an exported PDF document—playing a movie or a sound.

To create a button:

1. Select the object you want to use as a button and choose Object > Interactive > Convert to Button.

2. In the Buttons panel (**Figure 91**), enter a name for the button in the Name panel, and then choose a mouse action—On Release, On Click, On Roll Over, On Roll Off, On Focus, or On Blur—from the Event menu that will trigger the action associated with it. If you want the action to occur when the user releases the mouse button after clicking, choose On Release.

3. Click Add new action for selected event (⊕) to display a menu of available actions, and then choose an action.

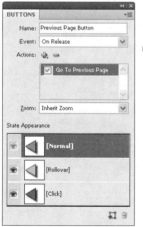

Figure 91 The controls in the Buttons panel determine what happens when a user of the exported file interacts with the button. In this example, the left-pointing triangle at the top has been configured to work as a Go To Previous Page button in the exported SWF and PDF files. .

Button States

If you want to make a button in an SWF file or PDF document look and behave more like a real-world button, you can configure it to display differently when a viewer moves the pointer over it or clicks it.

A button has three states:

1. Normal is when the pointer is not over the button.

2. Rollover is when the pointer is over the button.

3. Click is when a viewer clicks the button with the mouse.

To specify the appearance of a particular state for a selected button, select a state (Normal, Rollover, or Click) in the State Appearance section, and then modify the color, stroke, fill, and so on of the object.

You don't have to create different appearances for all three states. For example, you could configure a button that ignores a rollover and changes appearance only when a viewer clicks it.

Sample Buttons

The Sample Buttons panel (Window > Sample Buttons) offers an easy-to-use alternative to building buttons from scratch. You can click and drag prebuilt buttons from the panel to your layouts. The panel includes a variety of buttons for going to URLs and navigating to other pages. Many of the buttons come in matching pairs (for example, Go To Previous Page and Go To Next Page), and they include different appearances for Normal and Rollover.

4. Some actions display additional options that let you control one or more aspects of the action. For example, if you choose any of the go-to-page options (for example, Go To First Page), you can also choose the Zoom setting that's applied when the button is used. If you choose Go To URL, the URL field lets you specify a URL.

If you want, you can add multiple mouse events with different actions to a single button, and you can add multiple actions to a single mouse event. For example, you could configure a single button that plays a sound when a user of the exported SWF or PDF file moves the pointer over the button (Rollover) and plays a movie when a viewer clicks the button (Click). Click Add new action for selected event ( ) each time you want to add an action to the selected mouse event.

If you've included buttons in an InDesign document, make sure that when you export the file as SWF or PDF you check Interactivity: Include Buttons in the Export SWF dialog box and you check Include Interactive Elements in the General pane of the Export Adobe PDF dialog box.

#92 Adding Page Transitions

The ability to add animated page transitions that users will see as they navigate between pages in the SWF and PDF files you export is new in InDesign CS4. You can preview the built-in page transitions in InDesign as Flash animations, and you can experiment with different speeds and transition directions. Among the dozen page transition options are Curl, Wipe, Dissolve, and Split Window.

When a viewer of an exported SWF or PDF file navigates from page to page—for example, by clicking Previous Page and Next Page buttons—the page transitions you specify determine what happens visually when one page replaces another onscreen.

To specify the visual effect that's used when a page is displayed in an exported SWF or PDF file:

1. Select a page in the Pages panel (Window > Pages). Select multiple pages to apply a transition to all of the selected pages.

2. Choose Window > Interactive > Page Transitions to display the Page Transitions panel (**Figure 92**) .

3. In the Page Transitions panel, choose an option from the Transition menu. For most options, you can also specify Direction and Speed.

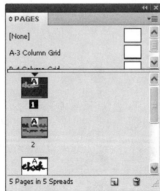

Figure 92 When you choose a page transition, it's applied to the pages that are currently selected in the Pages panel. In this example, pages 1 and 2 are selected, so the dissolve transition will display at medium speed—as specified in the Page Transition panel—when these pages are displayed after the file is exported as SWF or PDF.

Displaying Page Transition Previews

When you move the arrow pointer within the preview rectangle at the top of the Page Transitions dialog box, an animation of the currently selected transition is displayed.

Apply a Transition to All Pages

To apply a page transition to all of the pages in a layout, make sure that you're not currently viewing a master page, choose an option from the Transition menu in the Page Transition panel, and then click the Apply to All Spreads button at the bottom of the Page Transition panel or choose Apply to All Spreads from the Page Transition panel menu.

Unfortunately, you can't actually see the page transitions you've applied until you view the exported Flash or Adobe PDF file.

To clear all of the page transitions you've added to a layout, choose Clear All from the Page Transition panel menu.

#93 Exporting Documents as Flash and PDF

When you've finished adding buttons, page transitions, and hyperlinks to a rich interactive layout, you're ready to export it as a Flash (SWF) file or PDF file. Once you've exported an SWF or PDF file, you should open the file and test your interactive elements. (Note: SWF files can be opened and viewed using Adobe Flash Player, a free utility available at the Adobe Web site [www.adobe.com]. PDF files can be opened and viewed using Adobe Reader, also available for free from the Adobe Web site.)

To export an InDesign layout as a Flash file:

1. Choose File > Export.

2. In the Export dialog box, choose SWF from the Save As Type menu (Windows) or the Format menu (Mac OS), and enter a name in the File name field.

3. Use the controls in the Export dialog box to choose a storage location for the exported file, and then click Save.

4. Modify the settings in the Export SWF dialog box (**Figure 93a**). Make sure you check Include Buttons, Include Hyperlinks, and Include Page Transitions in the Interactivity section.

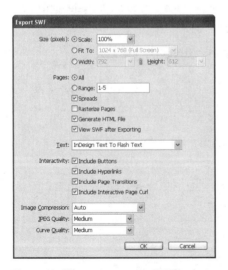

Figure 93a When you export an SWF file, the controls in the Export SWF dialog box let you determine how the exported file is displayed when opened and which interactive elements are included.

Exporting XFL Files

In addition to the ability to export SWF files, InDesign also allows you to export documents as XFL, a new document interchange file format that can be opened with Adobe Flash CS4 Professional.

A Flash developer can open an InDesign layout that's been exported as XFL and then add video, audio, animations, and ActionScript programming to create visually rich online documents with sophisticated interactivity.

Adding Movies and Sounds to PDF Files

If you want to use InDesign to create a rich interactive document that Includes not only hyperlinks, buttons, and page transitions, but movies and sounds as well, you can export the document as PDF.

Working with movies and sounds in InDesign is much like working with imported graphics. You can use the Place command to import video and audio files. Once you've imported a multimedia file, you can modify it in many ways. For example, you can configure a movie to play once or continually or a sound to play automatically when someone displays the page when viewing the PDF.

5. When you're done making changes, click OK.

If you select Generate HTML File in the Export SWF dialog box, an HTML page that contains the SWF file is created, and you can view the page in your Web browser. If you also select View SWF after Exporting, the HTML file automatically opens and plays the embedded SWF file in your default browser. (Note: View SWF after Exporting is available only if Generate HTML File is selected.)

Exporting a PDF file that contains interactive and multimedia elements (see sidebar at left) is much the same as exporting an SWF file:

1. Choose File > Export.

2. In the Export dialog box, choose Adobe PDF from the Save As Type menu (Windows) or the Format menu (Mac OS), and enter a name in the File name field.

3. Use the controls in the Export dialog box to choose a storage location for the exported file, and then click Save.

4. In the Export Adobe PDF dialog box (**Figure 93b**), choose Smallest File Size from the Adobe PDF Preset menu. Make sure you check Buttons, Hyperlinks, and Interactive Elements in the Include section of the General pane. Click OK when you're done making changes.

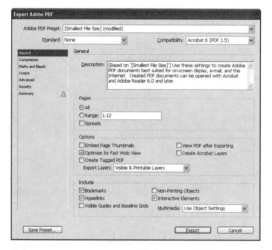

Figure 93b When you export a PDF file, the check boxes at the bottom of the Export Adobe PDF dialog box let you include interactive elements.

CHAPTER ELEVEN

Preflight and Output

As you work on a publication, you'll probably print several proofs to one or more desktop printers before the publication is completed. After you've added the final touches and the publication is ready for final output, you or your print service provider will print the finished document, probably using a high-resolution printer. If you're producing a color publication for print on a printing press, *final output* means printing color separations that will be used to print the document on-press.

One of the main advantages of page-layout software is that it lets you view publications onscreen before you print them. However, displaying a publication onscreen and printing it are very different processes. InDesign includes several features for troubleshooting potential printing problems before they occur, as well as an abundance of print-related controls that help ensure you get the results you want when you print a document.

In this chapter you'll learn how to preview color separations onscreen, how to preflight a document throughout its life span to identify and avoid potential problems, and how to gather all the files required to print a document. You'll also learn how to export documents to PDF, as well as how to export InDesign objects, pages, and documents for use in other InDesign documents and media. Finally, you'll learn how to print documents.

#94 Preflighting Documents

The term "preflight" comes from the aviation industry and refers to the checklist that pilots use to confirm that everything is ready for takeoff. In print publishing, when you preflight a publication you check the electronic file for potential printing-related problems, such as missing fonts or graphics or the use of color in a black-and-white publication.

In the past, preflight was generally performed immediately before a file was printed—which is not always the best time to find problems. The new Preflight panel in InDesign CS4 lets you preflight a document throughout its life span and identify potential printing problems as they occur. You have the option to use the default preflight settings, which warn you about overset text, missing and modified graphics, and missing fonts, or you can create custom preflight profiles that are appropriate for the publications you create.

To turn on preflight:

1. Choose Window > Output > Preflight to open the Preflight panel (**Figure 94a**).

2. Click the On check box. When a green check mark is displayed, preflight is enabled. By default, the [Basic] (Working) preflight profile is used.

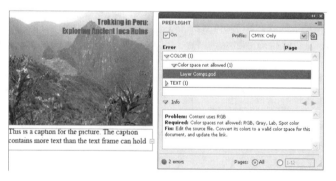

Figure 94a In this example, a custom preflight profile named "CMYK Only" is selected. Two errors are reported: 1) The picture uses the RGB color space; and 2) The text frame contains overset text.

If a document does not have any preflight problems, a green dot and "No errors" is displayed in the lower-left corner of the Preflight panel, as well as at the bottom left of the document window. If you violate any of the conditions of the current preflight profile, the green dot turns red and the number of errors is displayed. All errors are listed in the Preflight panel. If you select a specific problem, detailed information about the error is displayed in the Info area.

Creating custom preflight profiles

Although the default preflight profile [Basic] (working) warns you about the most common printing-related problems, you'll probably want to create your own custom preflight profiles.

To create a custom preflight profile:

1. Choose Window > Output > Preflight to open the Preflight panel.

2. Choose Define Profiles from the Preflight panel menu.

3. In the Preflight Profiles dialog box (**Figure 94b**), click the New preflight profile button ( ), and then enter a name in the Profile Name field.

4. Use the controls for Links, Color, Images and Objects, and so on to specify what you want to allow and exclude.

5. Click OK to save the profile.

6. If you want to use the profile you just created, select it from the Profile menu in the Preflight panel.

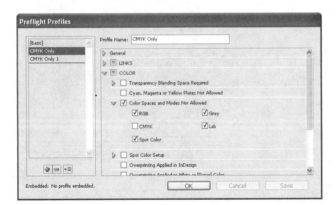

Figure 94b The "CMYK Only" preflight profile does not allow RGB, spot color, grayscale, and Lab colors. Importing a graphic or creating a color swatch that uses any of these color models will generate an error warning in the Preflight panel.

Working with Preflight Profiles

The Preflight Options dialog box provides several options for working with preflight profiles. For example, you can choose a profile to embed in new documents, and you can choose to use the embedded profile or the currently selected working profile when opening documents. To open the Preflight Options dialog box, choose Preflight Options from the Preflight panel menu (Window > Output > Preflight).

#95 Previewing Color Separations

InDesign includes several features that let you preview and prepare documents before you print final versions or send them to a print service provider for high-resolution output. The Separations Preview panel (Window > Output > Separations Preview) is one of the most useful production tools for color publications. It lets you show or hide individual colors, display color values for objects and graphics, and show areas that exceed a specified maximum ink coverage.

To preview color separations onscreen, open the Separations Preview panel (**Figures 95a** and **95b**), and then choose Separations from the View menu. The color list in the panel includes process colors—cyan, magenta, yellow, and black—as well as any other spot colors in the Swatches panel regardless of whether you've used them.

Preview Overprinting

To see an accurate onscreen representation of how objects that are set to overprint will look when printed, check Overprint Preview in the View menu. (Use the controls in the Attributes panel—Window > Attributes—to overprint an object's fill, stroke, or both.) Enabling Overprint Preview can slow down screen display, so you should use it only to check overprinted areas. Disable Overprint Preview when you return to working on a document.

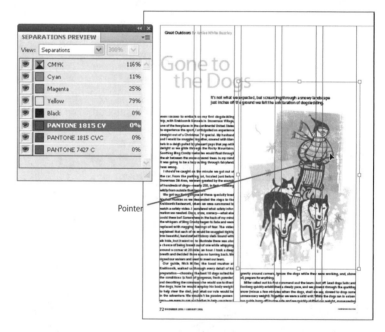

Pointer

Figure 95a The Separations Preview panel includes a list of process and spot colors, and lets you show and hide individual colors. In this example, the pointer is on the sweater of the person in the graphic. The values in the panel show the color makeup of the pixel that the pointer is on.

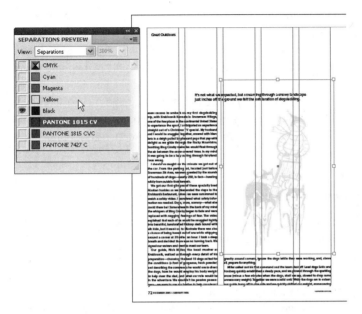

Figure 95b In this example, all colors in the Separations Preview panel are turned off except Black. Only objects that are black or contain a percentage of black are displayed on the document page.

The Separations Preview panel works as follows:

- Clicking the small square to the left of a color name shows or hides the color. Clicking CMYK shows or hides all process colors. You can show or hide whatever colors you want, although at least one color must always be displayed. The Show Single Plates in Black command in the Separations Preview panel menu lets you control how a color is displayed when all other colors are hidden. When it's checked, single colors are displayed as black.

- As you drag the pointer over a page, the values associated with the colors in the Separations Preview panel change to reflect the color of the pixel that the pointer is over.

- When you're done previewing separations and areas that exceed maximum ink coverage (see sidebar), choose Off from the Separations Preview panel menu to return to normal view.

Checking Ink Coverage

Because too much ink on a page can cause drying problems, you may also need to know if the colors in a layout exceed the maximum ink coverage value suggested by your print service provider. To highlight areas that exceed maximum ink coverage, choose Ink Limits in the panel menu, and then specify a maximum ink coverage value in the accompanying field. (Check with your print service provider for the suggested percentage.) Areas that exceed the specified maximum ink coverage value are displayed in shades of red. The more an area exceeds the maximum allowable ink coverage, the darker the shade of red.

#96 Packaging Documents

When it's time to send a finished InDesign document to a print service provider, you need to gather all of the font and graphic files used in the document, as well as a copy of the InDesign file, into a single folder for easy transport. Fortunately, InDesign can do this file management work for you.

In addition to collecting font and graphic files, the Package command (File menu) scans a document for potential printing problems and warns you if it finds anything amiss. (See #94 for information about preflighting documents.)

To package a document:

1. Choose File > Package.

2. The Summary pane of the Package dialog box displays information about the document's Fonts, Links and Images, Colors and Inks, and External Plug-ins. Yellow warning triangles are displayed next to potential printing problems. The other panes display details. You may want to click Cancel and resolve the problems; however, if you decide to ignore them, click Package to display the Printing Instructions dialog box. You'll be prompted to save the document if you've made changes since you last saved it.

3. The information you enter into the various fields of the Printing Instructions dialog box is saved as a text file that's included in the package. After you've entered the information you want to include, click Continue.

4. In the Folder Name field of the Package Publication dialog box (**Figure 96**), enter a name for the folder into which files will be copied and specify the location of the folder.

5. Use the check boxes at the bottom-left of the Package Publication dialog box to specify the files you want to include. You'll probably want to check Copy Fonts (Except CJK) and Copy Linked Graphics, and you should check Update Graphic Links in Package so that the InDesign file copied into the package folder is linked to the graphic files that are copied to the package folder and not to the original files. (Linked graphics are placed in a folder called Links within the package folder; fonts are placed in a folder called Fonts.) Click Package to create the package folder and include the files you've chosen.

Packaging a Book

To package a book, open the Book panel, and choose Package Book from the Book panel menu. You also have the option to package the documents selected in the Book panel.

Figure 96 The Package command creates a folder into which the files you specify in the Create Package Folder dialog box are copied. Send the package folder to your print service provider for final output.

After you've packaged an InDesign document, you'll probably want to compress the package folder and then e-mail the compressed file to your print service provider, upload the file to your provider's FTP site, or copy the file onto a CD or portable drive for delivery to your provider. Package folders are also useful for storing and archiving InDesign documents and all of the files required to print them at the end of the production cycle.

#97 Exporting Print Documents as PDF

Exporting a Book as PDF

If you've used InDesign's book feature to combine several layouts into a book, you can export all documents or selected documents to PDF. (For more about books, see #84 and #85.) To export all documents in a book as a single PDF file, open the book file, click a blank area in the Book panel, and then choose Export Book to PDF from the Book panel menu. To export some but not all documents, select the documents you want to export in the Book panel, and then choose Export Selected Documents to PDF. The rest of the process is the same as exporting a document to PDF.

At many publishing sites, publications in progress are exported as PDF documents for electronic markup and review, and finished publications are exported as PDF for final, high-resolution output. When it's time to export an InDesign layout to PDF, you have many options for controlling the size and many other characteristics of the file. The choices you make when you export to PDF depend on how the PDF will be used. For example, if you want to distribute a PDF via e-mail to colleagues or clients for electronic review and markup using Adobe Acrobat or Adobe Reader, you should save a compact, low-resolution PDF that's well suited for electronic distribution and review. If you intend to send a PDF file to a print service provider for high-resolution output, you should save a high-resolution file.

To export a layout to PDF:

1. Choose File > Export.

2. In the Export dialog box, enter a name for the PDF file and choose the folder in which the file will be saved.

3. Choose Adobe PDF from the Format menu (Mac OS) or Save as Type menu (Windows), and then click Save.

4. In the Export Adobe PDF dialog box, you can simply choose a PDF preset in the Adobe PDF Preset menu, and then click Export, or you can choose a preset, customize the settings in the various panes of the Export Adobe PDF dialog box (**Figure 97**), and then click Export. If the document contains any missing fonts or any missing or modified graphics, alerts are displayed. You can ignore any alerts and continue export by clicking OK, or you can click Cancel to cancel export and return to the document. If you change a setting, "(modified)" is displayed to the right of the preset selected in the Adobe PDF Preset menu.

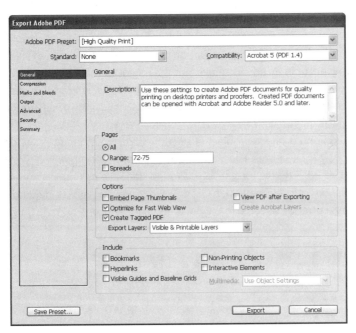

Figure 97 When you export an InDesign document to PDF, the settings you make in the panes of the Export Adobe PDF dialog box determine the characteristics of the PDF document and the size of the file that's generated.

When you make changes in the Export Adobe PDF dialog box, the new settings are saved with the application and used the next time you export a layout to PDF.

Exporting Interactive, Multimedia PDFs

When you export a PDF document that contains bookmarks, hyperlinks, buttons, and multimedia files (pictures and sounds), make sure you check Bookmarks, Hyperlinks, and Interactive Elements in the General pane of the Export Adobe PDF dialog box. For more information about creating interactive documents, see Chapter 10, "Creating Rich Interactive Documents."

Copying Objects as PDF Data

You can also use PDF to copy objects from InDesign to PDF-aware programs like Illustrator and Photoshop. For example, if you've created a graphic in InDesign and you want to use it in a Photoshop image, you can copy the object in InDesign and then paste it into Photoshop. If you check Copy PDF to Clipboard in the File Handling pane of the InDesign Preferences dialog box, PDF data is copied to the clipboard when you choose Edit > Copy or Edit > Cut. To use copied objects in a PDF-aware program, switch to that program, and then choose Edit > Paste.

#98 Exporting Documents in Other Formats

Sometimes, you may want to use InDesign pages, objects, or text in another application or in another InDesign document. For example, if you've created a magazine cover, you may want to use a reduced version of the layout in an advertisement for the magazine. Or you may want to include an image of the cover on a Web page. InDesign lets you export objects, text, pages, spreads, and documents in a variety of different file formats.

To export a selected object or multiple objects, selected text, or document pages, choose File > Export. The Export dialog box is displayed (**Figure 98**). The file formats displayed in the Save as type menu (Windows) or Format menu (Mac OS) and what you can export depend on what's currently selected in the document: nothing, one or more objects, a text frame, or text.

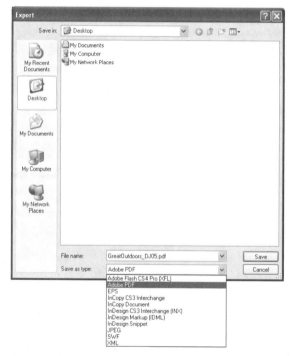

Figure 98 The Export dialog box, showing the formats available when an object is selected. When a text frame is selected, the insertion point is blinking, or text is highlighted, the Format menu in the Export dialog box includes text file formats, such as Rich Text Format and Text Only, as well as graphic formats, such as EPS and JPEG.

The Save as type menu (Windows) and Format menu (Mac OS) in the Export dialog box offer the following choices:

- **Adobe Flash CS4 Pro (XFL):** If you export an XFL file, you can edit the file using Adobe Flash Pro. Interactive elements such as hyperlinks, page transitions, and buttons are not included in exported XFL files.

- **Adobe InDesign Tagged Text:** This text file format saves all InDesign text-formatting codes. If you open a tagged text file in a word processing program, the formatting codes are displayed along with the text. If you import a tagged text file into InDesign, the formatting codes are applied to the text and are not visible. This option is available only if text is highlighted or the insertion point is blinking.

- **Adobe PDF:** This option lets you export a page, multiple pages, or a document to PDF. See #97 for more about exporting as PDF.

- **EPS:** If you need to use an InDesign page in another program or another InDesign document, the EPS file format is the best option. When you export to EPS, you can export a page, a spread, a range or pages, or all pages. Each page or spread is saved as a separate EPS file.

- **InCopy CS3 Interchange:** If your workflow includes Adobe InCopy CS3, a word processing and editorial application closely integrated with InDesign, you can export content (text and graphics) in the InCopy CS3 Interchange format (.inx). InCopy CS3 users can check out and modify these files. A link is maintained between the exported file and the InDesign document so that modifications made to the exported file are reflected in the InDesign document.

- **InCopy Document:** Lets you export InDesign content in .icml format that can be opened and modified using InCopy CS4.

- **InDesign CS3 Interchange (INX):** If you, a colleague, or a client needs to open an InDesign CS4 document using InDesign CS3, you can export the InDesign CS4 document using the InDesign Interchange format. If any objects use features that are new in InDesign CS4, they may be modified or omitted when the file is opened in InDesign CS3. Copies of InDesign CS3 may need to be updated to be able to open .inx files.

Exporting for Digital Editions and Dreamweaver

The File menu contains two additional commands for exporting InDesign documents for electronic repurposing:

- **Export for Dreamweaver:** This option lets you export the content of an InDesign layout for use on the Web. After exporting, you can open the resulting HTML file with Adobe Dreamweaver and make changes.

- **Export for Digital Editions:** This option lets you export a document or book as an eBook file (.epub) that can be opened using the free Adobe Digital Editions reader software.

- **InDesign Markup (IDML):** This format is useful for saving documents that were created in other page layout programs (QuarkXPress or PageMaker) or when you're having problems with an InDesign document. Developers can use standard XML tools to assemble and disassemble .idml files.

- **InDesign Snippet:** A snippet is an electronic file with an .inds extension that contains one or more InDesign objects. Snippet files are much like graphic files—for example, you can import (File > Place) or drag and drop snippet files into InDesign layouts.

- **JPEG:** The JPEG file format is often used for images in Web pages. When you export to JPEG, you can export an object, a page, a spread, a range of pages, or all pages, and you can specify the resolution of the file. Each page or spread is saved as a separate JPEG file.

- **Rich Text Format:** The Rich Text Format (RTF) converts all text formatting to text instructions that other programs, particularly Microsoft Word, can recognize. Not all of the text-formatting features in InDesign are supported by RTF. For example, horizontal/vertical scaling, optical kerning, and shear are not supported. This option is available only if text is highlighted or the insertion point is blinking.

- **SWF:** You can export SWF files that include page transitions, buttons, rollovers, and hyperlinks. SWF files can be opened and played using Adobe Flash player.

- **Text Only:** This option saves a .txt file and removes all paragraph and character formatting and is available only if text is highlighted or the insertion point is blinking.

- **XML:** Similar to HTML files, XML files include tags that describe text and graphic content, but do not include information about how the content is displayed or formatted. The XML file format is particularly useful for using the same content across different media. There's no point in exporting a document as XML without first assigning XML tags to the objects in the document.

#99 Printing Documents

While you can use InDesign to produce nonprinted documents, such as interactive multimedia PDFs, chances are you'll print most of the documents you create. Whether you need to print proofs of a layout to an inkjet or laser printer or send a finished layout to a high-resolution printer, such as an imagesetter, you can use InDesign's extensive printing controls to ensure that you get the results you want.

Before you print a document, it's a good idea to preflight it (Window > Output > Preflight; see #94) to determine whether there are any potential printing problems and, if so, fix them. You should also make sure that the correct printer drivers and PostScript Printer Descriptions (PPDs) are installed on your computer. When you're ready to print, choose File > Print.

To specify the printer, choose a print preset from the Print Preset menu in the Print dialog box (**Figure 99**; for more about print presets, see the sidebar on the next page), or choose Custom if you want to modify settings in any of the Print dialog box panes. You can also choose a printer from the Printer menu.

If you choose a print preset, all you have to do is click Print. All of the settings in the General, Setup, Marks and Bleeds, Output, Graphics, Color Management, and Advanced panes of the Print dialog box are automatically set based on the settings in the selected preset. You can specify custom print settings by making changes in any of the panes. When you modify default settings for a print preset or choose a different printer from the Printer list, "[Custom]" is displayed in the Print Preset menu.

Printing Transparency

When you print a document that includes transparency effects, such as soft drop shadows, InDesign performs a process called *flattening* before it sends transparent objects to the printer. During flattening, areas where transparent objects overlap other objects are either rasterized or converted into vector data that the printer can understand. Flattening doesn't affect objects on pages; it affects only the information sent to the printer. If you send your InDesign documents, or exported PDF versions of your documents, to a print service provider, it's a good idea to let the provider know if the files contain transparency.

Sending PDF Files to a Print Service Provider

Some print service providers prefer to receive PDF files rather than native InDesign files. If that's the case, you'll need to save the document to PDF before sending it to your provider. (For more information about exporting PDFs, see #97.)

Printing a Book

To print a book, choose File > Open and open the book file. Make sure no books are selected in the list of files, and then choose Print Book from the Book panel menu. The Print dialog box is displayed.

Using Print Presets

A print preset is a saved collection of print settings that lets you quickly print a document to a specific printer without having to manually specify settings in the Print dialog box. The easiest way to create a print preset is to select a printer in the Print dialog box, adjust the settings in the various panes of the Print dialog box, and then click Save Preset. Name and save the preset. To use a print preset when printing a document, choose the preset from the Print Preset menu in the Print dialog box.

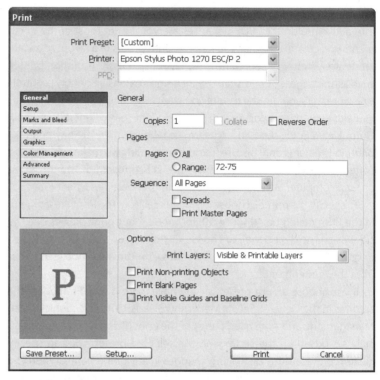

Figure 99 The Print dialog box contains several panes of controls for specifying printing settings. Here you see the General pane, which lets you choose a printer and specify the pages to print, and also provides options for printing objects, blank pages, and guidelines and gridlines that wouldn't otherwise print.

The Print dialog box contains several dozen controls—too many to attempt to explain here. It's a good idea to examine the controls in each pane so that you know what's available. You probably won't need to change many of the controls very often, but, if you do, familiarity will come in handy.

#**100** Creating Printer Spreads

When you create multipage documents with InDesign, the pages are displayed in the document window in the same order that a reader would read them. Page 1 is the first page, followed below by pages 2 and 3 (displayed together), then pages 4 and 5, and so on. Each facing-page spread is called a *reader spread*. However, before a multipage document is printed at a commercial printer, the pages must be rearranged into printer spreads. For example, the first page of a document and the last page form a printer spread. Page 2 and the next-to-last page are a printer spread, and so on. The process of creating printer spreads from reader spreads is called *imposition.*

Choosing the Print Booklet command (File menu) displays the Print Booklet dialog box (**Figure 100**), which provides several controls for specifying how multipage documents are printed. In the Setup pane, choose a print preset, specify the pages you want to print, and then choose one of the five options in the Booklet Type menu:

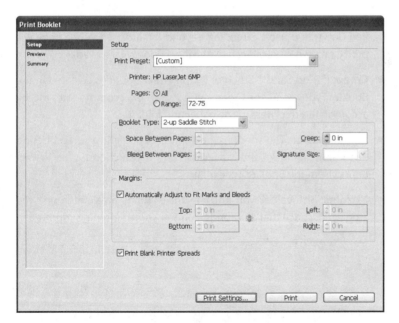

Figure 100 The Setup pane in the Print Booklet dialog box lets you control how multipage documents are printed. The Booklet Type menu provides five imposition options. The controls available in the Booklet Type section depend on what's selected in the Booklet Type menu.

- **2-up Saddle Stitch:** This option creates two-page, side-by-side printer spreads. The Space Between Pages, Bleed Between Pages, and Signature Size controls aren't available when 2-up Saddle Stitch is selected.

- **2-up Perfect Bound:** This option creates two-page, side-by-side printer spreads that fit within the specified signature size (see below).

- **2-up Consecutive, 3-up Consecutive, and 4-up Consecutive:** All of these options create multipage panels appropriate for a foldout publication or a brochure. The Bleed Between Pages, Creep, and Signature Size controls are not available when any of these options is selected.

Here's a brief description of the other controls in the Print Booklet dialog box:

- **Space Between Pages:** This specifies the amount of space between pages in a printer spread.

- **Bleed Between Pages:** This determines the distance within the specified Gap that objects extending beyond the inner edge of a page will print (somewhat like a bleed for the inner edges of a spread).

- **Creep:** If 2-up Saddle Stitch or 2-Up Perfect Bound is selected in the Booklet Type menu, the Creep value you enter accommodates for the accumulated thickness of the paper and folding.

- **Signature Size:** This specifies the number of pages in a perfect-bound document signature and is available only if you choose 2-up Perfect Bound from the Booklet Type menu.

- **Margins:** The values you enter in the Margins area determine the amount of space that surrounds a printer spread after it is trimmed.

Index